Macromedia®
Director®
Workshop

Hayden
Books

A Division of Macmillan USA
201 West 103rd Street
Indianapolis, Indiana 46290

Matthew Manuel

Macromedia Director Workshop

International Standard Book Number: 0-7897-2146-5

Library of Congress Catalog Card Number: 99-65675

Printed in the United States of America

First Printing: December 1999

01   00   99   4   3   2   1

Trademarks

All terms mentioned in this book that are known to be trademarks or service marks have been appropriately capitalized. Hayden Books cannot attest to the accuracy of this information. Use of a term in this book should not be regarded as affecting the validity of any trademark or service mark. Director is a registered trademark of Macromedia.

Warning and Disclaimer

Every effort has been made to make this book as complete and as accurate as possible, but no warranty or fitness is implied. The information provided is on an "as is" basis. The author and the publisher shall have neither liability nor responsibility to any person or entity with respect to any loss or damages arising from the information contained in this book or from the use of the CD or programs accompanying it.

Associate Publisher
John Pierce

Acquisitions Editor
Karen Whitehouse

Development Editor
Laura Norman

Managing Editor
Thomas F. Hayes

Project Editor
Nancy E. Sixsmith

Copy Editor
Kitty Jarrett

Indexer
Becky Hornyak

Proofreader
Maribeth Echard

Technical Editors
Julian Beak
John Warriner

Team Coordinator
Julie Otto

Media Developer
Brandon Penticuff

Interior Designer
Kevin Spear

Cover Designer
Karen Ruggles

Layout Technicians
Cyndi Davis-Hubler
Brad Lenser

Contents at a Glance

Table of Contents

About the Author

Matthew Manuel is a Senior Software Engineer for Disney Interactive, where he leads programming teams in the production of various Disney Interactive titles. He has worked extensively with Director for more than six years. Matt started out using Director in version 3, producing cross-platform multimedia products on CD-ROM. Matt also programmed in C, and produced backgrounds in Autodesk 3D Studio during the production of "The Riddle of Master Lu," a critically acclaimed CD-ROM adventure game.

Other titles that Matt has helped produce by using Director are "Disney's Winnie the Pooh and Tigger Too Animated StoryBook" and "Disney's Winnie the Pooh Kindergarten Learning." His latest title is "Disney's Winnie the Pooh Activity Center."

Dedication

To Kim: for support, encouragement, and patience.

Acknowledgments

Creating a book like this is the work of many people, most of whom labor behind the scenes.

Many thanks to Karen Whitehouse for giving me the opportunity to create this book. Laura Norman was always patient, helpful, and seemed to have just the right suggestions. Julian Beak was my safety net on technical issues.

Ward Makielski encouraged me along the way and provided a sounding board for my ideas. Without Patrick Blattner, I never would have thought that I could do this.

To my family, thanks for always being there and providing a touchstone for what is important.

Tell Us What You Think!

As the reader of this book, *you* are our most important critic and commentator. We value your opinion and want to know what we're doing right, what we could do better, what areas you'd like to see us publish in, and any other words of wisdom you're willing to pass our way.

As Associate Publisher for Hayden Books, I welcome your comments. You can fax, email, or write me directly to let me know what you did or didn't like about this book—as well as what we can do to make our books stronger.

Please note that I cannot help you with technical problems related to the topic of this book, and that due to the high volume of mail I receive, I might not be able to reply to every message.

When you write, please be sure to include this book's title and author as well as your name and phone or fax number. I will carefully review your comments and share them with the author and editors who worked on the book.

Fax: 317-581-4666

Email: hayden@mcp.com

Mail: Associate Publisher/Hayden Books
           201 West 103rd Street
           Indianapolis, IN 46290 USA

Introduction

About Macromedia Director

Macromedia Director is the grandfather of multimedia authoring programs. Its history dates back to before CD-ROMs, when it was primarily a presentation tool. Over the years, Director has matured and improved, adding many features and capabilities.

The latest version of Director, version 7, is one of the most significantly upgraded versions Macromedia has produced. Director version 7 is fast and flexible, it supports many media types, and it embraces the Internet with a new version of Shockwave.

Director includes behaviors, which are powerful tools you can use (even if you're not a programmer) to create interactive, interesting, and fun programs without using Lingo, Director's scripting language. As you work through the book, you'll get plenty of practice with behaviors. Of course, creating new behaviors is another exciting way to make a project interactive; this book introduces the basics of Lingo programming so that when you are ready, you can make your own behaviors.

Director provides two ways to distribute your creations. You can generate a projector application that contains your movies, which is playable by anyone with a Macintosh or Windows computer. You can also save your movies as Shockwave movies, which can be downloaded from the Internet and played inside a Web browser. The unique considerations of both methods are covered in this book.

Who This Book Is For

Macromedia Director Workshop was created for artists, designers, and people new to Macromedia Director. Major Director concepts are introduced in each chapter, along with specific ways to use them. Examples abound to reinforce the concepts so you can start making movies immediately.

If you're new to Director, this book will give you an appreciation for why it is such a successful product used for making CD-ROM and Internet multimedia. Especially if you're a nonprogrammer, you will be amazed at how easy creating real interactivity can be when you use Director's behaviors. If you are already familiar with Director's features, you'll be able to extend your knowledge of the program by working through the book's practical examples.

How to Use This Book

Macromedia Director Workshop was written with both beginner and intermediate Director users in mind. Each chapter is meant to build on the material from earlier chapters. You will start by learning how to plan a Director project, proceed to building the movies and casts, and then learn how to finish the project and distribute your program.

Many examples in each chapter reinforce the important concepts. I encourage you to follow along by performing each example's steps within Director. Director is such an interactive environment that as you follow along with the book's examples, you will probably be tempted to explore on your own. This is a very good way to learn more about the program and determine how you can best use Director to meet your individual needs.

Tips, warnings, and notes appear throughout the book. The information contained in them is often not covered in the program documentation, and are based on my experience using Director. They will save you time and aggravation.

To integrate all the various concepts in the book, Chapters 3 through 11 end with a project section. If you follow along with the project throughout these chapters, at the end of the book you will have a portfolio to show off what you know about Director. The portfolio project starts with an introduction, continues with an interactive menu that links to various areas of expertise, and ends with a contact information screen. All the files required for the project are contained in the project folder on the book's CD-ROM. See Appendix A for more details on the book's CD-ROM.

About *Macromedia Director Workshop*

Macromedia Director Workshop explores the principles and features of interactive content creation using Director. It covers the most important information that you need to know to start and finish a project. There is always more to learn about Director, and you will have an understanding of where to go next after you finish this book.

The book is intended to be read sequentially because each chapter builds on the material from earlier sections. The multimedia creation process is mirrored in the organization of the chapters. **Chapter 1, "What Is Director?"** introduces the software and covers its history, as well as some of its many uses.

Chapter 2, "Why Director?" presents the reasons why Director remains the best multimedia-authoring environment. Besides being very interactive and offering good execution performance, Director has a large and helpful developer community on the Internet that can be useful for support.

In **Chapter 3, "Planning Your Director Project,"** you will learn about the documents that serve as planning tools for your project. These include the concept document, design document, functional specification, and project schedule.

The concept of Director casts is introduced in **Chapter 4, "Working with Casts."** A *cast* is a holding area for all the elements that will appear onscreen in your project. Images, text, audio, and scripts are all stored in casts. External casts are also covered in this chapter.

Chapter 5, "Creating the Score," shows you how to use the score to create noninteractive animations. A *score* is a timeline that determines where and when elements show up on the Director stage. It is a powerful tool that, like a piece of music, becomes easier to read with experience.

The main Director file, the movie, is introduced in **Chapter 6, "Working with Movies."** A *movie* is the container file that stores all the various parts of a Director production. Projects can use multiple movies for even more flexibility.

Behaviors are explained in **Chapter 7, "Using Behaviors."** A *behavior* is a specialized Lingo script that you attach to an onscreen element. It controls the actions of the element based on messages that Director sends. For example, a behavior might tell an image to change whenever the mouse rolls over it.

More detailed information on scripting in Director's Lingo language is provided in **Chapter 8, "Understanding Scripts."** Parent scripts, frame scripts, cast scripts, and movie scripts are introduced, along with information on where they are best used. Lingo is such an important part of Director that you should spend some time becoming familiar with it.

One of Director's strengths is the variety of media that it can use. Details on common media types are explored in **Chapter 9, "Integrating Various Media Types into Director Projects."** This chapter explains the concepts behind bitmap images, vector images, text, sound files, QuickTime movies, and Flash movies.

In **Chapter 10, "Working with Xtras,"** you will learn about Xtras, which are plug-ins that expand Director's capabilities. You can use Xtras to do things such as add more transitions, support different media types, and extend the Lingo language. This chapter also shows you where to find Xtras on the Internet.

The last chapter, **Chapter 11, "Shipping a Title,"** demonstrates all the steps you need to take to distribute your project. To provide the best experience for end users, you need to keep in mind different considerations, and you will use different methods for creating a projector application on CD-ROM and a Shockwave movie on the Internet.

Appendix A, "What's on the CD-ROM," discusses the files you will find there.

Don't forget the project section at the end of Chapters 3 through 11. Throughout the project, you will learn to apply the concepts presented in each chapter by working through specific examples. The project is a continuous exercise throughout the book that will help you create a full Director application. You are encouraged to customize the project along the way to reflect your specific needs and strengths.

From planning a project to final distribution, *Macromedia Director Workshop* gives you the information you need to accomplish your interactive multimedia goals.

What Is Director?

Director is the premiere multimedia-authoring package available for Windows and Macintosh computers, developed and published by Macromedia, Inc., a public company formed in 1992. Director dates back to 1985, when Macromind, the predecessor to Macromedia, created it.

Director was originally used to create multimedia projects before anybody knew what *multimedia* was. People used Director to collect various types of media (such as text, images, and sound) and create presentations. With Director, personal computers were capable of exciting visual and aural creations.

Director gained popularity with the CD-ROM revolution of the early 1990s. The large amount of storage space on CD-ROMs made multimedia distribution practical in the general marketplace. Many multimedia companies got started with Director at that time and still use it today.

Macromedia has kept Director current for the needs of multimedia developers. With the explosion of the Internet, Director has become a key development tool for the World Wide Web. According to Macromedia's Web site, more than 350,000 people around the world use Director today.

To help reduce the size of projects created by Director for the Internet, Macromedia developed Shockwave. Director movies are *shocked*, or compressed, before being distributed on Web sites. Users can then play back these files by using the Shockwave plug-in.

Shockwave has become a standard medium for interactive multimedia on the Internet. Since 1996, Macromedia reports more than 70 million successful downloads of the Shockwave plug-in. Additionally, Microsoft and Apple now include Shockwave in the latest versions of their operating systems. For consumer use, Shockwave is now considered to be ubiquitous.

With Director's prowess at Internet connectivity, a new medium of delivery has emerged: the hybrid CD-ROM. A hybrid CD-ROM (or DVD-ROM) can contain Director movies and other large files, and the movies can also reach out onto the Internet and download data. This means that the application can run quickly because it doesn't have to download large amounts of data, and it also never becomes outdated because it can continually update itself from the Internet.

As an example of the power of hybrid CD-ROMs and Director, imagine a world atlas that always has the latest information. The CD-ROM product sold on shelves includes data that was current when the product was created. As long as there is updated information available on the Internet, a properly engineered product can access the most up-to-date online information to stay current.

A Brief History of Director

The best way to understand the evolution of Director is by looking at the important new features that have appeared in each version. In many ways, Director parallels the multimedia industry itself. A timeline of Director releases follows.

1985: VideoWorks by Macromind

In 1985, Macromind releases the first version of Director's predecessor, VideoWorks. Macromind eventually merges with two other companies in 1992 to form Macromedia.

1990: Version 2

In 1990, Macromind renames VideoWorks II to Director 2.

1993: Version 3

Now part of Macromedia, the Director Player for Windows is released. This is the first time Director movies can play on the Windows platform.

Director has 24 score channels in this version, meaning that only 24 sprites (that is, multimedia elements) can be onscreen at once.

1994: Version 4

Version 4 marks the first time that cross-platform development is available for Director. The authoring environment is released for Windows.

Lingo becomes object-oriented when parent scripts are introduced. This makes Director more programmer-friendly and expands its capabilities immensely.

Now at 48 score channels, this version also allows a maximum of 32,000 cast members, up from 512 in earlier versions.

1996: Version 5

Shockwave is introduced, enabling Director movies to play in browsers with the Shockwave plug-in. Interactivity is now possible on the Internet, with little programming knowledge required.

NetLingo, a collection of additional Internet-oriented Lingo commands, is introduced with Shockwave. This enables Lingo programmers to use Internet functions in their code.

Macromedia introduces Xtras, which are Director plug-ins that allow third parties to extend the program's capabilities.

1997: Version 6

Behaviors, which allow nonprogrammers to add even more complex and interesting interactivity to Director, are introduced with this version. Although behaviors can be created more easily than Lingo scripts, they have all the benefits of Lingo for advanced tasks.

The number of score channels more than doubles to 120. Director's graphic engine, combined with faster computers, allows more sprites to be animated onscreen at once. To complement this, a 500 frames-per-second tempo is available, although reaching this playback rate is generally unrealistic for animation.

To counter the criticism that Director is too Macintosh- and Windows-oriented, the Save-as-Java option appears. Limited-function Director movies can be converted to Java with a single command. This allows playback of Director movies on any computer that can run Java applets, such as those using UNIX-based operating systems.

1998: Version 7

Director's playback engine is completely overhauled for this release. Speed and capability increases are achieved almost everywhere in the product. Now, sprites can be rotated and skewed in real-time, a task that was essentially impossible in earlier versions. Vector graphics are added as a native cast member type, allowing even more efficient memory and bandwidth (the amount of data transferred per second) usage.

The score channel supports 1,000 channels and an essentially unlimited number of cast members.

Multiuser Xtra is introduced, adding more Lingo commands for Internet functions. Director movies, as Shockwave movies or projectors, can communicate with one another and a server. Applications such as chat rooms and multiplayer games are now possible with Director.

A Brief Overview of Director

Tasks in Director are loosely based on the metaphor of producing a play or a movie, which is useful for people getting started with the program.

Imagine that you are charged with making a movie for a major Hollywood studio. First, you want to know what the movie is about and what is going to happen in the movie. Think of this as the movie definition, or synopsis.

After you define what the movie is about, you determine where you're going to film the movie. The right locations can make the movie great.

The actors you want in the movie are also very important. A good cast can help turn a movie into a blockbuster. And don't forget the props the actors will use; they're part of the cast, too.

Finally, you need a strong script. A script defines what happens and when. The script determines everything from the dialogue and the stage directions to the surrounding environment.

Director uses all these same ideas and enables you to use them to create a multimedia project. This is similar to the way a real director makes a movie.

> **Note**
>
> The process of using Director to create a movie is often referred to as *Author mode*. Similarly, when a Director movie is playing back inside a projector, it is called *Projector mode*; it is called *Plugin mode* inside a browser.

The Movie

All the parts that make up a project in Director are called a *movie*. A movie contains the information needed to play the project for an end user. All Director projects start with a movie; some projects need only one movie; others use several movies.

The movie is the main file stored on disk. A Director movie has the filename extension `.dir`. Even if created on a Macintosh, the movie should have this extension because it is easier for Windows machines to use the movie.

A *projector* is created from a movie file for playback on the end user's computer. It can also be shocked, or compressed, into a Shockwave movie for distribution on the Internet.

> **Tip**
>
> A Shockwave movie contains the same playback information as a regular movie, but it is compressed. Movies on a CD-ROM project, as well as movies for the Web, can be shocked to reduce the load times from the CD-ROM.

The Stage

The *stage* is what the eventual user of the movie will see (see Figure 1.1). It is where all the text and images appear. All objects on the stage are called *sprites*. The score, described in the next section, controls their position and timing.

Figure 1.1   The stage is where the author of the movie places sprites that should appear when the movie is played back.

When you are creating the Director movie in Author mode, the stage is its own window within the Director application. Remember that the end user of the movie will see the stage only when the projector or Shockwave movie is played on his or her computer.

The stage's background color is either a palette position or an RGB (red, green, blue) value. Its dimensions, or width and height, are expressed in pixels. Common sizes for movies are 512×384, 640×480, and 800×600. They match typical desktop sizes and maintain the standard 4:3 aspect ratio (the ratio of the width to the height). The stage can have almost any dimensions, however. One restriction is that the width must be divisible by 16. This is for efficiency and contributes to Director's capability to show images quickly.

The movie author can also determine the position of the stage onscreen. The position is commonly defined by the location of the upper-left corner of the stage on the screen, also in pixels. Most often, the stage is centered onscreen.

> **Note**   CD-ROM projects tend to use typical screen sizes such as 640×480 or 800×600 pixels to match the end users' typical desktop sizes. Shockwave movies don't have standard sizes, but they are designed to fit in browsers.

The Score

Sprites on the stage are defined by their parameters in the Score window. The vertical dimension of the score defines the layers, which are called *channels* in Director. By default, sprites in higher-numbered channels appear on top of sprites in lower-numbered channels on the stage (for example, character sprites on top of a background sprite). With version 7, up to 1,000 channels are available. There can be only one sprite in each channel per frame of the movie.

Time progresses from left to right in the score, and is defined by frames. When a movie is played, the playback head moves from lower-numbered frames to higher-numbered frames. The time that a sprite is on the stage, defined by its start and end frames, is called the *span of the sprite*, or simply the *sprite span*. A sprite span can range from one frame to all the frames in a movie (see Figure 1.2).

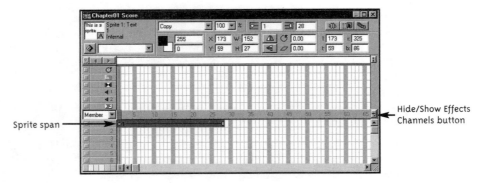

Figure 1.2   Sprite spans appear as horizontal bars in channels in the score.

> Director plays back frames in increasing numerical order. By using behaviors or Lingo, the movie author can control the order in which frames are played. For example, it might be useful to loop on a series of frames until some condition is met, such as the user clicking the mouse or some amount of time elapsing.

The score also has special channels at the top. These are for the movie tempo, current palette, transition effects, and sounds. The script channel, channel 0, is just above the frame strip that separates the special upper channels from the sprite channels. You can hide or reveal the upper channels with the button showing two arrows on the right side of the Score window. Figure 1.2 shows this button.

The Cast

Various assets, or *cast members*, appear in the Cast window for a movie (see Figure 1.3). The Cast window is like an offstage holding area for any object that will appear in the movie. The cast can contain images, sounds, movies, text, and Lingo scripts. Cast members are either created in Director or imported from external files.

Figure 1.3   Cast members for a movie are contained in Cast windows.

A movie can contain multiple casts, and each cast can have an unlimited number of cast members. Casts can exist internally, or they can be external to the movie as separate files. External casts can be shared between movies, which provides a lot of flexibility.

 There is no playback performance penalty for using multiple casts, although the movie may take slightly longer to start playing. So, using multiple casts, both internal and external, is a very effective way to organize your cast members.

Wherever possible, you should name the cast members in your casts. If a cast member changes position in the cast, the score will automatically update to reflect the new position. However, Lingo code and behaviors that refer to the cast member number instead of its name will fail if cast members are moved in the cast. Named cast members help in organization as well.

An additional organizational method is to group cast members in different casts according to their usage. For example, all the cast members used to show an environment (the background and foreground elements) might be stored in a cast called *static elements*. Frames of animation for different characters could be stored in casts named after each character. This helps the movie author keep track of where different cast members are located. Much more information on cast organization can be found in Chapter 4, "Working with Casts."

Inspector Windows

Different types of sprites have different *Inspector windows*, which display pertinent information about text, images, and behaviors. Some properties can be changed directly in the Inspector windows. This is more accurate, but less interactive, than changing them visually on the stage.

 Refer to the Director movie "Chapter01.dir" from the CD-ROM for the examples in this section.

The Sprite Inspector

Explore the Sprite Inspector window by changing values and watching their effects:

1. Click on the sprite on the stage, and then open the Sprite Inspector window by selecting Window, Inspectors, Sprite (see Figure 1.4).

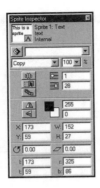

Figure 1.4   The Sprite Inspector window allows direct access to sprite properties.

2. Select the X value field and type 50 to replace the number already there. Press the Tab key to update the sprite properties. Notice that the sprite moves toward the left side of the stage.

3. Select the rotation field (the arrow pointing counterclockwise) and type 85. Notice that the sprite is now rotated 85 degrees clockwise from the horizontal axis.

4. Select other fields and enter values. You can load the movie again to start from the initial properties.

The Sprite Inspector provides access to all the properties of the selected sprite. It is a useful tool, both for reference and adjustment of these properties. The movie author can easily see the important information about the sprite at each frame of the sprite span.

The Text Inspector

Now, examine the Text Inspector window by changing properties and watching the results on the stage:

1. Make sure that the sprite is selected. Display the Text Inspector window by selecting Window, Inspectors, Text (see Figure 1.5).

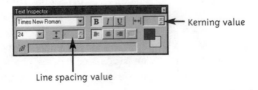

Line spacing value

Figure 1.5   Text properties can be changed quickly in the Text Inspector window. The kerning and line spacing values are adjustable only when Text window is open with the selected cast member or when the text is being modified on the stage.

2. Select and deselect the bold, italic, and underline modifiers by repeatedly clicking on the B, I, and U buttons, respectively. Notice that the text on the stage changes immediately.

3. Choose different fonts and font sizes in the two pull-down menus. Notice that you can type a value in the font size field, but it defaults to the closest allowed value when you update the Text Inspector window by clicking somewhere else.

4. Change the foreground color and background color of the text by double-clicking the color chips on the right side of the Text Inspector window.

Like the Sprite Inspector, the Text Inspector provides access to all pertinent information about text sprites. Because it is smaller than the Text window, it can be left onscreen to modify the properties of text sprites more easily.

The Behavior Inspector

Behaviors from the cast or attached to sprites are visible in the Behavior Inspector window (see Figure 1.6). From here, you can rearrange the order of behaviors on sprites, access the properties of a behavior, or edit the underlying Lingo script.

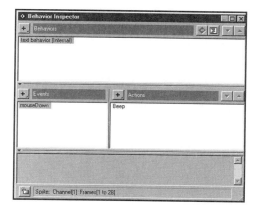

Figure 1.6   Behaviors on a sprite, along with their properties and scripts, are available in the Behavior Inspector window.

Simple custom behaviors can be created directly in the Behavior Inspector, with no Lingo scripting. Simply choose events and actions for the new behavior. Behaviors are covered in more detail in Chapter 7, "Using Behaviors."

Choosing to Use Director

Development teams should perform due diligence on all available multimedia tools in the marketplace before starting a project. Each application has strengths and weaknesses that affect its suitability for a given project. The following two sections cover Director's weaknesses and discuss competing tools.

Limitations of Director

With all the advances in capabilities over the years, Director still has some limitations. Most of these limitations are by design: Director is already a general-purpose tool, and adding more features might lead to degradation in quality and performance. Given the intended development audience, it is important to know what Director can't do.

So that it can be used on a variety of platforms, Director is separated from the low-level hardware of the computers on which it runs. The main functions of the product are even abstracted from the operating system to allow flexibility. Therefore, a developer can never get the same performance from a Director movie as with hand-tuned code in assembly language or C/C++.

Movie playback is available only on Windows and Macintosh computers, even with Shockwave. Director can make projectors only for these operating systems, and Shockwave plug-ins work only with them as well. This is mitigated somewhat with the Save-as-Java function, but this function does not allow the full palette of Director features.

There is no real-time 3D capability with the base Director product. Prerendered 3D artwork can be handled like any other bitmap cast member, though. More products are using real-time 3D, and several third-party plug-ins have been created to fill this need. Refer to Chapter 10, "Working with Xtras," for more information.

To ship projector applications on both Windows and Macintosh platforms, a developer needs two copies of Director—one for each platform. Because it is always a good idea to test and debug movies on both platforms, this isn't a major limitation. Either platform can be used to create Shockwave movies that work on both.

Other aspects of Director can be seen as limitations or constraints. For example, 1,000 score channels might not seem like enough for some users. In practice, however, these properties are not real limitations. At this stage, with such a capable and mature product and a little talent, experience, and vision, Director can be made to do almost anything. Like any good tool, its only real limitation is the craftsperson using it.

Director's Competition

Director is a somewhat unique application, and its strengths have helped it dominate its market. Also, Director is a niche product aimed at a relatively small market, compared with general-purpose software such as word processors and spreadsheets. It is difficult for a new product to make inroads into Director's market. However, Director has a few direct competitors in the marketplace, each of which has strengths and weaknesses. It is important to understand which tool is suitable for a particular project.

Authorware, another Macromedia product, is also a multimedia production tool. It is aimed more toward the education and training markets, and is less of an all-purpose multimedia development platform than Director. It is also significantly more expensive than Director. To find out more about it, check out http://www.macromedia.com/software/authorware.

A product called *mTropolis* was intended to compete with Director. Originally developed by mFactory, it was bought by Quark in 1997 and then cancelled in early 1998. It used more of an object-oriented metaphor to build applications. It was primarily a Macintosh program, but did have Windows playback capability. Version 2 was released by Quark and then officially abandoned. Several third-party mTropolis developers still exist, as does a small but loyal user community.

Bill Appleton, the creator of Hypercard, started Cyberflix to produce a multimedia development tool called *DreamFactory*. DreamFactory is a cross-platform environment that specializes in creating navigable nodes and paths from prerendered 3D artwork. It was never available as a shrink-wrapped product, only by license. Cyberflix created several commercial products entirely in DreamFactory (see `http://www.cyberflix.com`).

IconAuthor and Toolbook are two other multimedia and training tools that are still available. Both are published by Asymetrix (`http://www.asymetrix.com`), and are well supported. These tools can produce projects only for Windows and some UNIX platforms. Like Authorware, they are designed for creating interactive learning and courseware products.

Macromedia has spent considerable time and money to make sure that Director is the best available multimedia development tool. Feedback from Director developers is actively solicited by the company, and suggestions are often incorporated into the next version. Because of this constant refinement and its broad range of features, Director is the choice of more developers than any competing product.

Why Director?

Any software development tool worth using has to provide the three key project factors of software development: time, cost, and content. There are several compelling reasons to use Director to develop interactive multimedia, but the main attractions are that Director offers direct benefits relating to each of those key project factors.

First, Director offers time benefits because it doesn't require a lot of arcane knowledge, nor does it have a tremendously steep learning curve. Developers new to the program can be productive in just a few days.

Director is also cost-effective. Although its price tag may seem high compared to those of other commercial software packages, it is really a bargain for software development because it provides broad coverage of extremely well-supported features. Considering what it would cost to create a tool such as Director from nothing, Director is a steal.

With the rate that computer technology is improving in speed and capabilities, development environments such as Director become more useful. Director is general-purpose, so it's not optimized for one particular task. Although this does have some performance drawbacks when compared to custom programming, with current computer technology, a general-purpose tool such as Director is very often fast enough. Most types of content are reasonable to develop, and many development teams have proven that commercial-quality software products, both on CD-ROM and the Internet, are possible with Director.

Time Benefits of Director

Director has numerous aspects that make it a more efficient development environment than others. The immediacy of the interface encourages experimentation and improvement. It also makes prototyping very easy. The cross-platform nature of Director allows development for Macintosh and Windows within the same time frame. The large and helpful user community can be relied on for solutions and ideas, as well as a ready source of talent. Finally, Director itself is a stable application, so projects developed with it tend to require less testing time and fewer expenses. These benefits are discussed in the following sections.

Prototypes

Quite often, a multimedia production starts with prototyping. General ideas for the interface and interactivity are mocked up to see how they look and behave. Because Director is an integrated environment that includes layout, graphics, and scripting, prototyping is easy. The immediate feedback that Director provides promotes experimentation and creativity.

A more traditional development environment requires the separation of asset creation and programming. Because these two aspects are more closely integrated within Director, changes can be executed more quickly. Additionally, Director does not require the compilation times associated with other programming environments. After a script is edited, the movie author can play the movie to immediately see the effects of any changes. This leads to more experimentation with different ideas and ultimately to a better title.

A good prototype means that the team can see the product shaping up earlier than in more traditional development environments. Because it is easier to change direction earlier in the development cycle, effective prototypes can save time in the schedule. It is far better to find and solve potential problems in a prototype than to discover problems when an entire production team is creating assets and code for a product.

> **Note**
>
> There is a saying in software development: "Get ugly early." Team members should work on the difficult and time-consuming tasks first, such as interface definition and process development. The time it takes to complete these sorts of tasks is often hard to estimate, so getting them finished first helps meet deadlines.

Prototypes built in Director can sometimes become the final product, saving even more time. After the integration of final assets, performance tuning, and bug fixing, a prototype is essentially a finished product.

Cross-Platform Development

Cross-platform development is an area in which Director excels. By using Director, two products (one for each operating system) can be produced almost as quickly and inexpensively as one. Even with the disparity in market share between Windows and Macintosh computers, it is often worthwhile to produce a cross-platform CD-ROM. With Apple on an upswing, due in part to the overwhelming success of the iMac line, it makes even more sense.

Even though full copies of Director for each operating system are required for cross-platform development, it is still only an incremental cost to ship a product for both platforms. The author's experience shows that less than 10% additional effort is required. This effort typically increases sales by at least 10%; possibly more in common multimedia markets such as educational software and children's software.

Given the importance of the Internet today, it can be considered to be a third platform. Although it wouldn't be wise to just make a CD-ROM title accessible for playback from a Web site (because of bandwidth issues), Shockwave provides an efficient way of producing multimedia for the Web, especially from projects being developed in Director. Part of a product could be finessed to be more Internet-friendly (usually with a smaller file size), and then be used on a promotional Web site.

Community of Developers

The worldwide development community consists of more than 350,000 users. This means that it's likely that somebody has already encountered and solved a problem before your team even realizes that there is a problem. Having ready access to these solutions will save the duplicated time of solving problems in isolation. The discussions within the community can also lead to the generation of new ideas; this leads to a better product within the original schedule.

User groups, Web sites, email discussion lists, and newsgroups are all sources for this sort of information. It is important to remember to contribute positively to this community. People generally get back what they put into it.

These Internet links are good places to look for ideas, help, and camaraderie:

- Direct-L—An email discussion list for general Director information. To subscribe, send an email message to `listserv@uafsysb.uark.edu`, with SUBSCRIBE DIRECT-L *Firstname Lastname* in the body of the message.

- Lingo-L—An email discussion list for Lingo-specific issues. To subscribe, send an email message to `Lingo-L@listserv.tamu.edu`, with `SUBSCRIBE LINGO-L` *Firstname Lastname* in the body of the message.

- Xtra-L—An email discussion list for information on Xtras, both included with Director and third party. To subscribe, send an email message to `listserv@trevimedia.com`, with `SUBSCRIBE XTRAS-L` *Firstname Lastname* in the body of the message.

- Macromedia newsgroups—A set of Usenet newsgroups hosted and maintained by Macromedia for all products. You can find them at

  `news://forums.macromedia.com/macromedia.director.basics`

  `news://forums.macromedia.com/macromedia.director.exportforjava`

  `news://forums.macromedia.com/macromedia.director.lingo`

  `news://forums.macromedia.director.multiuser`

- Director Web—A broad and deep reference site for all Director-related information, at `http://www.mcli.dist.maricopa.edu/director/`.

- Director Online—A news- and reference-oriented site for Director, at `http://www.director-online.com`.

- Macromedia—The central site for official Director information, at `http://www.macromedia.com/software/director`.

- Director7.com—A source for tips, tricks, and tools for making Director more productive, at `http://www.director7.com`.

- Clevermedia's Resource Page—A collection of forums, lists, and links to help people use Director, at `http://www.clevermedia.com/resources/`.

- UpdateStage—News, bug lists, and some Xtras organized for easy access. The address is `http://www.updatestage.com`.

- Macromedia User Groups—An explanation of the user group concept and a source for finding one, at `http://www.macromedia.com/support/programs/usergroups/`.

Having a large user community also makes available many potential team members. Because Director is so widely used, even in some college courses, the talent pool is large and readily accessible. In fact, Director's multifaceted nature leads to the availability of well-rounded people from a variety of disciplines. Often, the greatest schedule risk for a project is gathering the full team. Director's excellent talent pool helps minimize this risk.

Stability and Compatibility

Macromedia does extensive feature and compatibility testing of Director on both Windows and Macintosh platforms, and in browsers. It is generally a stable product, and it performs as expected on a wide variety of hardware and peripherals. This can reduce product testing time and schedule risk because incompatibilities are infrequent. The downside is that Director is a proprietary tool, and developers are dependent on Macromedia for fixes to any problems that do arise.

Given the well-tested nature of Director, a development team needs to concentrate only on testing the contents of the product. More attention can be given to making the product better and testing time is minimized.

Cost Benefits of Director

All the timesaving benefits of Director indirectly save costs as well. If a regular-sized team is able to produce a project in a shorter-than-usual time frame, a company will realize cost savings in salaries as well as other areas.

The large talent pool of Director users allows a team to become fully staffed and efficient more quickly. Having properly trained and experienced team members leads to fewer mistakes and a solid product.

As mentioned in the introduction to this chapter, even Director's price is a relative bargain. It seems expensive for individual users, but is very reasonable for companies. From a business point of view, the cost of Director packages is virtually irrelevant. Consider the true cost of developing a high-quality, feature-rich multimedia authoring system. Director's maturity, feature set, and stability would be difficult to duplicate for any amount of money in a reasonable length of time.

Another benefit of Macromedia's attention to compatibility testing is that each developer need not maintain a full compatibility lab. Teams can be relatively sure that computers with different configurations will not create problems. For extra security and to avoid possible customer support costs, external-configuration testing companies are available. This is less expensive than creating a full testing lab and keeping it staffed and up-to-date.

Tip

When it comes to bugs in a product, remember this: Nobody remembers if you ship a day late, but everybody remembers if you ship with bugs.

Applications Suited to Director

As mentioned in Chapter 1, "What Is Director?," Director has some limitations and constraints. The content of a product is dependent on the development tools, but Director places few limits on the type of content it works with. Rather than fight against its limitations, a developer should aim to harness Director's myriad strengths to produce a successful product. Each of the following software categories is well-suited to being developed in Director.

Developing Reference Applications with Director

Reference applications are typically distributed on CD-ROMs because of the large amount of information they are designed to present. As DVD drives become more popular, DVD-ROMs will likely become the preferred method of distribution. Some reference works available now span multiple CD-ROMs, but will fit on one DVD-ROM to make accessing the information more convenient.

Although the type of information in reference titles can vary, these applications typically have one purpose: to quickly present information to a user. Because this type of application does not need to be entertaining, the interface can be fairly spartan while more energy is spent creating and presenting great content.

Director is well-suited for producing reference works. Its built-in tools and objects make creating a functional interface relatively easy. All different types of media (such as video, sound, text, and images) are directly readable by Director, so there is no restriction on the types of information for presentation.

No database of information is ever complete or finished. With Director's Internet capabilities, it is possible to create a reference product that is never out of date. As long it is designed with this function in mind and a server is maintained somewhere, the product can continually update its information.

Examples of this type of product are the following:

- General or specialized encyclopedias
- Historical archives of photos, sounds, and text
- Style guides or media guides for entertainment properties
- Catalogs of items to purchase, courses available, or movies to rent

Developing Educational Applications with Director

Rather than present information simply as a reference title does, educational titles intend to teach information. Some products also track progress and recommend areas of the curriculum that students need to improve their understanding.

Depending on the type of information taught, an educational title could be suited for CD-ROM, the Internet, or both. Some organizations convert textbooks to CD-ROM–based projects because they can enhance a textbook with hypertext links, real-time searching, animation, sound, and even video. Rather than being a static experience, the material can engage the student and make learning enjoyable. Students will tend to stick with the material longer and, if it is presented properly, they will recall it more easily.

Internet learning is becoming more popular and more important. People want to continue learning all their lives, but often don't have the large blocks of time to invest in taking a traditional course. A good Internet course has many of the advantages of a CD-ROM textbook, but is still subject to the bandwidth limitations of the Internet. However, the ability to network with an instructor and other interested students is a major advantage. A well-designed course might integrate a Shockwave-based textbook with live lectures, email assignments, and a chat room for students and the teacher.

> **Note**
>
> It's important to remember that just because information is on a computer does not necessarily make it easier to learn. Care and thought must be used to make computer learning effective and efficient. Teaching is an art and science that takes time to master.

The following types of educational projects are all possible with Director:

- A textbook conversion for distance or home-based learning that is always current, using updates from the Internet
- Instructional simulators to teach specific processes such as operating hazardous machinery or mixing dangerous ingredients
- Drill and practice exercises that are presented at a custom pace, according to past achievements
- Live Internet broadcasts of seminars and lectures, with accompanying slides and audio
- Group brainstorming sessions in a specialized live chat application

The possibilities of using Director, CD-ROMs, and the Internet to teach and inspire are amazing and continue to improve with developers' imaginations and experience.

Developing Edutainment Applications with Director

The word *edutainment* was coined to describe a class of software that's somewhere between educational and entertaining. No specific curriculum is taught nor are overall goals set. Playing educational games emphasizes general problem solving, creative abilities, and coordination skills. The entertainment portion is intended to keep the audience, usually children, interested.

Over the past several years, an important trend has emerged in the edutainment software industry: Families have purchased new computers and kept the older ones around for children to use. This means that many seemingly obsolete computers are still in use, and it presents an opportunity for Director developers because, although Director's performance has increased, the expectations of the target audience have not. It is still possible to make engaging products for first-generation Pentium and PowerPC computers. Windows 95 and MacOS version 7.5 are the oldest operating systems that Director still supports.

Edutainment products are intended for these older computers used by young people. Director's strengths in 2D animation (or playback of prerendered 3D animation), sounds, and interactivity are ideally suited for this demographic. The products do not have to be state-of-the-art, fast-paced games—instead, they can be slower-paced, simpler activities that keep kids entertained while they're learning something.

A storybook metaphor is often used for this type of software. Recognized characters, mostly animated, act out a story at a pace directed by the user. Periodic activities are presented to engage the viewer, enhance the story, and possibly teach a lesson.

Why Director?

Sometimes, an existing media property from a television show or movie is enough to base a product on. The characters are put in a situation that leads to a natural grouping of activities. The user is invited to cooperate or compete with his or her favorite characters in games of skill or problem-solving activities.

The structure and organization of edutainment titles is well-suited to Director. Each of the story screens or activities translates naturally into a Director movie. A hub, navigation, or menu screen—itself a Director movie—brings collections of these movies together. Director's capabilities are so appropriate for edutainment, in fact, that Director has partially defined the category.

Traditional real-world games sometimes make good activities in edutainment software. Checkers, tic-tac-toe, and concentration games can often be used without much customization. Other types of games can be brought to life only on a computer, such as a maze game that never has the same maze twice or exists only in three dimensions.

Ideas for edutainment products are as follows:

- A collection of educational and fun activities with the theme of a movie, television show, book, or original situation
- An interactive adaptation of a story from another medium to the computer
- A series of related challenges that must be mastered to solve an imaginary problem, such as helping heroes catch a villain

Two examples of edutainment titles made with Director are "Casper: A Spirited Beginning Activity Center" by Wayforward Technologies, and "Mindstorms Robotics Invention System" software by Lego. The Casper product is an example of movie characters appearing on CD-ROM. The Lego product is a companion CD-ROM to the Mindstorms Lego kit that contains instructions and challenges.

The edutainment market will continue to evolve as each generation of computer equipment is handed down to the younger generation. As the capabilities of these machines become greater, so does the promise of "stealth learning" through fun and games. It is also an ever-renewing market because another group of children is only a few years away.

Developing Puzzle Adventure Games with Director

Although this category is difficult to describe succinctly, one incredibly successful product can be used as a touchstone: Myst by Cyan Software and Red Orb Entertainment. Myst is a first-person adventure game, in which the user solves many small puzzles in order to solve the overall puzzle of the game. Creating games such as Myst or even its more advanced sequel, Riven, are particularly well-suited to Director.

> **Note**
>
> Although Myst and Riven were not developed in Director, other products in this genre have been. See the section, "Titles Created Using Director," for some examples.

Typically, these puzzle adventure games use hand-drawn or rendered 3D backgrounds and animation. The first-person perspective is used so the player's character does not have to be represented onscreen. Static backgrounds or animated paths and virtual nodes are easy to implement using QuickTime because it is particularly well-integrated with Director.

Even the interactivity of the puzzles is a natural for Director implementation. Although the pace is not as frenetic as that of an action game, smooth animation and interface controls are required—both of which Director excels at. The object-oriented nature of many puzzles is a particularly good fit for Lingo scripting.

Developing Internet Games with Director

The number of people using the Internet continues to grow incredibly, as does the diversity of people on the Internet. Studies and surveys show that Internet use is increasing as a form of entertainment while television use is decreasing.

With the advent of Shockwave, Director became a prime development tool for Internet games and entertainment. Its amazing capabilities, coupled with a relative ease of use, have created a whole new category of games that can be played in Web browsers (such as custom animated greeting cards and classic arcade game remakes).

The bandwidth available to the average consumer hasn't increased at nearly the same speed as the rest of the computer's components. Technology is now in the interesting situation where the processing power available on a consumer-level computer far outclasses the bandwidth of most consumer-level Internet connections.

Shockwave is positioned perfectly to take advantage of this situation. Users need to download the Shockwave playback engine (a browser plug-in) only once. All Shockwave movies play in the same plug-in. This means that only the content and specific game logic need to be downloaded over the slow modem connections.

Many Web sites are using Shockwave games to promote products, or entertain and engage Internet users. Sometimes, a game is created to draw attention to a new movie or television show. Sometimes, games are created just for people to enjoy. Whole sites are appearing that are dedicated to browser games, and most are built with Director and Shockwave.

Check out these sites for good examples of Shockwave games:

- Clevermedia's Shockwave Arcade, at http://www.clevermedia.com/arcade, has simple classic games that are quick to download.

- Macromedia's Shockwave.com site, at http://www.shockwave.com, has a diverse assortment of games and activities (see Figure 2.1).

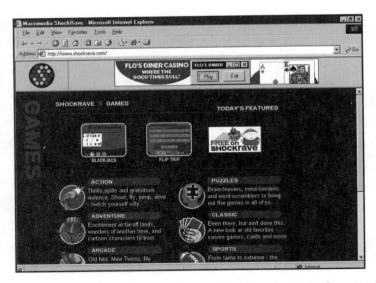

Figure 2.1 The Shockwave.com site offers a collection of games and activities for entertainment-minded Internet users.

Shockwave Internet games cover many of the categories already discussed in this chapter. Examples include the following:

- Reinterpretation of classic arcade games
- Single- or multiplayer trivia games
- Parodies of well-known people, places, movies, or games
- Card games and games of chance

Now, multiplayer Shockwave games are possible because of the Multiuser Xtra included with Director. It enables movies to communicate with one another and central servers. Again, Director's strength of providing useful capabilities to movie authors without requiring complicated implementations is realized.

Developing Internet Sites with Director

Shockwave has become a standard of interactivity on the Internet. It is so fundamental to today's Internet use that both Windows and Macintosh operating systems include Shockwave plug-ins in their default browsers. In addition, end users have downloaded Shockwave more than 70 million times.

The idea of building whole Web sites in Shockwave was almost unthinkable a short time ago. Now it is a viable option, and Windows and Macintosh users are the prime audience. All the benefits of Shockwave (such as interactivity, multiuser options, and animation) can be used to build an entire Web site.

Even if a complete Shockwave Web site is still too radical, Shockwave is perfect for specific components, besides games, of a site. Menus that react creatively to user input are one idea, and live image maps are another possible application.

Shockwave portions of a Web site can receive updated information from the Internet the same way as CD-ROMs built with Director. Imagine a main page implemented in Shockwave that relies on server text files for its information. Daily updates would consist only of changing a few simple files rather than having to edit HTML code.

Many of today's large and popular sites are database-driven. This means that their presentation is determined in real-time, based on user input and queries. Shockwave can do similar tasks by querying other servers on the Internet and presenting the information in a customized inter-face.

Examples of the possible uses of Shockwave on general Web sites are the following:

- Multiuser chat applications
- Custom stock quotes or weather information presented in creative ways
- Advertising banners that react to input such as mouse positions and the time of day

The ubiquity of Shockwave is virtually assured because Macromedia has such a lead over any of its competitors. Its inclusion in the two most popular consumer operating systems makes it accessible without a separate complicated download and installation procedure. If Macromedia chooses to release plug-ins for more browsers and operating systems, it will be even better. Shockwave sites will be positioned to benefit from more users looking for entertainment and enlightenment on the Internet.

Titles Created Using Director

Many commercial and custom multimedia titles and games have been developed in Director. The interactive multimedia industry succeeded in some ways because of Director's strengths and ease of use. The following is a brief selection of the hundreds of products developed by using Director:

Real Pool by Digital Fusion and Wizard Works (http://www.wizardworks.com/realpool.htm)

This real-time, three-dimensional pool game uses a custom Xtra for its amazing graphics. The entire game logic and interface uses Director's native features. It is available for Macintosh and Windows.

Disney's Winnie the Pooh and Tigger Too Animated StoryBook by Creative Capers and Disney Interactive (http://disney.go.com/DisneyInteractive/Pooh/wtpttasb/index.html)

A classic story brought to life on the computer, this product is for children from three to six years old. It presents Winnie the Pooh and his friends in the Hundred Acre Wood and contains several activities that tie to events in the story. The Macintosh and Windows versions are on the same CD-ROM.

Walt Disney World Explorer by Disney Interactive
(`http://disney.go.com/DisneyInteractive/WDWExplorer/index.html`)

The Macintosh version of this reference guide was developed entirely in Director in half the time as the custom-coded Windows version. It is a planning tool to use before visiting Disney World and a souvenir to help guests relive their experience.

Buried in Time by Presto Studios and Sanctuary Woods
(`http://www.prestostudios.com/bit/index.html`)

This is a first-person adventure game that continues the story of The Journeyman Project. The player is a wrongly accused time-police agent who must clear his name by finding the real culprit. It uses computer animation to present a virtual reality experience of several time periods, historic and futuristic.

Director should be considered a viable development tool for a wide variety of applications. Its capabilities fit the requirements of software such as adventure games, reference tools, and educational software.

The additional capability of Director to reduce both time and expense of product development is another strong advantage. Prototypes are easy to develop, a helpful development community exists, cross-platform development is simple, and testing requirements are reduced.

Planning Your Director Project

It is tempting to start working on a Director project right away. Keep in mind that upfront planning makes the production process smoother and results in a better product. The earlier and better you plan, the fewer mistakes your team will make.

This advice assumes that you intend to produce a commercial product with some fixed budget and timeline. If you are just experimenting with Director to explore its capabilities, however, you probably don't need to do as much planning because innovation and inspiration can come at any time.

This chapter does not detail the entire process of planning a multimedia project, but provides an overview of how planning relates to Director projects. The documents that are necessary to properly plan are explained. Deciding on the target platform for the title is explored. After these initial steps, setting up a project schedule is introduced. Finally, you will learn how to develop an effective asset production process.

Creating Planning Documents

In order to build a product, you need a few documents. Often, these documents seem like a waste of time to create, but their benefits outweigh the effort required to make them. These documents include the following:

- Concept document
- Design document
- Functional specification
- Schedule

Tip

Be careful not to go overboard and spend too much time and energy preparing any of these documents. Remember that the team's primary purpose is to produce the end product, not the documents.

Even for small teams, the process of writing the documents is as important as the documents themselves because it forces the team to think in a structured manner about what it's trying to build. A genuine effort at producing these documents will identify areas of concern before they become problems.

Note

Another important reason to create these documents is that they become touch-stones for the team. They keep the vision clear and the intent of the project the same in everyone's mind.

Concept Document

The first document you should create, the *concept document*, defines the overall goal of a project. It should always be short and clear. After the initial idea and discussion, the thoughts about the project should become the concept document. Ideally, it should fit on one or two pages.

In the concept document, you should describe the project in one paragraph or even one sentence. Of course, this leaves some details out, but it does focus on what is important about the project. The following are some examples:

- "The purpose of this CD-ROM multimedia title is to take the characters and story from *Alice in Wonderland* and present them on the computer in an imaginative, entertaining, and engaging way."

- "This Shockwave component will provide visitors to our corporate Web site with a brief introduction to our products and our company philosophy."

- "The textbook *Strength in Materials* will be converted to a DVD-based computer application with additional animations, audio descriptions, videos, and interactive exercises. The progress of the student will be assessed and tracked at the end of each chapter to provide additional study options."

In order to get funding and approval for a project, you often need to present a concept document to the appropriate management structure, potential software publishers, or other financial backers. It should provide estimates of costs and schedules, as well as a clearly stated description of the end product.

You should think about the potential audience when creating the concept document. It does not have to be produced in a word processor, but if the situation warrants, the concept document itself could be a Director movie, a Web site, or a multimedia presentation. When done well, a nontraditional concept document proves the capabilities of the team to potential sources of funding or approval.

Design Document

After the concept document is created and the project is approved, it's time to design the project in more detail. The next document you need to create is a *design document*.

Most multimedia projects can be broken down into discrete screens. Typically, they have different purposes and different background art. For example, a product could start with an introduction screen, proceed to a menu screen, and then proceed to individual topic-related screens. Multiple designers can work on different screens at the same time. If there are many screens in the product, early screens can be designed first and put into production while the later screens are still being designed. This will reduce the overall development time. This is a good way to organize a design document, too.

> **Note**
>
> Typically, a word processor is used to create individual files, one for each screen. This works well because any member of the team will have easy access to the design document for reference.

An individual screen design might be organized like this:

- Overview of the screen, including a sample screen mockup or layout

- Introduction sequence to occur when the user enters the screen, with instructions if necessary

- Normal behavior of the screen

- Game play description, if required
- Exit sequence to occur when the user leaves the screen
- Interface elements with their behaviors, such as rollover animations or dialogue prompts

As progress is made on the design, watch for common elements on each screen. These parts of the design should be collected in one place for reference across the entire project. Global design ideas that are separated like this make updating the design document much easier. The designers don't have to change them for each screen.

The chapters that follow describe efficient ways to implement global design elements within Director. As in the design document, the advantage of this is that implementation needs to occur only once for the project. Also, changes are easier to implement because the team needs to update only one part of the project, and it then cascades automatically throughout the project.

The overall structure of the design document consists of individual files that cover some or all of these topics:

- Introduction
- Educational goals (if applicable)
- Back story (if applicable)
- Flowchart or diagram showing links between screens
- Screen designs
- Global elements

Functional Specification

The design document includes more detail than the concept document, and the *functional specification* provides more depth than the design document. All the details required to produce the project should be included here because the team refers to the functional specification as the final word on implementation.

> Another way of thinking about the functional specification is that the team should be able to complete the project based solely on the functional specification if left alone on a desert island.

All asset names must be included in the functional specification (often referred to simply as the *spec*). The spec lets the artists know what to call the assets as they create them, and lets the programming team know what assets to use to accomplish the design. A file-naming convention should also be created so that filenames are consistent throughout the project.

For small- and some medium-sized projects, it is often satisfactory to create the spec in a word processor as you do the design document. However, for projects of broad scope, the spec should be built as a database because databases are much more flexible than text documents.

It is relatively easy to find custom information from a database. For example, the audio engineer might need a list of all the voice-over audio files for the project. This would be difficult to obtain if the spec were spread across many files with little organization. In contrast, you can use one command to generate the information using a properly formatted and prepared database.

Using a database rather than a text document for the functional specification can involve more work during the design phase, especially if the team is not familiar with databases. However, the time you'll save later, during production, outweighs any penalty at the start of a project.

The basic element of a spec database is the asset. Assets are covered in more detail in later chapters, but for now consider an *asset* to be any file that must be created for the project. Examples are background drawings, animation frames, and sound effects. Each record of the database should contain enough information about each asset for it to be produced by the team, independently of the designer.

Assets in the database should have a structure that links them to different screens where they are used. For example, the same piece of dialogue may be used in more than one screen. Rather than having to create this asset more than once, it contains a reference to all the screens where it is used. This also allows the database user to create custom reports of all the assets necessary for each screen.

Additional information that makes the database more useful are items such as the following:

- Creation date
- Asset type, such as audio, animation, background, or text
- Complementary assets, such as an audio file that must always be played with an animation
- A language-dependent flag to signal this asset needs to change for translated versions of the project

More information on assets, the building blocks of the spec, and the production process to create them is covered later in the chapter.

Schedule

As the design is progressing, the project manager should be building and maintaining a schedule. The concept document often contains some schedule components, but a standalone schedule document with much more detail should also be created.

A project schedule fulfills two main purposes. First, it communicates to the team when each member needs to have his or her individual contributions complete. Second, the project manager uses it to continually track progress and the projected completion date.

It is important for the project manager, or whoever creates the schedule, to include team members as part of the process. Estimates for the length of time and number of people that are required to complete various tasks should come from the team first. The people doing the production are best able to estimate the amount of work on a project. Also, by including them in the process, the project manager creates a greater sense of teamwork and buy-in to the project. People are less likely to question estimates that they provide themselves.

The first level of detail for a schedule should include the various phases of a production. For example:

- Concept approval
- Project design
- Asset production
- Programming
- Testing

Within each of these phases, the schedule should define milestone dates. *Milestones* are quantifiable objectives for the progress of the project. These milestones might apply to a project:

- Design starts
- Green light—concept approved
- Fully staffed
- Prototype complete
- Demo ready for trade show
- Alpha version ready—content complete
- Beta version ready—content frozen
- Final candidate—no known problems
- Release to public

It is very important that each of the milestones be well-defined and communicated to the entire team. The achievement of a milestone depends on a clear understanding of what that milestone means. For example, the alpha milestone can be defined in many different ways. One definition might be: "The Alpha version will have all functions and features operating fully, all content will be integrated even if the asset is not final, and no new features or content will be implemented."

The needs of the project, organization, and team will often determine these definitions. There is no need to find the absolute best correct definition in just have everybody agree on one.

For more details on the timelines of a Director project, refer to the "Planning the Project Timeline" section, later in this chapter.

Determining the Target Platform

A vital component of any project plan is to determine which platforms the project is intended for. This is more complicated than just selecting an operating system to support; it involves thinking about the installed base of potential users, the playback performance required, and the storage needed for all the assets.

One choice regarding the target platform is easy because Director is limited to providing playback on Windows and Macintosh operating systems, regardless of the medium chosen for distribution. Even on the Internet, the Shockwave plug-in exists only for these two operating systems.

It is important to keep your intended audience in the forefront of the target platform decision. Too restrictive a platform (such as Pentium III and G4 only, for example) will severely limit the available audience. Use the minimum platform available to your audience as a guide.

> **Note**
>
> The success of Apple's iMac provides an excellent opportunity for Director developers. Because of its consistent design and capabilities, it is almost like a game console system, and compatibility issues are almost nonexistent. Therefore, the iMac provides a relatively large and easy-to-service target audience.

The Internet

With Shockwave, the Internet has become a viable target platform for Director. Because the end user needs to download the Shockwave plug-in only once, Shockwave movies can be relatively small, which is a big advantage on the Internet.

In fact, the popularity of the Internet has changed the performance bottleneck of many Director applications. Since the multimedia industry began creating products for personal computers, the processor speed has been paramount in determining the performance of a title. Now, the bandwidth of the user's connection to the Internet has become the more important aspect.

All computers sold in the past several years have enough processor power and memory to provide fast performance. But the majority of Internet users are still using analog modems, which offer minimal bandwidth. It has become incredibly important to optimize the size of a Director movie—even more important than to optimize its runtime performance. If the movie is too big to easily download (over 300KB, for example), few people will see it.

One of the major drawbacks of using Shockwave is that the user must download the same Shockwave movie on every visit to a Web site (unless it is still in the browser cache). This limits the usefulness of Shockwave for commonly used applications. However, the site shockwave.com (http://www.shockwave.com) by Macromedia provides a solution.

Along with shockwave.com, a new supersite for Shockwave content, Macromedia has produced a tool for using Shockwave movies more easily. The Shockwave Remote, shown in Figure 3.1, is a small application that can download and store up to five Shockwave movies from the Internet. The user does not even have to connect to the Internet to use the Shockwave movies that have already been downloaded.

Another aspect of Shockwave movie performance is how smoothly it plays after it has downloaded. Because Shockwave movies play back inside a browser, they do not get the complete attention of the host computer. As such, they run more slowly than the same Director movie made into a projector or played back inside Director.

 To demonstrate this difference in performance, open the movie "performance.dir" with Director. It is a fairly simple movie that has three vector shapes animated onstage. It also provides feedback about the frame rate of the movie.

Figure 3.1   The Shockwave Remote is free software from Macromedia that enables users to find Shockwave content easily and download up to five movies to their hard drives for use while offline.

When you run the movie, the stage's Set FPS (frames per second) number shows what playback speed Director is trying to achieve. The Actual FPS number is the actual speed at which the movie is playing (see Figure 3.2). Director refers to the frame rate (FPS) of a movie as the *tempo*.

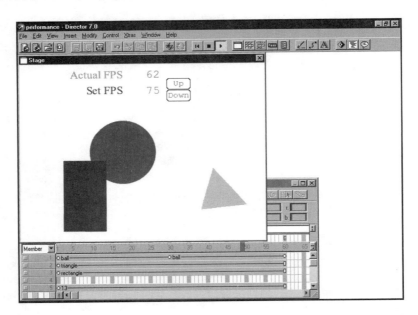

Figure 3.2   With Director running the movie in Author mode, the Actual FPS number matches the Set FPS number, up to a reasonably high number.

Run the movie and watch the two numbers. The movie is set to attempt playback at 60 FPS. The Actual FPS number will vary, depending on the speed of your computer and the other applications running.

Two Up and Down buttons beside the Set FPS number allow you to change the tempo setting for the movie. They modify it in 15-unit increments. Click each button a few times, and watch what happens.

You should be able to increase the tempo setting so much that Director can no longer keep up with it. No matter how high you set the tempo, the movie can run only at a certain maximum speed.

 Now, try running the same movie in a browser (see Figure 3.3). Open the file "performance.html" with your usual browser. If you do not have the Shockwave plug-in installed, you will see a dialog box, prompting you to install it from Macromedia's site.

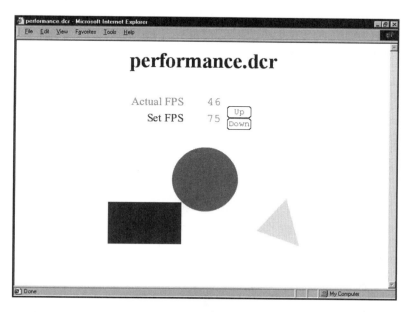

Figure 3.3   The Shockwave movie running inside Internet Explorer does not match the performance of the movie in Author mode. The Actual FPS number stops increasing when it reaches a lower number.

Try clicking the buttons again, and notice how the tempo changes. The maximum tempo here should be substantially lower than the tempo Director could achieve in Author mode. Again, this is because the browser is using some of your computer's processing power, and the Shockwave movie gets only what is left over.

If you want to investigate this phenomenon in more depth, you can try two more steps. First, you can make the movie into a projector and check its performance. (For more information on how to make projectors, refer to Chapter 11, "Shipping a Title.") You should notice that it is close to the performance when in Author mode inside Director. Second, you can try running the Shockwave movie inside another browser and check its performance. You will likely notice a difference in performance between browsers on the same computer.

An important area to consider when using the Internet as a multimedia platform is security. Shockwave is designed to offer users complete data security on their local storage devices. Unlike normal Director movies (or projectors), a Shockwave movie cannot access arbitrary files on a host computer. This means that all the data for a Shockwave movie must reside within the movie or in other locations on the Internet. As you'll see in the next section, a CD-ROM–based Director movie can access data on the Internet, but Shockwave does not allow the reverse.

CD-ROMs

CD-ROMs have become a ubiquitous medium for multimedia distribution. Practically every PC sold today comes with a CD-ROM drive, so the market for projects published on CD-ROMs is large.

The primary advantage of a CD-ROM is that it can hold 400 times more information than a normal 3.5" floppy disk: 650MB compared to 1.44MB. The most significant limitation of the CD-ROM format is its speed. Although performance has increased greatly over the years, CD-ROM drives are still much slower than any modern hard drive.

Besides capacity, which cannot be exceeded, CD-ROM drives have two other critical performance measurements: transfer rate and access time.

Transfer Rate

Transfer rate is the amount of data that the drive can read from a CD-ROM in a fixed amount of time. The original CD-ROM specification provided a transfer rate of 150KBps (kilobytes per second). Transfer rates of drives today are measured in multiples of this rate, reaching as high as 40 times, or 40X, the original rate. This translates to roughly 6000KBps, or 6MBps.

Keep in mind that the transfer rate refers to a best-case performance scenario. In most cases, the real-world performance is significantly less. Most multimedia titles are created to work with CD-ROMs of 4X speed or higher.

The data on CD-ROMs starts at the center and progresses toward the outer edge. Modern CD-ROM drives are able to achieve high transfer rates by reading data from different areas of the disc at different rates. The peak rate occurs at the outer edge of a disc, but this is also the last area to be used on a normal disc. If you put your large transfer-rate-dependent asset files on the disc last, they will benefit from this quirk of performance.

Access Time

The access time of a CD-ROM drive measures the number of milliseconds (thousandths of a second, usually shown as ms) that it takes the drive to start reading data after it receives the request. This means that an access time of 250ms will delay all your assets by one quarter-second when they're loading off the CD-ROM.

In many cases, access time can actually be a more important performance characteristic of a drive than its transfer rate. No matter how quickly a drive can read the data after it gets started, the perceived performance is dependent on starting to read the data quickly.

Fortunately, modern CD-ROM drives have much better access times than previous generations did. A typical drive today has an access time in the range of 50ms to 100ms. But, when compared to a normal hard drive access time of between 5ms and 10ms, this is still quite slow. A CD-ROM, although excellent for distribution, is not always the best choice for a playback medium if absolute performance is required.

Because Director does not depend on any particular medium for storing its files, it is up to the designer to plan where the files will reside. Knowing the relevant characteristics of various storage media is important. When planning your Director project, consider storing some of the most-used and performance-critical files on the user's hard drive. Leave the larger files on the CD-ROM, where they will not burden a user with a large install requirement.

Note

Remember that Director can link easily to files on the Internet. Even though the Internet is generally much slower than either CD-ROMs or hard drives, it has one important advantage: flexibility. Using files on the Internet for information that is likely to change can be a powerful tool; it enables you to keep your title up-to-date after the user has installed it.

DVD-ROMs

DVD-ROMs are similar in many ways to CD-ROMs. They have very large storage capacities, ranging from about 5GB (gigabytes) up to 17GB. DVD-ROM drives are at least as fast as modern CD-ROM drives for both access times and transfer rates.

Because DVD-ROM is a newer technology than CD-ROM, far fewer computers have DVD-ROM drives than CD-ROM drives. But the technology is growing rapidly and will surely overtake the number of CD-ROM drives within a few years. An advantage of recent DVD-ROM drives is they can read CD-ROMs as well as DVD-ROMs.

Unlike CD-ROMs, the equipment required to make DVD-ROMs is still very expensive. Writable DVD-ROM machines cost several thousand dollars, compared to a few hundred dollars for CD-RW (CD rewritable) drives. Based on historical data, however, these prices will continue to fall over time until the cost of DVD writers is on a par with that of CD writers. For right now, however, this makes DVD-ROM development more expensive than CD-ROM development.

Note

DVD-ROM drives are typically installed on higher-performance, more modern computer systems. Therefore, if you target DVD-ROM as a delivery medium, your target audience will generally have more capable computers as well. This might be desirable for a performance-intensive title such as an action game.

Planning the Project Timeline

For any professional Director development project, planning the *timeline* is essential. An experienced and efficient development team can provide accurate estimates and achieve these milestones, which can also contribute to cost savings and timeliness to the market.

Estimating the amount of time required to complete tasks is a critical skill. It involves both art and science. With experience, estimating becomes easier until it is second nature. It's a good idea to start with short tasks when working on estimates for a project timeline. They are often easier to estimate, and provide building blocks for larger tasks.

While working on a project, it is vital to track the time spent on a task against the estimate. This is the best way to learn how to estimate better for next time. It also gives a clear understanding of the team's progress.

Do not measure progress in terms of percentage complete because it has little meaning and can lead to problems with the schedule. Often, the tasks involved in a Director project have never been accomplished before, so it is impossible to accurately know what percentage is complete until the task is finished. Instead, use the concept of days remaining for progress tracking. (If the tasks are very short or very long, you can use another unit, such as hours or months.) This method involves re-estimating the time required to complete the task and is always more honest and accurate than a percentage-complete measurement.

Tip

Often, tasks in Director seem to conform to the 90–10 rule: 90% of the work takes 10% of the time, and the last 10% takes the next 90% of the time. Of course, this is facetious, but the point is that it is often easy to get a project mostly done, but finishing the details can take an inordinate amount of time. Keep this in mind while estimating.

Be careful of dependencies within the project. Some later tasks are dependent on the results from earlier tasks, and you should make sure to schedule them in the logical order. For example, a Director movie for your project cannot be completed until all the assets are ready for inclusion.

Always include in your timeline estimates of time at the end of the project for testing and quality assurance. Even small Director projects can become so complicated that the interdependencies of the components are hard to predict. The product testers should be given enough time to find problems and verify that they are fixed before the title is delivered.

Finally, consider including time in the schedule (or even after the project is complete) to verify the functional specification against the product. Often, there is just not enough time during the production to keep the spec current with the rapidly evolving product. Future work on the title, such as revisions or translations, is much easier with an accurate functional specification.

The Asset Production Process

The asset production process is a vital component to any Director project. Efficient planning before the project starts will result in fewer misunderstandings and mistakes. The quality of the assets will be higher and the schedule will progress more smoothly.

The three steps to the asset-production process are generating the source assets, preparing them for use, and integrating them into a Director project. Version control is important throughout the process.

Source Assets

Source assets are any assets that need to be manipulated before they can be used with Director to create the project. Artists, musicians, designers, and others create them in various media, both physical and electronic, such as the following:

- Videotapes of live action
- Hand-drawn frames of animation
- Musical performances
- Sculptures or models
- Paintings or illustrations

Source assets should be created with just enough quality for their application. When the quality level is high enough, expensive cleanup work is avoided in the preparation phase. To keep the process efficient, avoid using overly high-quality source assets; the extra details will be lost and only cause unnecessary delays. For example, do not use film to capture a scene that will appear only at quarter-screen size in the product.

Note Devise a proper archival strategy for all the source assets for a project. Because of the time and expense required to create the assets, they are quite valuable. Good organization standards make them accessible when they're needed again.

Asset Preparation

Inexperienced Director developers often overlook or underrate the asset preparation step in the production process. Before a source asset can be used in a Director movie, it must be prepared by using a variety of methods, including the following:

- Videotapes need to be captured digitally, edited, and compressed for playback.
- Animation frames need to be scanned digitally, colored, and assembled in the proper order.
- Music must be digitized into audio files of the proper format, bit-depth, and sample rate.

- Sculptures could be photographed or scanned in three dimensions, depending on the application.

- Paintings can be scanned, retouched digitally, made the proper size, and reduced to the correct bit-depth if necessary.

The first time you prepare a new type of source asset for production, you have to develop a new process. Trial-and-error, research, and previous experience will lead to the optimal procedure. Experimentation with different methods, tools, and parameters is essential. Ideally, this experimentation is complete before production starts.

As with the design stages, asset preparation must be properly documented. Keeping track of the state of all the assets makes progress-tracking possible. Assets should flow through the processes efficiently to make the best use of time.

Tip

Consider using spreadsheets or even a database to track assets. Few things are more frustrating than not knowing where the latest approved asset resides. With proper tracking, assets are not lost and everyone knows what assets to use.

Integrating Assets into a Director Movie

After the assets are created, they need to be incorporated into Director casts and movies. Proper file formats are essential at this stage because Director can import only certain formats for each type of asset. Refer to Director's documentation and help files for a comprehensive list of these formats for each development platform. If your team is developing a cross-platform title, it is important to agree on common formats that both Macintosh and Windows versions of Director can use.

The most common method of asset integration is to import the files into Director casts. There are several other options available, though. For example, Director can reference assets in external files while running. The exact method of integration depends greatly on the specific application. Refer to Chapter 4, "Working with Casts," for more information.

Version Control

Very rarely is the first version of an asset supplied for Director integration the one used in the final product. It may have been a placeholder asset, intended for a prototype; or design changes may have necessitated a different asset. This is a fact of multimedia development, and it is best to account for it when planning the project.

Version control refers to the procedures used to track various iterations of the assets. Proper version control means that everyone is confident that they are using the latest asset. New versions should replace older assets easily so that no time is wasted.

Team members are more likely to experiment with making the assets better if they have a version control system. That way, if the changes integrated into the project do not work any better than a previous version, it is easy to roll back to the best earlier version. When changes are tracked, it is also easier to find where mistakes are made so they can be prevented later.

The exact process of version control can be hotly debated within a team. Some prefer including the version in the filename. This can cause problems because it means that Lingo code and behavior properties have to be changed every time a new version is supplied. If the same filename is used throughout a project, these sections need never be updated.

A simple method of tracking versions is to use subfolders to store assets. As long as the team understands that current versions will always be in one place, this system works well. Older versions are put into subfolders named with the version number or description, so you can easily revert to an older version simply by copying the file from the correct folder.

Large, complex projects benefit from a professional version control system, which is basically a specialized database with set rules and procedures. Users access the database by using supplied client software. They can be operated over a network and can make version control very easy.

Microsoft and Metrowerks make version control software called Visual SourceSafe. Microsoft provides clients (special programs for accessing the version control database) for Windows systems, and Metrowerks provides them for Macintosh systems. Only one database is required because it is platform-independent; the clients are compatible. This software is relatively easy to set up, learn, administer, and use. Teams with projects containing more than a few hundred assets should seriously consider making the investment in such version-control software.

Note

Information on Visual SourceSafe is available on the Internet at http://msdn.microsoft.com/ssafe/ and http://www.metrowerks.com/desktop/mwvss/.

Planning the Interactive Portfolio

In this chapter, the process of planning a Director project was introduced. Tools such as the concept and design documents are invaluable for the early stages. It is vitally important to decide on a target platform before going too far into production. A good project timeline allows the team to track progress and estimate a completion date. Development of an efficient asset production process should occur before it is required. The three stages of production (source, preparation, and integration) make up this process. A version-control scheme will lead to a better project and less wasted time. Consider using a professional system such as Visual SourceSafe for the best results.

To apply the concepts from each chapter to a real-world project, you will create an interactive portfolio that you can easily customize for other uses by the time you have finished the book. At the end of each remaining chapter in this book, a set of steps will be provided to lead you through the creation of another aspect of the portfolio. This chapter starts with sample planning documents.

> **Note**
>
> Specific information relevant to the author is used to create the portfolio. Feel comfortable replacing this information with your own. This way, the final product will reflect your unique achievements.

Portfolio Concept Document

Any Director project should start with a concept document, however small. It provides initial direction for the project and helps the people working on the project think ahead to possible problems.

The following list of items outlines my concept document for the interactive portfolio project:

- "An interactive portfolio will be created to demonstrate the concepts learned in each chapter. The portfolio will integrate text and other assets to show the experience and skills of the movie author. Buttons and other interface items will respond to user actions."

- "Files used to make the portfolio are provided on the CD-ROM accompanying the book. Readers are free to replace files and information with more personal items."

- "There is no budget for this project except for the movie author's time. No commercial software, beyond Macromedia Director, is required to complete the project."

- "The schedule is variable, according to how the reader completes each chapter. Additional time may be spent between chapters on optional material, and at the end of the project for further personalization."

You should compose your own concept document by substituting any specific information to fit your own planning schedule.

Portfolio Design Document

Because this is a relatively small project, the corresponding design document is also small. It mainly expands upon the concept document by providing more details. Various areas of the project are introduced and more information about the target platform is covered.

Following is the sample design document for the portfolio project:

- "The purpose of the interactive portfolio is twofold. First, it will demonstrate practical applications of the concepts covered in each chapter. Second, it will provide the reader with a framework for creating their own portfolio in Director."

- "The target platform consists of low-end computers running either Windows or Macintosh operating systems. A 90MHz Pentium or 90MHz PowerPC processor, 640×480 color graphics, 16MB of RAM, and a quad-speed CD-ROM drive are the minimum requirements. An Internet connection is optional, but will provide more features."

- "A Shockwave version of the portfolio is possible, but it is beyond the scope of the sample project. Readers might want to replace any large files with smaller versions to make the portfolio Internet-friendly."

- "The portfolio will consist of the following main areas (see Figure 3.4 for a sample state diagram):

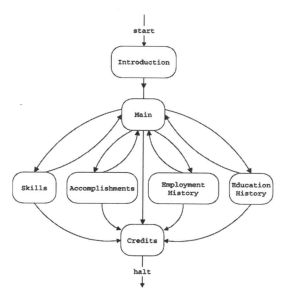

Figure 3.4   This state diagram shows the main areas of the interactive portfolio and the program flow between them.

Introduction screen with animation—This screen is noninteractive, and introduces the subject of the portfolio with score-based animation.

Main hub screen with navigation buttons and idle animations—This screen is the gateway to all other areas of the product. Buttons are presented that allow the user to jump to each area in any order. Idle animations play continuously to keep the screen alive. Rollover highlights provide immediate feedback.

Skills screen with a list of specific knowledge and experience—A concise list of important skills are shown on this screen. Internet links are provided, if possible.

Accomplishments screen with a list of completed projects—This screen lists the major projects that the movie author has worked on. Links to relevant Internet information are provided where applicable.

Employment History screen outlining previous and current jobs—A list of relevant work experience appears on this screen. Titles and responsibilities from each position accompany Internet links to the company's Web site.

Education History screen with information on degrees, certificates, and qualifications—Courses, university or college degrees, and certifications are shown on this screen. Internet links provide an avenue for more information about each institution and course.

Credits screen with contact information—The screen is vital so the end user knows how to contact the movie author. It will pause to allow time to copy the information. Additionally, the Made With Macromedia logo is displayed immediately before the movie terminates."

- "There will be several global elements that are used in a majority of the screens. A Quit button, Return to Main Menu button, screen border, and interface sounds are examples. These should be stored in a shared section of the project so each screen uses the same source element."

- "No significant preprocessing is required for this project. All needed files are supplied on the CD-ROM accompanying the book."

- "The stage size is 640 pixels wide by 480 pixels high. The color depth is 24-bit (true color). The tempo is 30 frames per second. The stage background color is black."

This sample design document is obviously intended for the project that goes along with this book. A real interactive portfolio would have some differences. For practice, try writing your own design document as if you were creating the portfolio without the aid of this book.

Portfolio Functional Specification

The functional specification is specific for this project because the portfolio is built from instructions in each of the following chapters in this book. The project section at the end of each chapter is, in effect, the functional specification.

The naming convention will also be provided in the project section. Asset filenames for import, and movie and cast filenames will be specified in the associated step.

If you choose to deviate from the steps by using your own information or adding other asset files, the project section will no longer represent your portfolio. Formally track your additions and changes to simulate keeping the functional spec updated during production.

Portfolio Schedule

Because the portfolio is being created as part of the progression of concepts in the book, the schedule does not reflect a real-world project exactly. A sample schedule for this project follows.

- "This interactive portfolio project starts when the reader nears the end of Chapter 3. By the end of Chapter 11, the project will be complete as specified. Continued improvements to the project may take place when the reader is finished the book. A chapter-by-chapter schedule is outlined as follows."

Chapter 3, "Planning Your Director Project"—The project is introduced and documents describing the project are created. The basic structure of the project is defined and some global elements are introduced.

Chapter 4, "Working with Casts"—Casts for the movie are discussed and created. Several cast members are imported and created for the introduction movie.

Chapter 5, "Creating the Score"—The score animation for the introduction movie is discussed and created. This movie is noninteractive, and links to the main movie when playback finishes.

Chapter 6, "Working with Movies"—The structure of the project is created using separate Director movies for each section. They are linked together using basic Lingo behaviors.

Chapter 7, "Using Behaviors"—The introduction of behaviors allows greater interactivity to be added to the project. Different button states and scripted animation are added.

Chapter 8, "Understanding Scripts"—Some more advanced scripting is added to the portfolio. Behaviors are created to personalize the experience for the end user.

Chapter 9, "Integrating Various Media Types into Director Projects"—More media are added to the movies. Text fields are created with Internet hyperlinks to relevant sites. Sounds are added.

Chapter 10, "Working with Xtras"—The use of Xtras is explained in the context of a portfolio. Xtras required for the project are identified.

Chapter 11, "Shipping a Title"—The final preparation for shipping the portfolio is accomplished. A projector is created that contains all the Director files necessary for the portfolio.

- "The typical reader will require one evening to complete each chapter's project section. Additional time may be required to customize the project."

Using this schedule as a starting point, apply each stage of the process to complete the portfolio to your specific situation, and create a unique schedule for your project. Attach completion dates to each stage, and track your progress in terms of days remaining. Allow a bit of slack time between sections for customization and unforeseen circumstances.

Portfolio Version Control

All the source asset files that were used to create the portfolio are supplied in final form on this book's CD-ROM. Movie and cast files that are created throughout the course of the project need to be stored on your hard drive in a folder called "ChapterX," where X is the chapter number for the part of the project that you completed most recently. As the project section of each chapter is started, the previous files will be copied into the chapter folder for safekeeping.

Files that you choose to create for customization of the portfolio can be archived in a similar manner. Store older versions in successive folders, and keep the latest version in the current working folder. The size of the project does not require using a full-version control database. As an optional exercise, you are welcome to experiment with one, however.

Wrap-up

By the time you complete this chapter's project section, you should have a concept document and design document that is specific to your own portfolio. Any changes to the functional specification should be documented if you want to follow the customization route. A schedule with dates of completion for each chapter's phase of the project should be created and tracked.

Working with Casts

The cast in Director is an off-stage holding area where cast members reside. An asset—be it video, pictures, or audio—must be in the cast before it can be used onstage in the movie. (There are exceptions to this rule, but they have to do with Lingo coding, so they aren't covered in this chapter.)

Cast members are different from sprites in Director. A *cast member* is an object that does not appear onstage on its own, whereas a *sprite* is the onstage representation of a cast member. A cast member can be used by multiple sprites simultaneously, and each sprite is composed of only one cast member.

Cast member names can be critical because they can make casts and scores much easier to understand and manipulate. Consider the naming convention for cast members as carefully as you consider the naming convention for assets. Short, coded names are better than long, explanatory ones. For example, use IN01A rather than Introduction First Animation. Longer names seem easier to read, but are harder to automate and reference in Lingo. The short forms quickly become second nature.

Tips and Tricks for Importing Casts

The most common way to add assets to a cast is by importing them from files. The files for these assets can exist on a local disk, a network server, or the Internet. Open the File menu and select the Import command to open the Import Files into dialog box, as shown in Figure 4.1.

Figure 4.1   The Import Files into dialog box is composed partially of a typical operating system file management dialog box that you can use to navigate around the local and network drives. To import files directly into another cast, first select the desired cast window and then use the Import command.

Double-click files in the dialog box to add the selected file to the import file list. You can select multiple files to import, even from different directories and drives, in one step. The order in which the files appear is the same order in which the new cast members appear. You can change this order by using the Move Up and Move Down buttons.

It is important to keep in mind that files shown in the dialog box might not all import correctly or at all. Director does not filter the files shown based on their file types, so it is up to you to convert the files to types that Director can import. Refer to Director's help files under the heading "About Import File Formats" for a complete list of supported files.

The Media drop-down list includes an option for linking to external files. This is a powerful tool for creating innovative Director movies. Refer to the section later in this chapter titled "Integrating External Cast Members," page 66, for more information.

To import assets from the Internet, follow these steps:

1. Use the Internet button to bring up the URL dialog box.

2. Type in the exact link for the asset you want to import:
   `http://www.companyname.com/logo.gif`, for example.

Internet-based assets are most powerful when used in combination with the Link to External File media option because they are reimported every time the movie is played, which means the asset can change on the Internet, and the movie will automatically reference the updated asset. The section "Integrating External Cast Members," later in this chapter, explains linked assets in more detail.

For nonlinked assets, it is easier to download the asset file first to a local or network drive by using your browser, and import it normally from there.

After you click the Import button, you might get additional dialog boxes. For example, if you are importing bitmap asset files, you might need to import their palettes as cast members as well. Based on the selections you make on these dialog boxes, you can choose to have new palettes created or to use an existing palette from the casts. Figure 4.2 shows an example of this dialog box for a bitmap image file.

You should carefully plan before you import assets with palettes into Director. Be sure that you know the desired bit-depth of the assets before you begin to import them. Director presents the option to remap or dither images to an existing palette, but may not do the best conversion. It is much safer for you to preprocess images in a tool such as Equilibrium DeBabelizer (`http://www.equilibrium.com`) or Macromedia Fireworks (`http://www.macromedia.com`). These utility programs convert images between various formats and color depths. Their batch modes take a lot of the drudgery out of preprocessing images. Preprocessing ensures the highest-quality images and the least confusion while importing.

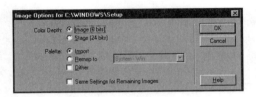

Figure 4.2 This dialog box appears when a bitmap image is imported. Director needs more direction on how to deal with the image as it is imported. The color depth and palette are selected. If more than one image is to be imported with the same settings, use the Same Settings for Remaining Images option.

Creating an Empty Cast Member

One of the features of Director for creating interactivity is its capability to change the cast member of a sprite on stage. This is the basis for animation that is controlled by Lingo. Also, button sprites that respond to mouse movement use this technique.

In the case of animation, it is sometimes desirable to start with a sprite that uses an empty cast member. This technique allows the sprite to stay on stage in its assigned spot without appearing to the end user. When the animation starts, the empty cast member is changed to the cast members of the frames of animation.

Sprites should maintain the same media type while this dynamic switching of cast members takes place. Therefore, an empty bitmap cast member should be used as a placeholder for other bitmap cast members. The following steps show how to create and use an empty cast member for animation:

1. Open the file "emptymember.dir" from the Chapter4 folder on the CD-ROM. This file contains one shape cast member and two behavior cast members. Figure 4.3 shows how this movie starts.

2. Select the first empty cast member position by clicking it. Use the Import command to open the Import dialog box. Navigate to the Chapter4 folder on the CD-ROM and double-click the file "earth.gif" to add it to the import list. Figure 4.4 demonstrates this step.

3. Click the Import button, and an options dialog box appears. Animated GIF files can be imported as an Animated GIF or as a Bitmap Image. For this example, you want all the frames of the animated GIF, so choose the Animated GIF option. This is shown in Figure 4.5.

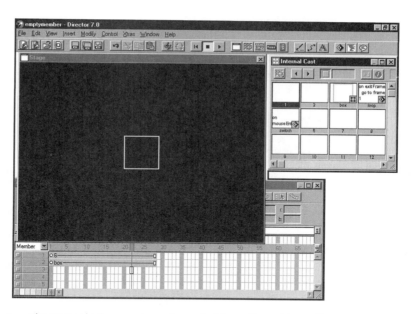

Figure 4.3   The rectangle shape cast member called *box* will provide a rollover target area. The two behavior scripts are provided to simplify the example.

Figure 4.4   Use the Standard Import selection from the <u>M</u>edia menu. This imports the entire contents of the image file into the cast.

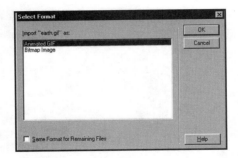

Figure 4.5 This dialog box allows the movie author to select what format the image file should be imported as. If Animated GIF is chosen, as in this example, all the frames of the GIF file are imported together. The Bitmap Image option imports only the first frame of the GIF file.

4. Click the OK button to complete the import. A new cast member called *earth* is created in the Internal cast. Figure 4.6 shows it in the first cast member position because you selected this before starting the import process.

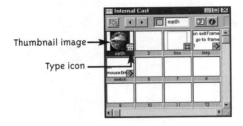

Figure 4.6 A thumbnail image of the cast member helps identify it in the cast window. The icon in the lower-right corner of the thumbnail identifies the type of this cast member.

5. Select the second cast member position in the cast. This is where you are going to create the empty cast member. Open the Paint window by selecting <u>W</u>indow, <u>P</u>aint. Figure 4.7 shows the empty Paint window with this cast member selected.

6. Because you want this to be an empty cast member, you will not create anything in the main Paint window. If you were to close the window at this point, no cast member would be created. If a name is given to the cast member, however, you will achieve the desired result of an empty cast member. Type *empty bitmap* into the cast member name area of the Paint window. This is shown in Figure 4.8.

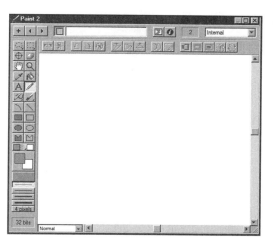

Figure 4.7   The Paint window is a built-in image-editing tool. Use it to create bitmap cast members from scratch or to modify members created by importing files.

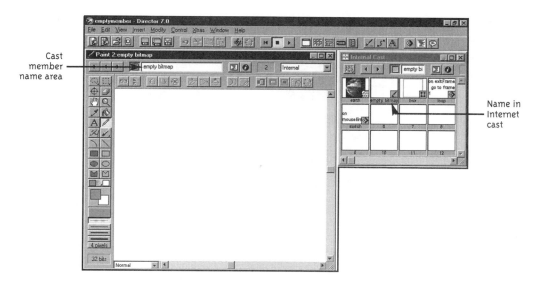

Cast member name area

Name in Internet cast

Figure 4.8   Notice how the cast member in the Internal cast window immediately reflects the new name of this cast member.

7. Close the Paint window to complete the creation of the empty cast member. Drag it to the score window, and place it in channel three just beneath the sprite called *box*. It is important to put it in the proper position because the "switch" behavior depends on this information. Figure 4.9 shows the correct layout. (More information about the score is contained in Chapter 5, "Creating the Score," page 81.)

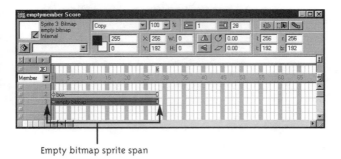

Empty bitmap sprite span

Figure 4.9 The horizontal bars in the score are called *sprite spans*. They represent the range of frames in which each sprite appears onstage.

8. Select the stage window to bring it to the front. Play the movie and notice that the yellow box stays empty. The "empty bitmap" cast member is on the stage, but it does not show anything because it doesn't contain any information. Roll the mouse cursor over the yellow box, and the animation of the Earth rotating appears inside it. Figure 4.10 shows what this looks like.

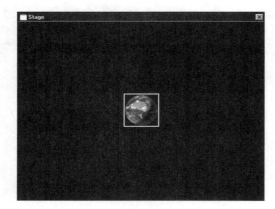

Figure 4.10 The "switch" behavior simply switches the cast member associated with sprite channel three whenever the mouse enters and leaves the yellow box. This has the effect of making the animated Earth appear only when the mouse is over the box.

Although rather simplistic, this example shows how to import an external file to use as a cast member. It also demonstrates the use of an empty cast member for creating interactivity. It was necessary to include some steps that have not been covered yet to complete the sample—that information on the more advanced topics is included in later chapters. A finished version of this movie is on the CD-ROM in folder Chapter4 with the name "emptymember_finished.dir."

Multiple Casts

For several versions, Director has supported the use of multiple casts. Originally, multiple casts provided a workaround for the limited number of cast members allowed per cast. Now, because a virtually unlimited number of cast members are allowed per cast, this allows better organization of individual Director movies and entire projects.

Because each cast can now hold 32,000 cast members, it is very easy for a cast to become disorganized. Using multiple casts lets you categorize the cast members in whatever way makes sense for the project. Well-organized casts not only help you, the original author, keep track of cast members, but also make it easier for another person to understand the movie's structure.

The method of organization you choose is not important, as long as it makes sense for your movie. You might choose to create different casts for different types of assets or for different sections of the movie.

For example, you can have cast names organized by media type:

- Behaviors
- Text
- Sounds
- Movies
- Images

Or, you can organize movie sections by cast names:

- Loading screen
- Introduction
- Options
- Game
- High-score list
- Reward sequence

Whatever method you choose, be sure that it makes sense for your project and, if applicable, for the rest of the development group.

  Refer to the files "media.dir" and "sections.dir" on the CD-ROM for examples of Director movies that use multiple casts.

There are two basic kinds of casts: internal and external. You'll learn more about these types of casts later in the chapter, but for now, you just need to know that organizing a movie's cast can involve using both types of casts.

Creating a New Cast

You can create a new cast using one of the following three methods:

- Select the New, Cast command from the File menu.
- Select Modify, Movie, Casts, and then click the New button in the Movie Casts dialog box that appears.
- In any cast window, select the New Cast item from the drop-down menu. Figure 4.11 demonstrates how to use this menu.

Cast selection icon

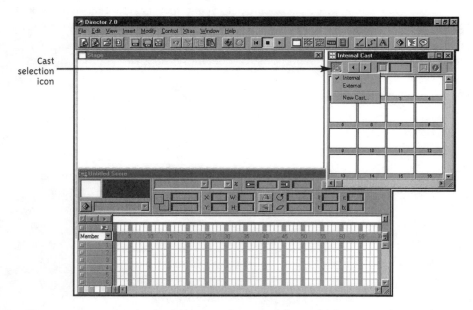

Figure 4.11   You can use the grid icon in the upper-left corner of a cast window to select another cast. If you hold down the [Alt] (Option) key before you click, the cast you select will open in a new window.

Moving Members Between Casts

It is possible to move and copy cast members between casts. Moving helps with cast organization. Copying a cast member is useful if you want to have several sprites that look exactly the same but are based on different cast members.

Follow these steps to move or copy a cast member:

1. Open both the source and destination cast windows.
2. Arrange the windows so it is easy to see the original cast member in the source cast and the desired position in the destination cast.
3. Drag the cast member from the source cast to its new position in the destination cast. You can hold down the [Alt] (Option) key to copy a cast member rather than move it.

When you move cast members, keep in mind that the score will automatically update to reflect the new position of each cast member. Behaviors and other Lingo scripts may not necessarily reference the cast member by name, however. Use caution when moving cast members, especially between casts, if they are referenced by scripts. If a cast member moves and the script references its old position in the cast, rather than its name, the script will not work correctly.

Exploring Internal and External Casts

Director offers two types of casts: internal and external. In practical use by the movie author, they are essentially the same. The main difference is that internal casts are stored within the movie file that uses them. External casts, in contrast, are separate files (with a `.cst` extension) that a movie file references. The next two sections detail these differences and provide sample uses for each type.

Internal Casts

The default type of cast in Director is *internal*. This simply means that the cast is stored internally with the movie. Whenever the movie is saved, the cast is saved with it. Internal casts are easy to manage because they do not create separate files.

There is no simple way for other movies to access members in an internal cast. You should use internal casts for cast members that are not used in any other movie in the project.

Internal casts are listed in the order in which they are created, and you cannot change this order easily. Figure 4.12 shows the order of casts in the movie "sections.dir," referred to earlier in this chapter.

Figure 4.12   The drop-down menu available from the cast window shows the order of casts in the movie.

The order is important for organization, for two reasons. First, you see this order every time you look at the cast list. Second, Director looks for cast members across casts in this order when the cast member is referenced by its name.

If a script refers to a cast member by name, Director finds the first cast member with that name (according to the order of the cast list) and ignores any other cast members with the same name. (It is possible to reference cast members by both their names and the cast that contains them, but not all scripts do this by default.)

The previous section, "Creating a New Cast," provides instructions on how to create an internal cast.

External Casts

External casts are created and used the same way as internal casts; however, Director saves *external casts* as separate files.

The main reason you use an external cast is to share cast members across multiple movies. Each movie in a project can access a shared external cast exactly as if it owned the cast completely. This simplifies production by encouraging reuse of cast members.

> **Note**
>
> In previous versions, Director had only one external cast available, called the *shared cast*. Now, Director can use many external casts, named as you choose. It's a good idea to use the standard filename extension .cst for clarity.

The cast members of an external cast can be modified independently of any Director movie. If a cast member must be changed or fixed, it needs to be done in only one place. All the movies that use that cast will automatically use the updated cast member.

This can be especially important when a team is working on a project. As some team members work on the movies, others can work on external casts behind the scenes at the same time. If done properly, this can save time and make the team more efficient.

External Casts for Multiple Languages

Projects that contain assets in multiple languages are ideal candidates for external casts. The same movie can be used with different casts, each containing assets for a different language. The movie will appear in the language determined by whichever cast is used. These steps illustrate the process:

1. Create an external cast with the name language.cst or something similar.

2. Place all the language-dependent cast members in this cast. This includes members that use text or audio in a specific language.

3. Use the external cast as normal to create the movie file.

4. Copy the files to a new directory to start work on the next language.

5. Replace all the cast members in the external "language" cast with their corresponding cast members in the next language. For example, the "title" cast member should be in the same place in both casts, only in different languages. Do not modify any other parts of the movie.

6. The same movie file can be distributed with different language casts, and it will appear in the corresponding language without extra work.

With a bit of planning, this can facilitate the often-arduous task of shipping a project in multiple languages.

Tip

Do not change the names or the order of cast members in shared external casts, if possible. Director often figures out the changes, but sometimes they cause problems. If you must do this, be sure to check the changes in every movie that uses the cast. As an example, two movies may expect to find a cast member named "logo" in a shared external cast. The movie author may change the name of this cast member and modify the current movie to work correctly. The second movie that uses the same cast will not work anymore unless it is also modified.

External Casts for Different Color Depths

Another reason to use external casts could be to make movies that work in different color depths. As when creating projects for different languages, you can create external casts with image assets for palette-based and true-color playback:

1. Create an external cast with the name images.cst or something similar.

2. Place all the true color (24- or 32-bit) image cast members in this cast. Typically, all the bitmap cast members should be included.

3. Use the external cast as usual to create the movie file.

4. Copy the files to a new directory.

5. Open the "images" cast window and select all the cast members.

6. Use the Modify, Transform Bitmap command to change the color depth of all the cast members. Figure 4.13 shows the resulting dialog box.

7. The palette you choose should be determined in advance. Shockwave movies intended for the Internet should use the Web 216 palette because all browsers support it.

8. The same movie file can be distributed with different image casts, and it will appear at the corresponding color depth with no extra work.

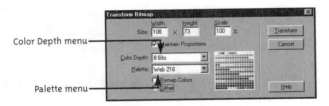

Figure 4.13   The Transform Bitmap command is used to modify the dimensions or color depth of cast members. In this case, select 8 Bits from the Color Depth menu. The Palette menu has a list of default palettes and palettes in casts. Choose the best palette for your movie here.

The Shockwave version of the movie can use the cast with palette-based (8-bit) cast members to keep compatibility high and download times short. The same movie could be used for a CD-ROM project. Substitute the higher-quality external image cast (using true-color assets), and the movie will look better.

Note

As mentioned previously in the chapter, other programs are better at color-depth reduction than Director. If the original image files that were imported into the external cast are available, consider using programs such as DeBabelizer or Fireworks to change their color depth, rather than the Transform Bitmap command in Director. The resulting image files can then be imported directly into an external cast and will look better.

Director's built-in behavior libraries are actually external casts, as you'll learn in Chapter 7, "Using Behaviors," page 149. Similarly, as development teams build collections of scripts and other assets, you will often want to store them in external casts. This will give you or another team a head start on the next project. You will learn how to add your own libraries to Director in Chapter 7 as well.

Managing Casts and Cast Members

There are two important aspects to managing casts and cast members:

- Casts have load priorities that Director references when loading cast members. The load priority determines when, during movie playback, a cast member is loaded from disk and into memory.

- Individual cast members have unload settings that help Director manage the available memory. Likewise, unload settings determine when a cast member may be unloaded (purged from memory) while Director plays the movie.

The following sections discuss these two aspects.

Refer to the file "castmanagement.dir" from the Chapter4 folder on the CD-ROM as you read the next two sections.

Cast Load Priorities

Director must always load a cast member into memory before it can be displayed on the stage. There are three levels of priority Director uses to load entire casts into memory, and they apply to both internal and external casts:

- When Needed—Individual cast members are not loaded into memory before they are referenced by either the score or scripts.

- After Frame One—All the members of a cast are loaded into memory after the first frame of the movie is displayed. If there is not enough memory to load the entire cast, loading stops when memory is full.

- Before Frame One—All the members of a cast are loaded into memory before any frame of the movie is displayed. Again, subject to available memory.

Figure 4.14 shows a movie with three casts to demonstrate their load priorities.

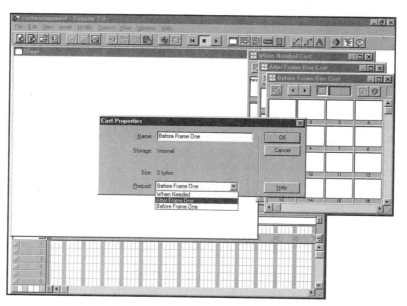

Figure 4.14   This movie has three internal casts, each with a different load priority.

To set the load priority for a cast, follow these steps:

1. Activate the window of the cast you want to modify.

2. Use the Modify, Cast Properties command to open the Cast Properties dialog box. This is shown in Figure 4.15.

Preload menu ——

Figure 4.15 The Cast Properties dialog box allows the cast name to be changed, and shows the amount of memory the cast uses.

3. Choose the desired load priority option from the Preload menu.

4. Click OK to confirm any changes.

These priorities help Director manage available memory and affect the playback of the movie. Loading any cast member (in terms of bytes or kilobytes) takes a finite amount of time. If a cast member is not in memory when Director needs it, Director loads it at that time, possibly inadvertently pausing playback of the movie.

Setting a Cast to Load When Needed

The default priority, When Needed, is typically used for casts that contain a variety of cast members. Often, it is difficult to make a generalization about when these members should be loaded. This setting effectively lets Director manage the loading of members while the movie is playing. A movie that uses casts with this priority starts playing more quickly, but may have frequent pauses for loading during playback.

Setting a Cast to Load After Frame One

Casts that have the After Frame One priority normally contain members that need to be loaded right away but are not used on the opening frame of the movie. The first frame might display a welcome message or progress meter that stays displayed until all the casts of this priority are loaded. This is useful for showing the user that something is happening when casts are loaded. It still involves a pause in playback during the loading process.

Setting a Cast to Load Before Frame One

Director does housekeeping and setup tasks behind the scenes before any movie starts playing. If a cast uses the Before Frame One priority, all its members are loaded during this phase. This can create an appreciable wait before the movie starts playing, if the casts are large. Playback during the movie is smoother if cast members are all loaded first because Director does not have to pause to load anything.

Optimizing Load Times

The most important factor to keep in mind when planning cast load priorities is that every cast member takes a certain amount of time to load. This causes unavoidable delays in the playback of movies. Nothing the movie author can do will reduce or eliminate these delays beyond a certain point.

Using the priorities effectively does allow the author to determine when the delays will occur. Experimentation and judicious use can lead to efficient movies that do not annoy users with misplaced loading delays. Clever authors will mask the inevitable delays by engaging the user in another aspect of the movie, such as reading text or listening to audio.

 Tip

If you know that all the casts in your movie will fit in available memory, use the Before Frame One priority. This sacrifices the startup speed of your movie for execution smoothness. On high-bandwidth media, such as CD-ROMs and hard drives, this works best because the casts load relatively quickly.

Cast Member Unload Priorities

When the amount of free memory gets low, Director unloads cast members to make room for more to be loaded. You can't determine exactly when a cast member will be discarded from memory, but you can influence Director's algorithms. Throughout this section, keep in mind that Director will never unload a cast member that is currently in use.

There are four levels of cast member unload priorities:

- Never (0)—The cast members assigned this priority are never unloaded under normal circumstances.

- Last (1)—Cast members with this priority are unloaded only if no other cast members with higher-numbered priorities are still in memory.

- Next (2)—These cast members are unloaded immediately when Director needs to free some memory.

- Normal (3)—This default priority tells Director to unload these cast members only after any with priority 2 are already unloaded.

The unload priorities for individual cast members are accessed via the Xtra Cast Member Properties dialog box. This is shown in Figure 4.16. It is accessed from the <u>M</u>odify, <u>C</u>ast Member, <u>P</u>roperties command, or by clicking the icon with the letter *i* in the blue circle in the Cast window.

 Note

Refer to the Director movie "castmanagement.dir" from the CD-ROM. The When Needed cast contains four cast members, each with a different unload priority.

Figure 4.16   The cast member unload drop-down menu is on the Xtra Cast Member Properties dialog box.

With no information to the contrary, Director unloads cast members somewhat randomly from memory when new cast members need to be loaded. This can create unwanted delays if a frequently used cast member is accidentally unloaded before it is used. Unload priority settings help avoid this situation.

You need to help Director unload the right cast members. Only you as the movie author have an understanding of the relative priorities of the cast members. For example, Director can't tell the difference between an interface icon that is used often and a text member that is used only once. By setting the priorities properly, you can tell Director to never unload members used constantly and to unload members next that are used only once.

An example of a class of cast members that might need the Never priority assigned is interface elements. They are used often enough to warrant this. Voice-over narration files that play only once are an example of cast members that should have the Next priority. Audio files that play repeatedly at certain intervals might be candidates for the Last priority.

Note   Do not spend too much time with the unload priorities. For most cases, the Normal setting works well. Other priorities should be assigned sparingly to special-case cast members.

Integrating External Cast Members

External assets are files that are linked to a Director movie rather than imported completely. These can be either linked cast members or assets referenced through Lingo code. This section deals mainly with assets as linked cast members. You need to distribute the linked files with the Director movie and any external casts.

External assets are different from external casts in that each has the equivalent of only one cast member per file. External assets also remain in their original file format. Imported cast members are converted to an internal Director format. Director cannot access any arbitrary external asset; the asset must be in a format that Director can recognize and read. Figure 4.17 shows an example import dialog box for external assets.

Figure 4.17 The Import dialog box provides a Link to External File option in the Media drop-down list. Cast members imported using this option do not have the entire asset file stored in the cast—they have only a link to the specified asset files.

For most purposes, Director does not treat linked cast members differently from imported cast members. All the same properties apply, and they can be used interchangeably.

Tip

Refer to the Director help section, "About Import File Formats," for a list of formats that Director supports. Note that some formats are exclusive to either Windows or Macintosh.

Note

Director uses Xtras to import files of different formats. If you choose to use external assets, you must distribute these Xtras with your movie. See Chapter 10, "Working with Xtras," page 267, for more details on this topic.

Externally linked cast members are useful for providing flexibility during development. They are easier than internal cast members to modify and update by various team members. If a file that is linked to a cast member changes, Director automatically uses the changed file the next time the movie is played, without the author having to explicitly reimport it. Of course, the file-name and directory location must stay the same for Director to know where the cast member is located.

Linked cast members are also useful for providing updates and expandability to a finished project. If the end user is connected to the Internet while the product is running, any linked cast members that point to Internet files automatically use the latest files. Another option is to have the product download files (for the external cast members) from a server to the user's local drive at various intervals. This removes the requirement that the user be connected to the Internet while using the product.

> **Note**
>
> In a Shockwave movie, this requirement is not so much a problem as it might be in a Projector application. Because most Shockwave movies run off the Internet, beginning with externally linked cast members is quite natural. The development team needs to update only the linked asset files on the server, and the Shockwave movie will be freshened.

Interactive Portfolio Project

In the previous chapter, you created the documents that helped plan and track the portfolio project. This chapter covers some of the main building blocks: internal and external casts.

Casts are the building blocks of any Director movie. They contain the cast members that appear when the movie plays. Internal and external casts should be used where appropriate. Internal casts are best suited to containing cast members that appear in only one movie. External casts can be shared between movies, and thus their cast members are accessible to any movie that uses the cast.

Internal casts are used only by the movie that contains them. For this project, the internal casts will primarily store text and graphic members specific to each screen. The internal cast for the introduction movie is created and populated in this chapter.

External casts may be used by any movie that links to them. They are an efficient method for storing cast members that will be used by multiple movies. Four external casts are required for this project, and the steps in this chapter show how to create them.

Setting Up the Internal Cast for a Movie

The introduction movie for this project is a self-contained movie that does not reference any external casts. It will consist of score and cast member animation, followed by a simple script that causes it to go to the main movie when complete.

Follow these steps to create the introduction movie:

1. Create a folder somewhere on your hard drive to contain all the files you create for the portfolio project. Name it *Portfolio_Project*.

2. Open the Portfolio_Project folder, and create a subfolder named Chapter04. This is where the version of the movie and casts created in this chapter will be stored.

3. Launch Director and arrange the windows to your liking. Director automatically creates a new empty movie when it starts. We're going to jump ahead slightly by specifying the properties for this first movie. This information is covered in more detail in Chapter 6, "Working with Movies," on page 113. Use the Modify, Movie, Properties command to open the dialog box shown in Figure 4.18.

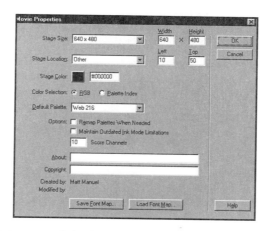

Figure 4.18   The Movie Properties dialog box sets the color model, stage size, and color and number of score channels for the movie.

4. Set the stage size to 640×480, the color selection to RGB, the stage color to #000000 (pure black), the default palette to Web 216, and the score channels to 10. Figure 4.18 shows all these settings as well. Most of these settings come from the design document that you created in Chapter 3. The default palette setting is not needed at this point, but sets the project for future Shockwave conversion. The introduction movie will require fewer than 10 score channels for its animation, so we limit it to this number. Click the OK button when the settings are correct. When Director asks whether it is okay to delete any sprites, choose Yes. There are no sprites in the score yet because this is a new movie.

> **Note**
>
> This stage size does not take into account the menu bar and sides of the window. The 615×430 setting is the size that fits perfectly in the 640×480 screen setting.

5. Select the cast window by clicking on its title bar or choose Window, Cast. Select the first cast member by clicking it. Figure 4.19 shows an example.

6. Open the text window with the Window, Text command. Set the width of the text area to around 6" by grabbing the right margin and dragging it to the proper position. Figure 4.20 shows the text window.

7. The opening animation will consist of four words that appear on the stage in an interesting way. To animate the words separately requires a separate cast member for each word. Type your first name in the text area of the text window. Select the entire word and choose a font you like. Make the text bold and select a font size of 48 (unless your first name is very long and will not fit in the width).

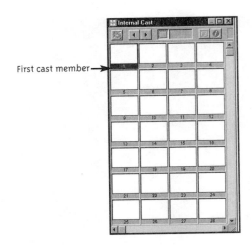

Figure 4.19 The internal cast is open, and the first cast member is selected.

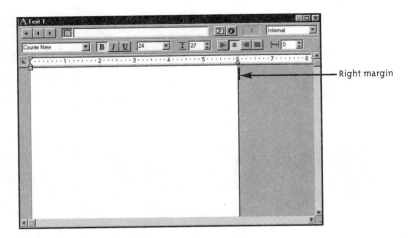

Figure 4.20 The text window is used to create text cast members in Director.

8. Open the tool palette with the <u>W</u>indow, T<u>o</u>ol Palette command. With the text still selected in the text window, click the foreground color chip, shown in Figure 4.21. From the pop-up palette, choose the leftmost yellow in the top row. (You may choose another color, but make sure that it contrasts with the black background.)

9. Give the cast member the same name as the one you entered in the text area. This will make it easy to track in the cast and score. Close the text window and return to the cast window.

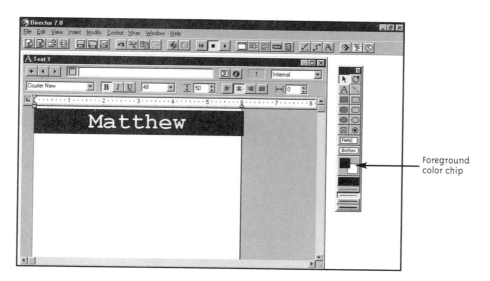

Foreground
color chip

Figure 4.21 One of the uses of the tool palette is to set the foreground and background colors
of text cast members.

10. Rather than create a new empty cast member for the next three words, we will copy
    this cast member and modify it. Copying the cast member helps keep the formatting
    consistent among cast members. Select the cast member, and choose the Edit, Copy Cast
    Members command. Select the next cast member, number 2, in the same cast. Paste the
    copied cast member here with the Edit, Paste command. Open the new cast member by
    double-clicking it.

11. Delete your first name and type your last name with the possessive "'s" at the end.
    Change the cast member name to the same text.

12. Repeat Steps 10 and 11 twice with the words *Interactive* and *Portfolio*. Be sure to rename
    the cast member each time. Figure 4.22 shows the internal cast after this step.

13. Next, import three cast members from the files on the CD-ROM included with
    the book. Select the next empty cast member, number 5, in the internal cast.
    Start the import process with the File, Import command. The standard Import
    dialog box appears (refer to Figure 4.1).

14. Navigate to the CD-ROM and open the Portfolio_Project and Chapter04 folders, succes-
    sively. Select three files: "lightning.gif," "missle.gif," and "rocket.gif." Click the Add but-
    ton to add them to the import file list, shown in Figure 4.23. Select the Standard Import
    option to completely import the files (not just link to them).

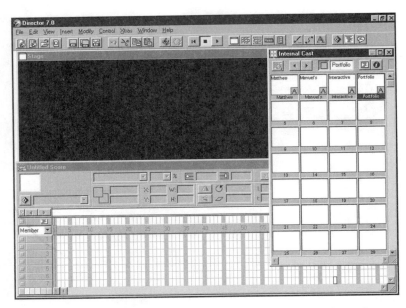

Figure 4.22 Four text cast members have been created, with one word in each member.

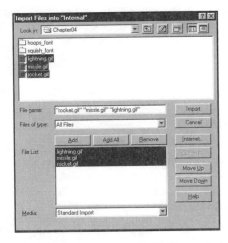

Figure 4.23 Three GIF files are selected and added to the file list, ready for import.

15. Click the Import button to start the import process. Because these are GIF files, Director can import them using two methods. The next dialog box, Select Format (shown in Figure 4.24), shows the two options. Import each of these files as Animated GIFs to preserve their animation frames. If Bitmap Image were chosen, only the first frame of the GIF file would be imported. Check the Same Format for Remaining Files option to speed up the import process slightly.

Figure 4.24 The Select Format dialog box is presented by Director if a file can be imported in multiple ways.

16. The three images are imported into the internal cast, as expected. The cast member names are the same as the source filenames without their file type extensions, as shown in Figure 4.25.

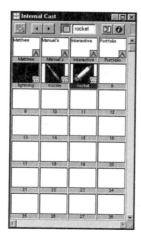

Figure 4.25 Thumbnail images of the three files appear with each corresponding cast member.

17. Save the movie with the File, Save command. Use the filename "intro.dir," and make sure that you are saving to the Chapter04 folder inside the Portfolio_Project folder on your hard drive. A finished version of this movie exists on the CD-ROM in the Chapter04 folder, where you found the image files for this section.

Creating the Global External Casts

External casts are often used to store cast members that are used globally in a project. In this sense, *globally* means in the majority of movies. The next three sections show you how to create the four external casts that will be used by many movies in the Portfolio project.

Macromedia Director

Font Casts

The title text on each screen of the portfolio uses a custom bitmap font. Each letter in the alphabet, plus a number of symbols, is a separate file that will be imported. This adds an interesting look to the project rather than just using Director text, which is limited to a single color for each letter.

The files that make up the individual characters in the font are animated GIFs. Each character has a small animation associated with it. This will be used to create some life to the title text by having each letter animate as the user rolls over it.

To accomplish this, you are going to create two different font casts, one with the character files imported as bitmap images (so just the first frame of the animation is imported), and one with the files imported as animated GIFs (with all their frames intact).

The following steps detail the process of creating these two casts.

1. Create a new cast with the File, New, Cast command. The New Cast dialog box, shown in Figure 4.26, appears.

Figure 4.26   The New Cast dialog box requires a cast name and enables you to select whether the cast will be internal or external.

2. Name this font StaticFont to denote that it will store the bitmap image versions of the characters. Specify an external cast, and deselect the Use in Current Movie check box. These settings are also shown in Figure 4.26.

3. Click OK to create the cast. A new cast window appears in Director with the name StaticFont, as you specified. At this point, the cast is created, but it has not yet been saved to a file.

4. With the new cast window still selected, choose the File, Save command and navigate to the Chapter04 folder inside the Portfolio_Project folder on your hard drive (the same location as the last section where the "intro.dir" movie was saved). The name of the cast you chose when you created the new external cast (StaticFont) is presented as the filename to save it with. Add the .cst extension and proceed with the save by clicking the Save button.

5. Select the first cast member in the StaticFont cast. Start the import process with the File, Import command. Navigate to the Chapter04 folder inside the Portfolio_Project folder on the CD-ROM. You will see two font folders in this chapter folder. The font images used in the rest of the book are in the hoops_font folder. The squish_font folder contains images for an alternative font that you may want to use instead. Open the chosen folder and click the Add All button to add all the files to the file list for importing.

6. Choose Standard Import again from the Media menu. You want the files imported completely, not linked. Click the Import button to continue.

7. As in the last section, a dialog box appears, asking what method to use to import the files. Because this is the StaticFont cast and you want just the first frame of each image, choose the Bitmap Image option, shown in Figure 4.27. Check the Same Format for Remaining Files box to speed up the import process. Click OK to continue.

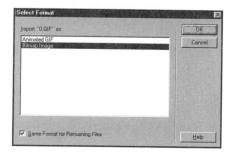

Figure 4.27 To import just the first frame of an animated GIF file, choose the Bitmap Image format option.

8. After selecting the format, Director requires the image options to be set for import. As shown in Figure 4.28, you want these images imported at the stage color depth (bit-depth) of 24 bits. As before, check the Same Settings for Remaining Images option to speed up the process. Click OK to continue.

Figure 4.28 The Import Options dialog box sets the color depth at which the images are imported.

9. After the import progress dialog box disappears, you will notice that the StaticFont cast has 47 new cast members. Each character image file became a new cast member with the name of the corresponding file. Double-click a cast member to verify that they were imported as bitmap images. The member should appear in the Paint window.

10. Save this cast again now that all the letters are imported.

11. Create another new external cast with the File, New, Cast command. Name this cast AnimatedFont, and make sure that Use in Current Movie is not selected, as with the StaticFont cast.

12. As seen in Step 4, save this new cast to the same folder (Chapter04) and use the name `AnimatedFont.cst`.

13. Start the import process again, and add all the same character image files for the same font to the file list. Click the Import button.

14. When the Select Format dialog box appears, use the Animated GIF option. You want these files imported again, but with all their frames of animation. Check the Same Format box again to import all the files with the same format, as shown in Figure 4.29. Click the OK button to continue.

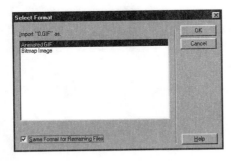

Figure 4.29   The Animated GIF import format is selected for the `AnimatedFont` external cast members.

15. Because you chose the Animated GIF format, Director does not need to be told what color depth to import the files with. All Animated GIF files are imported at 8-bit color depth, but will still play back correctly on a 24-bit stage. Again, the new cast is populated with 47 new cast members, corresponding to the character image files.

16. Double-click a cast member to open its properties dialog box. Figure 4.30 shows an example for the letter Z. Click the Play button to have the frames of the cast member played in a loop. This is a useful method of checking what the animation looks like. Leave all the settings at their defaults, and click OK to return to Director.

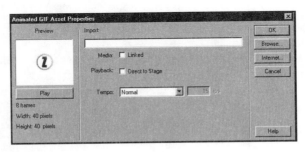

Figure 4.30   The Animated GIF property dialog box enables you to preview the frames of animation for the cast member.

17. Save the `AnimatedFont` cast again; you are finished with this section.

You have created two external casts, one with single frame images and one with animated images. The cast members in each cast correspond with each other, which will be very useful for the project steps in a following chapter. Finished versions of these casts are in the Chapter04 folder inside the Portfolio_Project folder on the CD-ROM.

Graphic Cast

Several bitmap cast members will be used in the main movies of this project. They are perfect candidates for inclusion in an external cast that is shared by these movies. This section leads you through the steps to create this cast and import the required files:

1. Make a new external cast named `GlobalImages`, and do not link it to the current movie.

2. Select the first cast member and start the importing process. Navigate to the Chapter04 folder inside the Portfolio_Project folder on the CD-ROM. Open the global_images folder contained there.

3. Add all five files to the file list, as shown in Figure 4.31. Use the standard (nonlinked) import method. Click the Import button.

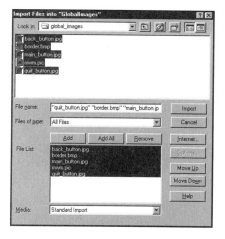

Figure 4.31   The five images that will be used in multiple movies are ready to import.

4. Even though the five files have three different file formats (JPEG, BMP, and PICT), you can import them in one step. Choose the Stage (24 bits) color-depth option, and check the Same Settings box. Click the OK button to complete the import.

5. All five images are in the new `GlobalImages` external cast. You may want to rearrange the cast members so that the buttons are colocated, just for ease of use. Figure 4.32 shows the cast after this step.

Figure 4.32   Five bitmaps are contained in the global images external cast, ordered for easy reference by the movie author.

6. Even though they are not images, you will store three text cast members in this global external cast, as well. They are the button labels for the Quit, Main, and Back buttons. Select the next empty cast member in the GlobalImages cast, and open the text window.

7. Type *Main* into the text area, and select the entire word. Change the font information to Courier New (or another font you like), set the style to Bold, and make the size 36 points. Use the tool palette to ensure that the foreground color is black and the background color is white. Name this cast member *Main*.

8. Close the text window, and copy this cast member twice to the next two free cast member locations in the GlobalImages cast. Edit one of these cast members so its text and name are *Back*. Edit the other so its text and name are *Quit*.

9. Save the cast in the Chapter04 folder in the Portfolio_Project folder on your hard drive. Remember to add the .cst extension to the filename. A completed version of this cast is in the Chapter04 folder in the Portfolio_Project folder on the CD-ROM.

Code Cast

As with the global images external cast, many of the movies use the same behaviors and scripts. It makes sense to store these in a global external cast as well. Any changes to the Lingo code will automatically carry over to each movie that uses one of the shared scripts.

The following steps show how to create this cast and insert several behaviors from the built-in library (the other scripts will be created in the project sections of later chapters):

1. Create a new external cast named GlobalCode that is not linked to the current movie.

2. Open the built-in behavior library window, shown in Figure 4.33, using the Window, Library Palette command. You will learn more about this window in Chapter 7, "Using Behaviors," page 149.

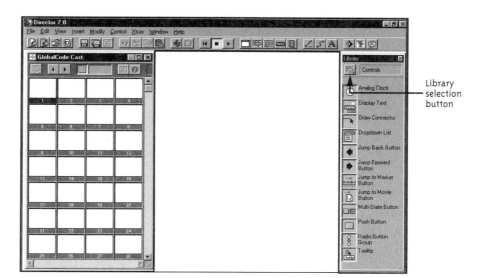

Figure 4.33   The behavior library is an organized collection of prebuilt behaviors that comes with Director.

3. Use the library selection button, shown in Figure 4.33, to choose the Controls library.

4. Drag the Jump to Movie Button behavior from the library window to the first cast member in the GlobalCode cast. This copies it from the library and stores the copy in the external cast.

5. Change to the Navigation library, shown in Figure 4.34, using the library selection button.

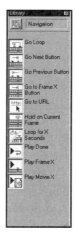

Figure 4.34   The navigation library contains behaviors for controlling the flow within and between movies.

6. Drag the Go Loop, Go to URL, Play Done, Play Frame X, and Play Movie X behaviors to the GlobalCode cast. Figure 4.35 shows the cast with all six behaviors in it.

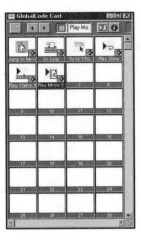

Figure 4.35   All six built-in behaviors that will be used in the project are now stored in the GlobalCode external cast.

7. Save the GlobalCode cast, with the .cst extension, in the Chapter04 folder in the Portfolio_Project folder on your hard drive. A finished copy of this cast is in the Chapter04 folder in the Portfolio_Project folder on the CD-ROM.

Wrap-up

In this chapter's project section, you created five casts for use in the interactive portfolio. The first, an internal cast, will be used to make the introduction movie. Two external casts were created to store one-frame and animated versions of bitmap image characters for an interesting font. The animated letters will be used to add life to the project. Two more global external casts for storing images and Lingo code were also created. The five images that will be used in multiple movies were imported from files. Six behaviors were copied from libraries.

Note that knowledge of what images and behaviors will be required in the development of the project was required for this section. If you were creating the portfolio from scratch, this would be more of an exploratory process as you decided what things would be needed in multiple movies. Nevertheless, the structure and planning of the external casts is a useful exercise.

The next step for the portfolio, covered in the project section of the following chapter, is to create the animated introduction movie using the score.

Creating the Score

The *score* is a symbolic representation of the sprites onstage. It is a tool that is unique to Director and provides impressive animation capabilities. The horizontal dimension shows a progression over time, called *frames*. The vertical dimension displays the layers of sprites, called *channels*.

The *stage* shows the actual images of the sprites for one frame, displayed in their proper locations. The score is a way of looking at multiple iterations of the stage over various frames that emphasize different properties (see Figure 5.1).

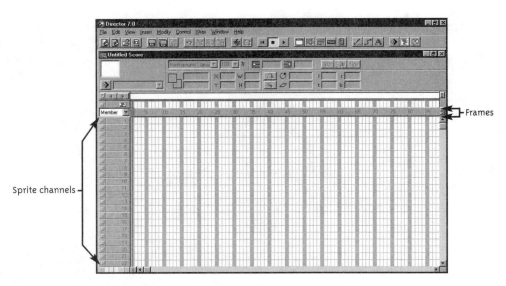

Figure 5.1   The score is one of Director's unique and powerful tools. Although initially it can be difficult to understand the nuances, it becomes indispensable once mastered.

A frame in the score is a snapshot of the movie at one specific point in time. A sprite's position is constant in a single frame, but it can move across multiple consecutive frames. This gives the illusion of movement—sort of like the flip-books kids like to play with.

Director normally progresses in order from lower-numbered frames to higher-numbered ones. There are, however, Lingo scripts and behaviors that can command Director to jump to a specific frame. Interactivity is created when different frames of a movie are played according to user input.

Understanding the Score

The score supports only one sprite per channel per frame. On a given frame, the channel number is synonymous with the sprite in that channel. A channel can have a new sprite each frame, or one sprite can span successive frames (which is called a *sprite span*). A sprite span is composed of only one cast member but it can contain animation information such as position, rotation, and scale changes over time.

Sprite Channels and Key Frames

Normally, sprites in lower-numbered channels appear behind sprites in higher-numbered channels on the stage. This allows sprites on top to mask sprites on the bottom or to create the appearance of perspective. It is possible to change the relative levels of sprites, called their *depth* or *Z-order*, on the stage without moving them between channels, but only through Lingo scripting. This is covered in Chapter 8, "Understanding Scripts," on page 183.

The relative depth of sprites on the stage is an important concept (see Figure 5.2). Sprites in front of other sprites obscure the ones behind them wherever they overlap. When a frame is prepared by Director to be displayed on the stage, all these layers are made into one composite image, following the rules of depth order.

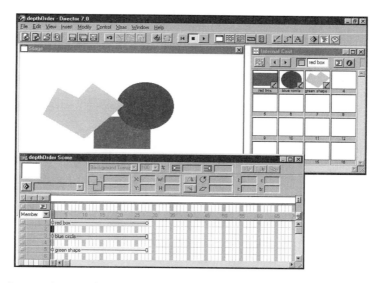

Figure 5.2 Three overlapping shapes are visible on the stage. The red box is in the lowest sprite channel so it appears behind the other two sprites. The green shape in the highest sprite channel appears in front of the other shapes.

 The following steps show the basic relationships between sprites in different channels. Refer to the file "depthOrder.dir" from the CD-ROM:

1. Notice that the depth of the sprites on the stage corresponds to their channels in the score. Drag the red box sprite in the score from channel 1 to channel 6 (see Figure 5.3). It will appear above the other sprites on the stage.

2. Move the red box sprite back to channel 1. Click on the red box sprite span near frame 14. Choose Insert, Keyframe. Notice that the sprite span is bisected where the key frame was inserted. The key frame enables sprite animation by telling Director to treat the frame in a special manner. Without key frames, each frame of the sprite has the same properties as the frame before it. A key frame signals a change in properties. Figure 5.4 shows what the key frame looks like in the score.

3. Locate the input box labeled Y: in the score. With the key frame of the red box sprite still selected, type the value 87 into this box and press the Tab key or click on the stage. The sprite has moved up 100 pixels from its previous location. Click on the last frame of the sprite, frame 28, and type 187 into the Y: position. The sprite returns to its original position (see Figure 5.5). The line extending down from the middle of the red box sprite shows that it animates. This is called the *animation path*.

83

Red box sprite onstage

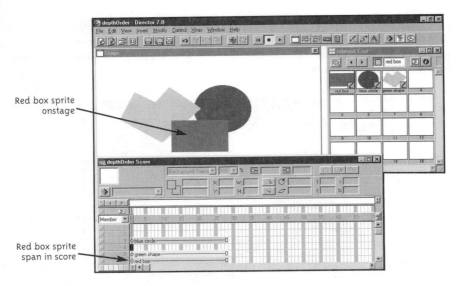

Red box sprite span in score

Figure 5.3   Now, the red box appears in front of the other two sprites on the stage. It is in a higher-numbered score channel.

Key frame

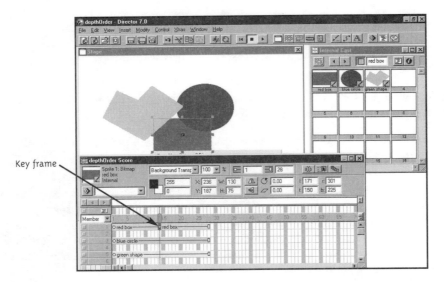

Figure 5.4   With the key frame inserted in the sprite span, it still remains one sprite span because it is based on one cast member.

4. Play the movie and watch Director animate the red box underneath the other two sprites. Notice that the correct areas of the red box are obscured by the sprites that are above it.

Animation path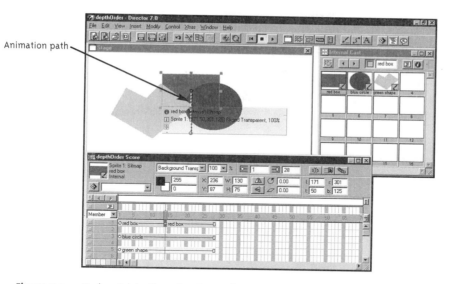

Figure 5.5 Each notch in the animation path represents a position that is automatically generated by Director when the animation is interpolated (automatically generated) between key frames.

5. Animate the other two sprites, using the same method. Click on the blue box's sprite span near frame 14 and insert a key frame. Change its X: position to 388. Notice that it is 100 pixels closer to the right edge of the stage. Select the last frame and type 288 as the X: position.

6. Click on the green shape's sprite span near frame 14 and insert a key frame. Change its X: position to 200 and its Y: position to 200 (see Figure 5.6). This will move the green shape diagonally toward the bottom right of the stage. Type 146 and 136 as the X: and Y: positions, respectively, on the last frame of the sprite to return it to its first position. Again, notice how the sprites move underneath and one on top of another. Refer to the "depthOrder_complete.dir" file in the Chapter5 folder on the CD-ROM for a finished version of this movie.

 Try dragging the middle key frame of each sprite in the score closer to the beginning or end of the span. Watch what happens to the animation. As the number of interpolated frames between key frames changes, Director must make the sprite move faster or slower to get to the key frame location by the correct frame.

Sprites are assigned to channel numbers 1 and up. Channel 0 is the script channel in which frame scripts are located. Channels above the script channel in the score are for special purposes; for example, you can use them to play sounds, create transitions, and change palettes.

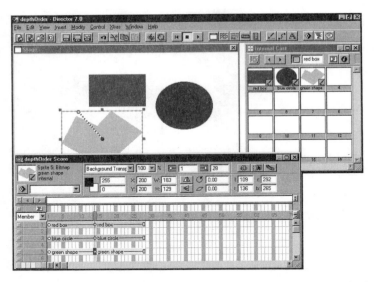

Figure 5.6   All three sprites are animated now. Setting the last frame of each sprite back to its original location creates the seamless looping effect.

The score provides a useful alternative to the stage for selecting sprites. A sprite may be hidden behind another sprite or even off the stage, making it difficult or impossible to select on the stage. Sprites are always easily accessible on the score because their depth and location onstage are irrelevant. Just scroll to the proper channel and click on the sprite in the desired frame to select it.

> **Note**
>
> Experienced Director authors tend to develop the ability to read the score much the same way musicians can read music. After becoming proficient with Director, people find the score an excellent visual representation of the flow of the movie. This is facilitated by good score organization.

Frame Markers

Above the channels is the marker area. Click on a frame in this area to create a named label for navigation and reference. Markers are useful for navigation and organization. Figure 5.7 shows several markers in the score.

Named markers help you locate sections of the score; they are a common form of movie documentation. The drop-down menu on the left side of this area shows all the current markers; clicking on a marker moves the playback head to the associated frame. This is a useful shortcut on scores that spread out over multiple screen widths.

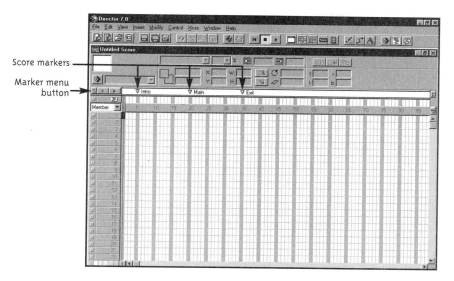

Score markers

Marker menu button

Figure 5.7   Markers for the Intro, Main, and Exit sections of the score have been added. Click a marker name to edit it.

Using markers instead of frame numbers in Lingo scripts makes them more flexible. This lets the author reorganize frames in the score with the knowledge that scripts will still work correctly. Many built-in behaviors use markers this way.

Tip

When using scripts that refer to frames, try to make the scripts work independently of the actual frame numbers by using markers instead. In programming parlance, try not to *hard code* the frame numbers into scripts. Reorganizing the score is much easier if scripts do not need to be updated for every change in frame numbers, such as adding frames to lengthen an animation.

Customizing the Score

Director provides several ways to customize the score to best suit the movie and your preference. Some preferences apply to all movies, and others are specific to each movie.

The size and position of the score affects its ease of use. Generally, a larger score window makes using the score more effective. The number of channels shown in the score affects the movie's playback efficiency. The score should use as few channels as possible to relieve Director of extra work. Magnification options allow you to zoom in on a particular section or zoom out to get an overall view of the score. Sprite span color-coding makes similar types of sprites easier to identify, and is useful for organization. The label showing information about each sprite in the score can also be customized.

Setting the Score Size and Position

The easiest way to customize the score is to size and position it for best use. In most cases, the score should be as large as possible. If your computer supports it, increase the desktop size (that is, resolution) of your computer to allow more information to be displayed. You might also want to use a larger monitor. A 17-inch monitor is the smallest practical monitor size for Director use. A 19-inch monitor or a 21-inch monitor is even better.

If you are limited to a desktop and monitor size, you may want to hide the score when you are not using it. There's a shortcut for accessing the score at any time: Press [Ctrl+4] (Cmd+4) to alternately display and hide the score. You can also hide the effect channels temporarily; this allows more visible sprite channels in a given size.

Tip

Consider investing in a dual-monitor configuration for your computer. This has traditionally been a Macintosh feature, but with the advent of Windows 98, even PCs can use two (or more) monitors. The extra cost will be paid back many times by the time savings. You will spend more time developing the project rather than repositioning windows and switching between them. A common configuration is to have the score on a monitor by itself and the rest of the windows on the other monitor (see Figure 5.8). Note that Windows 98 does not maximize an application across multiple monitors—you have to position it manually.

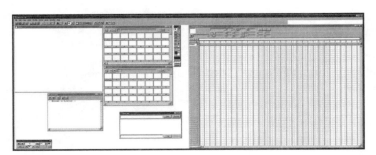

Figure 5.8   A sample configuration of a Director development environment, using a dual-monitor display.

Changing the Number of Score Channels

The number of score channels available has increased with almost every version of Director. Version 3 had 24 channels, and Version 7 has up to 1,000 channels available (see Figure 5.9). This increase is possible for two reasons: Computers are faster so they can handle the extra work of more channels, and Director's playback efficiency has been optimized with each version. This allows movie authors to use as many sprites as they require.

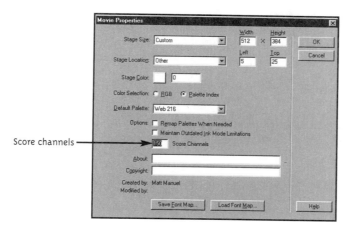

Score channels

Figure 5.9   You can set the number of channels (up to 1,000) in the Movie Properties dialog box, which you get by choosing Modify, Movie, Properties.

Keep in mind that every channel that Director uses slows movie playback to some extent. When the movie is running, Director must composite all the sprites onstage into one image for display onscreen. It's generally a good idea to keep the number of channels you use in your movies to a minimum. Even though Director supports 1,000 channels, it still pays to use as few as possible for efficiency reasons.

Choosing the Score's Magnification

Another customization feature in the score is its capability to scale to different levels of zoom, as shown in Figure 5.10. Access different magnification values from the View, Zoom menu or the button on the right-side frame strip of the score.

Normal magnification is 100%, and you can set the magnification as low as 12%. Using a smaller magnification percentage means you can see more frames in the same screen area. You can set the magnification as high as 1600%; using a high magnification percentage means you can see the most information about individual sprite frames. Zooming out is useful for getting an overview of the score, and zooming in displays a small section.

Score Scaling Menu

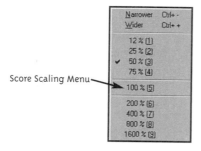

Figure 5.10   You use the Score Scaling menu to set the zoom level of the score's horizontal dimension.

Using Color Coding

The sample movie from the CD-ROM in the first section of this chapter, "depthOrder.dir," demonstrates another organization technique. You can assign key colors to sprite spans to provide a visual reference for related cast members. Director ignores these colors for playback; they are a guide for you only.

Individual sprite spans can be color-coded independently in the same score channel. This serves to visually separate the spans from one another. Using the same color for similar types of sprite spans helps you identify them at a glance. For example, the background sprite, button sprites, animation sprites, and text sprites may all use different colors (see Figure 5.11). The file "spriteColors.dir" on the CD-ROM shows an example of this score technique.

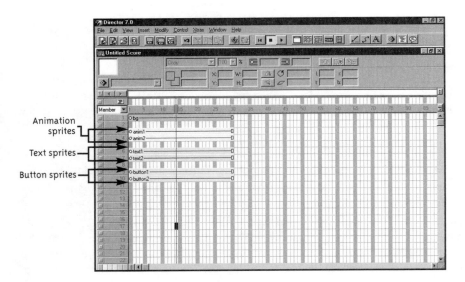

Figure 5.11   Each type of sprite span uses a different color in the score.

Changing Sprite Label Options

The sprite label option drop-down menu on the left side of the score is useful for understanding a movie's score (see Figure 5.12). It determines what information about a sprite is displayed in the score within each sprite span. Sometimes, it makes more sense to see the behaviors attached to a sprite rather than the cast member name, for example.

The score can display one of the following sprite attributes:

- Cast member name
- Behaviors assigned; multiple behaviors are listed horizontally
- Location on the stage of the sprite's registration point

- Ink assignment that determines the appearance of the sprite onstage and its corresponding bounding box
- Blend value (for transparency); similar to an alpha value for the entire sprite
- Extended information that displays all five of the preceding attributes but takes up five times as much screen space

Figure 5.12 You can customize the information about each sprite as you create a movie.

The Score As a State Machine

State machine is a computer science term that refers to a construct to describe the states (or situations) and actions (or events) of a system. It consists of various states of the system and actions that cause the system to move between states. A *state diagram* visually represents a state machine.

State machines are helpful for visualizing the structure of a system, and they apply easily to interactive multimedia. By creating a state machine diagram before starting to build a movie, you can explore the various combinations and variables of the movie. This leads to timesavings by reducing errors and rework.

Creating a State Diagram

You start making a state diagram by listing all the states and events in the proposed system. Lay out the states either randomly or in some order that makes sense for the system, maybe chronologically. Now, attach the events between states as directed arrows. Each event must start and end at a state, even if it is the same state.

States are usually shown as circles or ellipses, with captions inside. Events are shown with directed arrows between states. Their caption is adjacent to the arrow.

After all the states and events are represented on the diagram, the flow of control should be evident. Orphaned states or events will also be obvious. Are there any states with no events tied to them? Do any events not lead to other states within the system?

Often, a state diagram has an initial state (a *source*) and a final state (a *sink*). Each of these states has only one outgoing or incoming event, respectively.

The state machine illustrated in Figure 5.13 describes a typical interactive storybook screen. First, the narrator reads the text, and then the introduction animation plays. While the movie is in the interactive state, the user can choose to activate various animations by clicking on *hotspots* (areas of the screen that cause events such as animation or sound effects when clicked). When the user clicks on the Next Page button, the exit animation plays and the program moves on to the next screen.

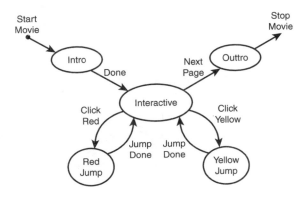

Figure 5.13   The state diagram for a story screen shows the flow of control clearly.

Refer to the file "storybookpage.dir" on the CD-ROM for a basic example of how to implement this. This movie uses the score and behaviors to make a simple storybook page. You can click on either ball in the movie during the interactive portion to see their animations (see Figure 5.14). Click on the Next Page button to start the exit animation. (For simplicity, this movie does not actually link to another page.)

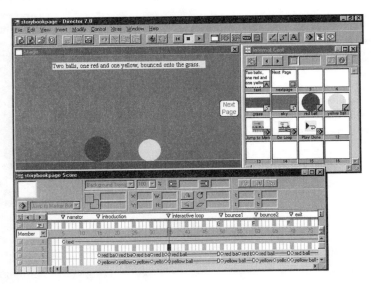

Figure 5.14   This simple movie demonstrates the necessary states and events for an interactive story page.

The movie "storybookpage.dir" was constructed entirely with behavior scripts that come with Director. Refer to Chapter 7, "Using Behaviors," page 149, for more information on using these built-in behaviors from the library.

Implementing State Machines

Director's score makes implementing state machines straightforward. You use markers to define the first frame of each state. Buttons and other sprites use scripts or behaviors to cause the events that move the movie (the system) between states.

As mentioned previously in the chapter, if you use good score organization, you can easily use the score as a visual overview of a movie. State machines implemented in the score reinforce this concept.

Often, movie authors feel they want to outsmart Director and use a lot of clever scripting. However, if something can be accomplished with a built-in feature, you should use that instead of creating needlessly complicated movies.

 The following steps show how to create a state machine in the score for a simple electronic brochure (see Figure 5.15). Start with the movie "ebrochure.dir" from the Chapter5 folder on this book's CD-ROM; it contains ready-to-use cast members:

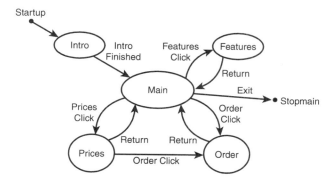

Figure 5.15 A state diagram that shows how the electronic brochure in the example is configured. Refer to it as you follow the steps to build the Director movie that represents the state machine.

1. Create frame markers in the score to represent the states (see Figure 5.16). To take advantage of playback starting at frame 1, put the Intro marker there. To change a

marker's name, click it and retype it. You can drag a marker off the score to remove it completely.

Marker area ——————

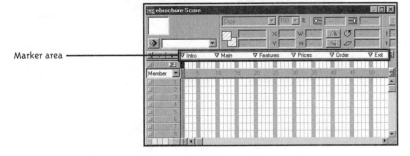

Figure 5.16 The score shows markers every 10 frames that correspond to states in the state machine. The capitalization of markers does not matter to Director, but makes it easier for people to read.

2. Drag the cast members' Intro title, Main title, Features title, Prices title, and Order title to the score in channel 2, and place them in their respective states. Assigning them to channel 2 leaves room for a background image in channel 1, although this example does not use one. Select all of channel 2 by clicking on the channel number on the left side of the score. Use the X: and Y: boxes to set the position of each sprite to (200,20). The numbers in parentheses are a shorthand way of representing the sprite's position, meaning (*x-position,y-position*). Figure 5.17 shows their final positions.

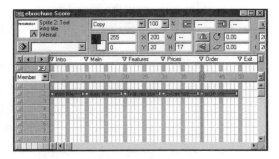

Figure 5.17 The title cast members are placed in the score within their respective states.

3. Place the photo art cast member in the score twice in channel 3, once in the Intro state and once in the Main state. Extend the sprite span from the Main state through to the end of the Order state. Set the position of both sprites to (130,192). Insert a key frame at the last frame of the Intro sprite. Click the first frame in this span to select it and set the rotation value to -90 degrees (see Figure 5.18). Set the position of the first frame to (0,192).

One of Director's preferences is to truncate sprite spans at markers when cast members are placed onstage or in the score. Access this setting with the File, Preferences, Sprite menu. If Terminate at Markers is not enabled, you have to manually contract or expand each span to the proper range of frames. Drag the last frame of a span to change its range of frames. If the span is only one frame long, use the [Alt] (Option) key in combination with a mouse drag to expand the span.

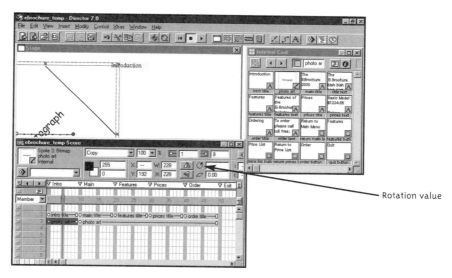

Figure 5.18 The photo cast member animates during the introduction. More frames allocated to the Intro state would allow a longer animation.

4. Put the text cast members for each state—Main text, Features text, Prices text, and Order text—in the score in channel 4. Select the entire channel and set their positions to (290,60). Selecting multiple sprite spans is a quick way of setting several positions at the same time (see Figure 5.19).

5. Drag the cast members' Features button, Price List button, Order button, and Quit button into channels 5 through 8 of the Main state. Set their locations to (415,275), (415,300), (415,325), and (415,355), respectively. Extend the quit button sprite span across all the states and three frames into the Exit state (see Figure 5.20). The Quit button is visible in all states except the introduction. Extending the sprite span across the states allows one behavior to be assigned to the button.

6. Put the return Main button cast member in channel 7 in the Features, Prices, and Order states. Extend the sprite across the states like the quit button sprite in Step 6. Set its position to (415,310).

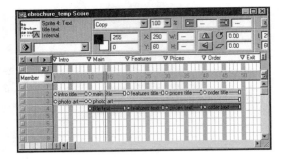

Figure 5.19 Because the text cast members are all the same width, using the same location onstage makes them automatically line up correctly.

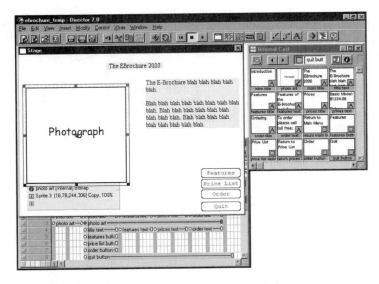

Figure 5.20 The buttons are lined up vertically on the right side of the stage.

7. Put the Order button cast member in channel 6 in the Prices state. This provides an alternative method of reaching the Order state. Set its position to (415,285).

8. Put the return Prices cast member in channel 6 of the Order state. It allows the user to go directly back to the price list from this state. Set its position to (415,265).

9. Put the Web site button cast member in channel 5 of the Order state. (Later, you will add a behavior that will allow the user to automatically open a Web site in the default browser.) Set its position to (415,240) (see Figure 5.21).

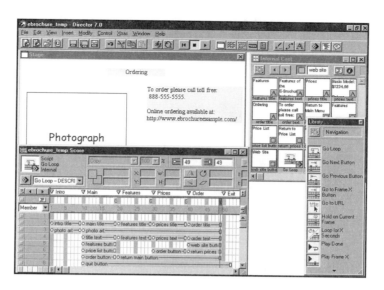

Figure 5.21 Now, all the cast members are in the score in their proper positions, channels, and states.

Note

Notice that the sprites in the score roughly parallel the positions of the sprites onstage. This helps with organization and understanding of the movie.

10. Open the Library Palette window from the Window menu and select the Navigation library. The first behavior in this library is called Go Loop, and it is used to send the playback head back to the previous marker in the score. Drag this behavior to the script channel (just below the markers, as shown in Figure 5.22) and assign it to the last frame of every state except the Intro and Exit states.

Tip

This part of the example uses behaviors extensively. Refer to Chapter 7, "Using Behaviors," page 149, for more details on behaviors.

11. Change to the Controls library. Drag the Jump to Marker Button behavior onto the quit button sprite in the score. A properties dialog box appears, with two drop-down menus and a check box. Choose the Exit marker from the first drop-down menu and uncheck the Remember Current Marker for Back Button? box (see Figure 5.23).

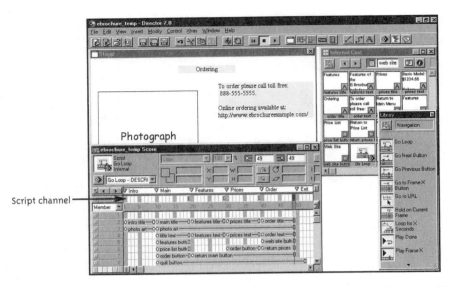

Figure 5.22   The Go Loop behavior makes the playback head remain within the range of frames for each state by sending it back to the previous marker.

Figure 5.23   A behavior that causes the playback head to jump to the specified marker when the mouse is clicked on the button it is assigned to.

12. Assign the same behavior to the features button, price list button, order button, return main button, and return prices button sprites. Choose the appropriate marker from the drop-down menu for each button. These are Features, Prices, Order, Main, and Prices, respectively. Don't forget that the order button sprite appears twice in the score: once in the Main state and once in the Prices state. The behavior must be assigned separately to each sprite because they are separate spans. These behaviors define the events that change the current state of the state machine.

Note

Notice how easy it is to refer to markers rather than to frame numbers. The behavior even presents a list of available markers, so you don't have to remember and type the marker name. This helps you organize scores well.

13. Choose the Navigation library again. Assign the Go to URL behavior to the Web site button sprite in the score. A dialog box appears, asking for an Internet URL (see Figure 5.24). Because this is a fictitious example, use the address `http://www.macromedia.com/` or another that you know is valid.

Figure 5.24   A behavior that launches the default Web browser and loads the assigned URL when the sprite is clicked.

14. Rewind and play the movie. Navigate around the states using the buttons. Try accessing the Web site from the Order state. Watch the playback head move around in the score as you click buttons onstage.

> **Note**
>
> Note that the movie will restart when you click the Quit button if Loop Playback is selected in the Control menu. If this movie were running as a projector (a self-contained application), it would exit to the desktop instead. Projectors are covered in detail in Chapter 11, "Shipping a Title," page 289.

Although this example uses simple and fictitious content, it demonstrates how to implement a state machine. Again, only behaviors built in to Director are used, along with simple buttons and markers. Refer to the movie "ebrochure_complete.dir," found in the Chapter5 folder on the CD-ROM, for an example of the finished movie.

Exporting from the Score

Usually, the score is used to create a Director movie that is distributed to end users. Director's export feature allows the score to be used as a powerful animation tool as well. Exported movies are typically digital video files and can be used independently of Director, a projector, or Shockwave.

The Export command in the File menu is used to create a file that corresponds to the playback of a movie (see Figure 5.25). In essence, Director plays the movie and copies each frame that is displayed on the stage into the exported file. Director ignores scripts, and plays back the score linearly over the range of frames selected. The resulting files can be either a series of still images (PICT on Macintosh and BMP on Windows) or a digital video file (QuickTime on Macintosh and Windows, and Video for Windows AVI on Windows).

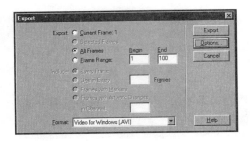

Figure 5.25   The Export dialog box uses a range of frames from the current movie as the source.

Because whatever appears on the stage (without the effect of scripts) is exported, all channel information that is controlled by scripts is lost. The sprites are composited according to normal Director rules, and the result is an image of one layer only.

For movies with many layers, the playback of the exported file can be smoother than the source Director file. This is because Director completes the composite work during the export. The export process may not happen in real-time; it may be slower or faster than the movie's frame rate, depending on the complexity. The resulting movie file will always play back at the specified frame rate, even if it has to drop frames to keep up.

Contrast this to a Director movie, in which the playback speed may decrease if the scene is too complex. Each frame must be composited just before it is displayed on the stage, possibly slowing it down. An exported movie has all its frames precomposited, so it is easier to play back.

The following steps illustrate how to export an entire score to a movie:

1. Start with the "ebrochure_complete.dir" file from the Chapter5 folder on this book's CD-ROM. This movie relies on scripting to jump around the score, based on user input. During the export, these scripts are ignored. Set the bit-depth (color depth) of your monitor(s) to 8-bit (256 colors). This is necessary for the actual export to work correctly.

2. Choose File, Export to display the Export dialog box. Select All Frames to include the entire score in the export. Choose Video for Windows (QuickTime Movie) from the Format drop-down menu. Figure 5.26 shows these selections.

Figure 5.26   The Export dialog box has All Frames and Video for Windows (QuickTime Movie) selected.

3. Click the Options button to bring up the Export Options dialog box. Because the movie was authored to play at 15 frames per second, enter 15 in the Frame Rate field, as shown in Figure 5.27.

Figure 5.27   The frame rate chosen is stored in the resulting movie file.

4. Click on the Export button to continue. The Save File(s) As dialog box appears. Choose a descriptive filename and click the Save button. The default name for the resulting file is the name of the movie.

5. An alert box appears, warning you to disable any screensavers that may activate. This movie will not take very long to export, so you can dismiss this dialog box.

6. The Video Compression dialog box appears next. You can select the method used to compress the information in the resulting exported file. Video for Windows and QuickTime have different options available. The Video for Windows options are shown in Figure 5.28. Choose Microsoft RLE as the Compressor and set the Compression Quality to 100. The corresponding compressor for QuickTime is Animation at full quality.

Figure 5.28   The options in the Video Compression dialog box affect how the exported file is stored and played back.

7. Click OK to continue. The movie is played back in the upper-left corner of the screen as it exports. Open and run the resulting Video for Windows (QuickTime) movie file to see the results.

The resulting exported file shows all the frames of the movie played back in order, with no regard for markers or scripts.

Applications for Exported Movies

A common use for the export feature is long, noninteractive sequences. You construct such a sequence as a normal Director movie, taking advantage of the layering of channels and the available ink effects. Then, the movie is exported to an external file. Another Director movie can now use that external file as a linked asset for playback. The advantage is that the external file will be streamed onto the stage during playback, not preloaded like normal cast members. This can reduce the memory needed to play back the sequence as well as improve the smoothness.

Note

Digital video file formats such as Microsoft Video and Apple's QuickTime are synchronized to a time track. If the host computer cannot play all the frames at the specified frame rate, some frames are dropped. This guarantees that frames are played at their assigned times, and tends to keep the video synchronized with any audio in the file.

When exporting a movie as a digital video file, Director presents a compression method dialog box, as shown in the example in the previous section. The choices are determined by the format (QuickTime or AVI) and the compressors installed on the system. Generally, it is best to export either uncompressed or losslessly compressed files. Uncompressed files use a lot of disk space but maintain quality for further processing. Lossless compression (Animation or Microsoft RLE) saves some disk space and maintains quality. (In lossless compression, no information is thrown away during the compression process, so the original content may be reconstructed completely. RLE stands for Run Length Encoding, a common method of lossless compression.)

Often, the exported file is processed further (in another program) to achieve some effect or it may have another layer of video put onto it. In these cases, you should use the highest-quality export option from Director so that the artifacts from recompression are minimized. When the final, highest-quality file is ready for use, you should compress it for final delivery as the last step. A tool such as Media Cleaner Pro from Terran Interactive (http://www.terran.com/) can be invaluable here: It allows experimentation with compression algorithms to achieve the highest quality-to-bandwidth ratio. More information on these sorts of options is available in Chapter 9, "Integrating Various Media Types into Director Projects," page 229.

Tip

The bit-depth (color depth) of the monitor determines the bit-depth of the resulting exported file. Be sure to set the monitor bit-depth to the desired value before exporting. Additionally, the export frame rate option is not stored between export commands; you must set this with every export.

Limitations of Exporting Scores

There are a few limitations of the export process. As already mentioned, Director completely ignores scripts and behaviors during an export. Sprites that are animated through Lingo are not animated in the exported movie. Any navigation scripts are also ignored; the score plays back linearly over the range of frames.

For sound to be exported with the movie, the sound files must be fully imported cast members. Externally linked cast members do not work. Also, the sound must be in one of the two score sound channels, not played through Lingo. QuickTime is the only export format that supports the inclusion of sound.

Transitions may not export exactly as intended. Experiment with the different transitions and try exporting just the frames around a transition before exporting the whole movie.

The entire stage is always exported, so cropping must occur after the export process in another program, such as Media Cleaner Pro or Adobe Premiere (http://www.adobe.com/). QuickTime does, however, support scaling of the movie on export, which can be useful for creating thumbnail references of the movie. QuickTime is the only choice for creating movies that will play back on both Windows and Macintosh computers.

Using the score and all its features is an excellent way to export linear sequences. You can use them for other purposes or to reimport them into Director to take advantage of the benefits of digital video file formats. The channels in the score provide a tremendously useful tool for experimenting with effects and assets before the final export.

Interactive Portfolio Project

Good score organization leads to a better overall understanding of the movie. State machines are useful tools for planning score organization and are easy to implement.

The export feature of Director allows movies to be used as media-creation tools. Whatever appears onstage during movie playback is output to an external file, according to the layout in the score. The resulting file can be played back in Director using Video for Windows or QuickTime more efficiently than the equivalent score.

In the previous chapter, you created the internal cast for the introduction movie. This movie is the first part of the portfolio that the user sees. It will contain noninteractive animation that informs the user about what they are about to see.

The project instructions to follow in this chapter consist of two main parts. First, you will create the animation of the text appearing on the stage. Then, you will add three animated GIF images to serve as small special effects.

Creating the Introduction Score

The internal score created in the last chapter is stored in the movie "intro.dir." You saved this movie in the Chapter04 folder inside the Portfolio_Project folder on your hard drive. If you do not create this movie, you may retrieve it from the equivalent folder on the CD-ROM. Follow these steps:

1. For version-control purposes, you will copy the movie created in the previous chapter into a working folder for this chapter. Create a folder called Chapter05 in the Portfolio_Project folder on your hard drive.

2. Copy the movie from the Chapter04 folder on your hard drive or the CD-ROM to the new Chapter05 folder. This ensures that a copy of the movie that is in a known state is safely stored, in case anything goes wrong with the movie in this chapter.

Text Animation

First, you will create the animation that brings the title of the project onto the stage. You start with a blank stage and then slide the words into their final positions over several frames using the score.

It is often easier to start with the elements in their final positions and then work backward. This ensures that the words will appear where you want them at the end of the animation.

The following steps show how to create the score animation for the four words in the title:

1. The design document states that all movies in this project should run at a frame rate of 30 frames per second. This is set from the Control Panel window inside Director. Open this window by choosing Window, Control Panel.

2. Change the frames per second setting for the movie by either selecting the existing value and typing 30 in its place, or by using the arrows to progressively increase the value. Figure 5.29 shows the Control Panel with these areas identified.

Current FPS setting — Setting arrows

Figure 5.29 The Control Panel shows the current tempo setting and the actual tempo while the movie is playing.

3. Position the internal cast window and the score window so the text members can be moved to the score easily. Drag each text member, starting with the first name, to channels 5, 6, 7, and 8 in the score; as shown in Figure 5.30. Position them so each sprite span starts in frame 1 of the score.

4. If you look at the stage now, you see that all four members are positioned with their upper-left corners in the center of the stage. They also appear with white backgrounds. Select all four sprite spans in the score and choose Background Transparent from the ink menu in the score. Now, the white areas of the sprites (the background colors) are transparent and the stage shows through from behind.

5. Position each sprite on the stage to be centered horizontally. Move the sprites vertically so the words appear as if they are on separate lines. Figure 5.31 has an example of this layout. The exact positions are not important; just arrange them so they look nice onstage.

6. You want the introduction movie to be long enough to have some interesting animation, but not too long to bore the user. Five seconds is a reasonable duration for this movie. At 30 frames per second, you need 150 frames of animation in order to last five seconds. Select all four sprite spans in the score. Click on the end frame entry and type 150 in place of whatever is there, as shown in Figure 5.32. Now, all four sprites last the entire duration of the movie.

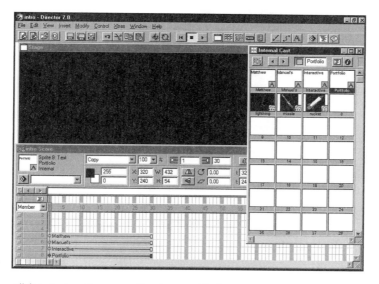

Figure 5.30 All four text sprites are on the stage and in the score.

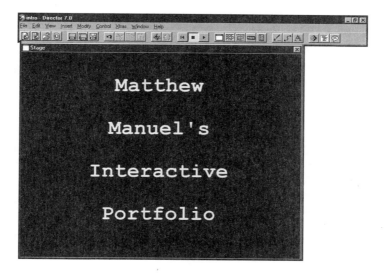

Figure 5.31 The title words are set to their final positions onstage.

7. For an interesting effect, try staggering the appearance of the words onstage. You will start with the first name and show each subsequent word a few frames later. Select the sprite span in the score for the last name and drag its start frame to frame 25. Repeat

this with the word *Interactive*, but move its start frame to frame 50. Do the same with the word *Portfolio*, but change its start frame to frame 75. This delays the appearance of each word by almost a full second (25 frames). The resulting score is shown in Figure 5.33.

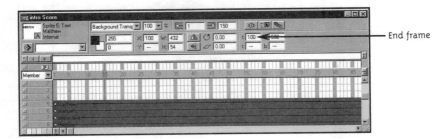

End frame

Figure 5.32 After setting the end frame, all four text sprites cover the entire duration of the movie, 150 frames.

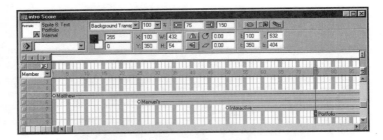

Figure 5.33 With their start frames moved to later in the score, the lower words appear onscreen progressively later.

8. Because you want the words to appear to slide on to the stage from offstage, you need to have their first frame position be offstage. Click on frame 25 of the first name sprite span in the score. Select the Insert, Key frame command and a new key frame appears at that frame in the sprite span. This ensures that the slide portion of the animation will last only 25 frames instead of the whole movie. Repeat this step on frame 50 of the last name sprite span, frame 75 of the Interactive sprite span, and frame 100 of the Portfolio sprite span. Figure 5.34 shows the results.

9. In this step, you will move the sprite offstage at the first frame of each sprite span. Select the first frame of the first name sprite in the score. Change to the stage window and move the sprite up until it disappears from the stage. You may drag the sprite with your mouse or use the up-arrow key. Holding the Shift key down while dragging constrains the movement to either the horizontal or vertical dimension. This can make it easier to keep the sprite at the same X position onstage while changing only its Y position.

Holding down the Shift key while using the cursor keys moves the sprite in increments of 10 pixels rather than just one pixel.

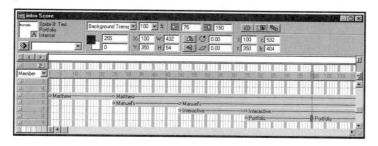

Figure 5.34 Key frames have been added—25 frames into each sprite span. The scale of the score has been reduced to 75% to show all the key frames.

10. Change back to the score window and select the first frame of the last name sprite (at frame 25 of the score). Switch back to the stage window again. This time, drag or move the sprite off the right side of the stage until it is not visible.

11. Repeat Step 10 with the Interactive and Portfolio sprites. Move the Interactive sprite off the left side of the stage and the Portfolio sprite off the bottom.

12. To test your animation, you may play the movie at this point. As the movie starts, each word should slide onto the stage in succession.

Tip

An optional enhancement is to have the words come in from the corners of the stage, or all from the same area offstage.

13. The words stop rather abruptly at their final positions. To give them a sense of momentum, you will need to have them overshoot their final positions and then settle back. Insert a key frame at frame 30 and 35 in the first name sprite. Select the key frame at frame 30 in the score and switch to the stage window. Move the sprite down slightly to have it move past the desired position. Because you inserted a key frame at frame 35 when it was still in the final position, the sprite will now move to that position automatically over the next five frames.

14. Repeat Step 13 for the other three sprites. Insert key frames at frames 55 and 60 for the last name, frames 80 and 85 for Interactive, and 105 and 110 for Portfolio. Move the last name sprite slightly farther left at frame 55, the Interactive sprite slightly right at frame 80, and the Portfolio sprite slightly up at frame 105. Figure 5.35 shows the score with these key frames added.

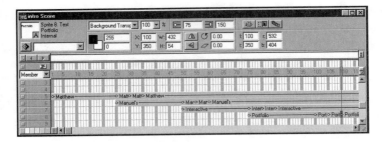

Figure 5.35 To give a sense of weight and momentum, a few more key frames are added to each sprite. This allows some overshoot animation to be inserted before they come to rest in their final positions.

15. Play the movie again to see whether the proper effect has been achieved. If you want to tweak the animation, be sure to select the middle key frame of each sprite span just before it comes to rest.

At this point, the animation of the text sprites is complete. You may want to add your own variations to the animation presented in these steps.

Adding Images

Now that the text is animated into its final position, it is time to add a bit of "eye candy" in the form of a few animated images that add some life to the stage. Three images were imported into the internal cast during the project steps in Chapter 4, "Working with Casts." These are the images that will be used in this section.

1. All three of the images that were imported to the internal cast in Chapter 4 will be added to score channels with lower numbers than the text sprites (this is so they appear behind the text during the movie playback). Open the internal cast window and position it so that score channels 1, 2, and 3 are visible.

2. Drag the lightning, missile, and rocket sprites to channels 1, 2, and 3, respectively, in the score.

3. Double-click on the lightning cast member to open its property dialog box. Figure 5.36 shows that this animated GIF has 12 frames. Press the Play button to preview the animation. Click OK to close the dialog box.

4. Select the lightning sprite in the score. Drag its end frame to frame 24 (assuming that its start frame is at frame 1), so its duration is 24 frames. This sets the duration of the sprite span to 24 frames, which is two complete cycles of the animation.

5. With the entire lightning sprite span still selected, either drag it onstage, or change its X and Y positions in the score until it is centered near the top of the stage. A Y value of 120 should accomplish this, as shown in Figure 5.37.

6. Drag the sprite span in the score until its start frame is around frame 100. This will make the lightning sprite appear and start animating just as the final word, Portfolio, settles

into place. You can play the movie again to view the lightning animation as it appears behind the words.

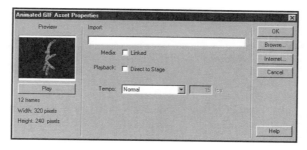

Figure 5.36 The cast member property dialog box shows the total number of frames in an animated GIF.

Figure 5.37 The lightning sprite appears centered horizontally near the top of the stage, behind the text sprites.

7. The two other images, the missile and the rocket, will slide from the bottom of the stage up to the left and right sides, respectively. Drag the missile sprite span so that its first frame is around frame 30 in the score. Drag its end frame (or set it in the end frame entry) to frame 115.

8. Drag the rocket sprite so that its first frame is around frame 45 in the score. Move its end frame to around frame 135. Figure 5.38 shows both sprite spans in the score.

9. Select the last frame of the rocket sprite span in the score. Switch to the stage window and move this sprite offstage to the right. Select the first frame of the same sprite span

in the score. Switch back to the score and move the sprite down until it is just off the bottom of the stage, still near the center.

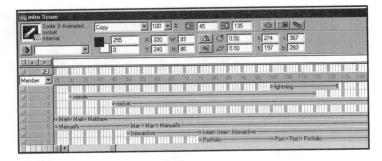

Figure 5.38 Both the rocket and missile sprites cover large portions of the score, offset slightly.

10. Repeat Step 9 with the missile sprite. Select its last frame in the score and move it off-stage, but to the left side this time. Select its first frame in the score and move it down off the bottom of the stage near the center.

11. Play the movie to see the missile and rocket animations slide up and off the screen as the text slides onto the screen. Figure 5.39 shows the movie at frame 100, just as the lightning appears. A finished version of the movie is in the Chapter05 folder inside the Portfolio_Project folder on this book's CD-ROM. Be sure to save your movie in the Chapter05 folder on your hard drive.

Figure 5.39 All three animated GIF sprites and the four text sprites are onstage at frame 100 in the movie.

Wrap-up

During this stage of the Portfolio Project, you have created the introduction movie. It consists of four text sprites that comprise the title of the project and three animated GIF sprites that add life to the movie. The text sprites are animated to their final positions using the score. Two of the animated GIF sprites are also animated in position using the score.

In the next chapter, you will create more of the movies that represent different screens in the project.

Working with Movies

Movies are the basic building blocks of any Director project. Every project needs at least one movie. A small project might need to include only one movie, but there are advantages to using multiple movies in most cases.

It is essential to plan and organize the structure of the movies associated with a multimedia product. For example, a team will have the easiest time working with multiple movies if it establishes and follows conventions on how to work with them.

Setting the properties of the stage is the best starting point for creating a new movie. The stage size, location, and color can all be customized. This chapter shows how to select the default palette for the movie and specify the number of score channels that will be used.

Multiple movies are essential to Director projects of any significant size. You will learn the advantages of multiple movies and how to link them together. The concept of a stub movie and some organization concepts are also introduced.

Setting the Stage

Before you start working on any movie, it is important to set the movie's properties. Setting these values first will save production effort because changes after the movie is partially built are much more difficult than those made up front. Figure 6.1 shows an example of the Movie Properties dialog box, accessible by selecting the Modify, Movie, Properties menu.

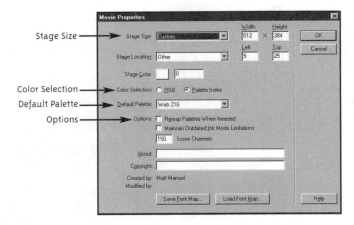

Figure 6.1   The Movie Properties dialog box contains basic parameters that affect important aspects of the movie.

Version control, covered in Chapter 3, "Planning Your Director Project," page 29, is another way to improve efficiency when planning a multifaceted project. To save time and aggravation as the project progresses, you should implement a version control system before you begin.

Tip

Stage Size

The stage size is one of the most important movie properties. Because all the sprite positions are dependent on the stage size, it is vital to set this before starting work in the movie's score.

Stage size is determined by a number of factors, mostly related to the end-user platform where the movie will eventually play. (Target Platforms are covered in detail in Chapter 3, "Planning

Your Director Project," page 29.) Large stage sizes use more memory and generally cause movies to play back more slowly than small stage sizes, given the same type of assets. Custom stage sizes are available, but the width must always be a multiple of 16 pixels. This helps Director increase a movie's playback efficiency because it is easier for computers to work with numbers that are multiples of 16.

> **Note**
>
> Typical stage sizes maintain an aspect ratio of 4:3. This ratio of the width of the stage to the height of the stage is used by the vast majority of applications and matches the aspect ratio of most monitor resolutions.

Available stage sizes are as follows:

- 640×480—A very common size for consumer multimedia projects. This size works with the widest range of computers. Figure 6.2 shows an example of this stage size in Director.

Figure 6.2   For maximum compatibility, a 640×480 stage size is the best choice.

- 800×600—A standard monitor size that is commonly available on consumer computers. It can display more information than the 640×480 size.
- 1024×768—Another standard size, but not commonly used. Older machines may not have this screen size available. Custom applications that must display a lot of detail are good candidates for this size.

Macromedia Director

- 1280×1024—The largest standard size commonly available. It typically requires at least a 17-inch monitor to be legible. Note that the aspect ratio is no longer 4:3, but 5:4 instead (1280:1024 simplified).
- QuickTime 160×120—A small stage size that can be used to make a QuickTime movie. It is $\frac{1}{16}$ the size of a standard 640×480 screen and therefore creates small movies that play back well.
- QuickTime 320×240—Another standard QuickTime movie size that is $\frac{1}{4}$ the size of a 640×480 screen, as shown in Figure 6.3.

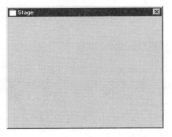

Figure 6.3   Exported files at this stage size can be played back on 640×480 stages by a technique called pixel doubling. Pixel doubling turns each pixel in the source movie into four identical pixels, forming a square when played back.

- Current Screen—This option sets the movie size to the size of the screen, which is useful for odd-sized screens.
- Custom—Any other stage size is a custom size. You enter the width and height in the dialog box. This is especially useful for Shockwave movies that must fit within the boundaries of an Internet page.

Tip

Advertising banners on the Internet are usually a custom size of 468×60 pixels. You should use this standard custom stage size to develop movies for ad banners.

Stage Location

The stage location is important only for development purposes. It lets you position the stage exactly within the Director application window. You can use the shortcuts Upper Left and Centered for those exact positions. You can also position the stage window interactively by simply dragging it around the screen.

Color Selection

The stage color is the background color of the movie. When a projector plays in full-screen mode, the stage color is used for the border between the edge of the stage and the edge of the screen, as shown in Figure 6.4. This color can be defined as a palette position for 256-color movies or an RGB (red, green, blue) value for RGB movies. If the movie uses a palette, the stage color changes as the palette changes. For example, palette position 19 in the Macintosh system palette (hot pink) is not the same color as palette position 19 in the Web 216 palette (tan).

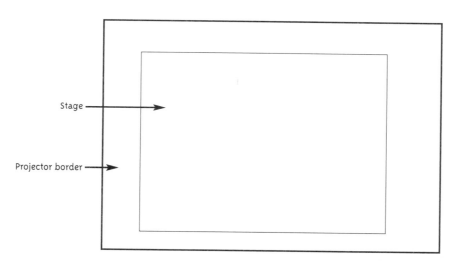

Figure 6.4   The white border surrounding the stage is the same color as the stage.

> **Note**
> The standard Web 216 palette is commonly used for movies that are intended to play on the Internet. The palette has 216 colors that are compatible with various Web browsers and operating systems. The rest of the colors, up to 256, are used by interfaces to maintain a consistent look. Use this palette to ensure that your Shockwave movie plays back with accurate colors.

Default Palette

The default palette is used in a movie unless another is specified. Alternate palettes can be set using the palette channel of the score or through Lingo. The related option Remap Palettes When Needed causes Director to automatically change cast members with different palettes to best fit the current palette in the movie. This is usually not advisable because it can signifi- cantly slow the playback of the movie. Also, the results may not be what you have in mind. It is much better to make sure that the palettes of all the sprites onstage match the current movie palette, even if this means having multiple versions of cast members with different palettes.

Tip

For cross-platform CD-ROM projects that use 256-color palettes, you should set each movie's palette to the Windows palette. This provides a common palette between movies, even if different palettes are used within each movie. Movies with palettes intended for the Internet should use the Web 216 palette exclusively.

The Score Window

As mentioned in Chapter 5, "Creating the Score," page 81, the number of score channels visible in the Score window can be customized. The default value is 150 channels and the maximum is 1,000. You should use the minimum number of channels required for each movie to help Director maintain efficient playback. A sample score with 150 channels is shown in Figure 6.5.

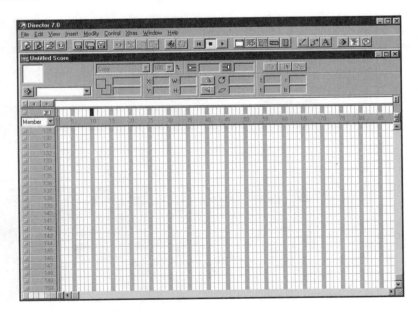

Figure 6.5   The number of channels displayed in the score determines the maximum number of unique objects that can be used onstage.

> After you set the movie's properties for a particular project, save the movie. Consider saving the movie separately as a template before adding any cast members. You can begin subsequent movies with this movie file, and thereby avoid having to duplicate the property setting procedure.

Creating Multiple Movies

Unless the project is very small and has only one person working on it, multiple movies are recommended. Using more than one movie requires more up-front planning, but the advantages are well worth it. Multiple movies make project organization much easier. Different team members can work on movies simultaneously to shorten the production schedule.

> Plan and test the organization of the movies in your project early. The navigation scripts that pass control between movies should be created first.

Linking Multiple Movies

In practice, using multiple movies is uncomplicated. Each movie passes control to another movie, when appropriate, using the new movie's filename for reference. In Lingo, the script consists of the `go to movie` command with the movie name in quotation marks as a parameter. Listing 6.1 shows an example.

> Note that the filename extension is not included in the filename. This makes the code function independently of the destination movie's extension. Shockwave and protected movies have different extensions than normal Director movies. (Projectors can play protected movies but their cast members are not accessible through Director.)

Listing 6.1 An example of the `go to movie` command.

```
on exitFrame me
    go to movie "Page3"
end exitFrame
```

Macromedia Director

Refer to Chapter 11, "Shipping a Title," page 289, for a complete explanation of Shockwave and protected movies. Basically, protected movies do not have any scripts or other cast members accessible from Director. They are used to ensure that end users can't see the scripts in movies that ship with a title.

A different method that does not require Lingo scripting is to use the Jump to Movie Button behavior from the Controls behavior library included with Director. (Refer to Chapter 7, "Using Behaviors," page 149, for more information on behaviors.) When attached to a sprite, this behavior asks for the destination movie in a standard file dialog box. Then, the dialog box shown in Figure 6.6 is displayed. The @ symbol signifies that the destination movie is in the same folder as the current movie.

Figure 6.6   The parameter dialog box for the Jump to Movie Button behavior shows the movie selected in the previous dialog box.

Note

The movie name cannot be edited within the Parameters dialog box. It must be reselected by canceling and reassigning the behavior. You can specify a marker name, and the destination movie will start playback at that marker.

Tip

Edit the destination movie name in the first dialog box to leave off the extension. If the .dir extension remains in the movie name, the behavior will not work correctly with Shockwave or protected movies.

The Jump Mode drop-down menu presents two choices: Go To, and Play and Return. Go To is the normal mode for transferring control to a new movie. The new movie does not know which movie called it. Play and Return is used to automatically return to the original movie when the first movie is finished playing.

Be cautious of sending the new movie on to other movies if Play and Return is selected. The logic can become confusing, and it can be hard to track what will happen when a movie finishes.

Finally, the Remember Current Marker for Back Button? check box is used in conjunction with the Jump Back Button behavior in the same library. If this box is checked, the behavior stores the frame of the movie before going to the new movie. The Jump Back Button behavior can then be used in the new movie to automatically return to the same point. This is similar to the Play and Return option, but allows the end user to return before the destination movie is finished.

Advantages of Using Multiple Movies

One major benefit of using multiple movies is that they contribute to good project organization. A project can be broken down into its component parts, with each part corresponding to a separate movie. The parts are therefore easier to manage.

Different team members can work on movies simultaneously when multiple movies are used. This is important when a schedule is short because work can be accomplished in parallel. This does require excellent communication and coordination between team members. There must be absolute understanding of and agreement on filenames and conventions.

Settling on and adhering to conventions is also good for the overall organization of a project. You should make sure that each team member knows how to implement common interface elements in their movies, for example. Also, common behaviors should be shared from one cast rather than included separately in each movie. This ensures that if they are changed in any way, the change propagates throughout the project. Refer to Chapter 4, "Working with Casts," page 49, for more information.

Tip Even though team members are working on separate movies, they should periodically test the links to other members' movies. They should link into their own movies from the previous movies and link to the movies that follow theirs. This verifies that the links work properly and that the project behaves as it should overall. Unwelcome surprises that might occur later in the project can be avoided this way.

The final advantage of multiple movies is that they keep the project from becoming cluttered. During development, movies stay small because they deal with only part of the project. Team members need worry only about the part of the project that pertains to their movies.

At playback time, each movie is in some ways like a separate application. Each starts with a clean environment. Cast members from the previous movie are purged from memory and new cast members are loaded fresh. *Global variables* persist between movies, however. (Global variables are accessible by any script from anywhere in the movie. Chapter 8, "Understanding Scripts," page 183, contains more information on variables.)

Getting Started with Stub Movies

It is common practice in Director projects to create a *stub movie*, which is a movie file that contains just one script or behavior, and whose sole purpose is to launch the first movie in the project with actual content.

Stub movies are used to make projectors or to start a sequence of Shockwave movies. They allow a very quick launch of either the projector or the Shockwave plug-in, respectively. End users are almost instantly aware that the experience has started. Without a stub movie, all the cast members required to start playback of the first movie must be loaded before anything begins onstage. Refer to Chapter 11, "Shipping a Title," page 289, for more information on making projectors and Shockwave movies.

Because a stub movie is so simple, it is unlikely to change during development. Therefore, the team needs to make the projector application only once from the stub movie. Without a stub movie, the projector would have to be remade each time the first movie changed, which can be frequently during normal production.

Making a projector is not especially difficult, but it is another element to avoid during the crunch time at the end of a project. Also, all the projector's settings are reset when it is remade. For example, the icon is set back to the default projector icon. On the Macintosh platform, the memory settings are also reset to their defaults. Remaking the projector unnecessarily can lead to errors and omissions that could jeopardize a deadline.

Making a stub movie is straightforward. You can use the template movie for your project or just make sure that the movie parameters match the rest of the movies. The following steps lead you through the creation of a new stub movie:

1. Create a new movie by selecting File, New, Movie. Choose to save or discard the current movie, as desired.

2. Set the movie properties from the Movie Properties dialog box. Figure 6.7 shows an example of this dialog box.

3. Open the score window by choosing Window, Score or [Ctrl+4] (Cmd–4). Select the frame channel (channel 0) in frame 1 of the score. Figure 6.8 shows where this is located.

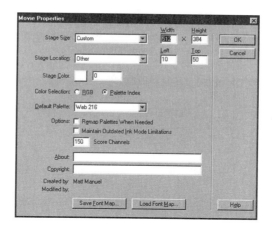

Figure 6.7   The movie in this example uses the custom size 512×384 and the Web 216 palette.

Frame 1 script location

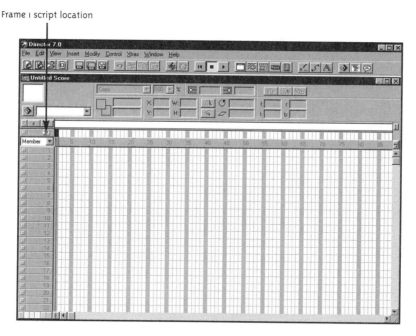

Figure 6.8   The script for the stub movie is inserted at frame 1.

4. Type `go to movie "first"` with this frame script still selected. The script window auto-matically opens with the default script `on exitFrame`, which is pregenerated when you start typing. The script window appears in Figure 6.9.

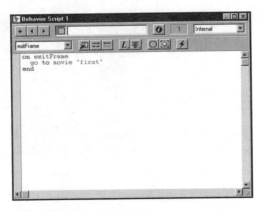

Figure 6.9   The only script in a stub movie calls the first movie in the project.

5. Close the script window and save the movie. Call it `stub.dir` or `projector.dir` for refer-ence. If you run the movie now, Director will ask where the movie called *first* is located, unless a movie with that name exists in the current directory.

Chapter 11, "Shipping a Title," page 289, shows you how to create a projector from any Director movie. This stub movie should be the first movie included in a projector that is built for the associated project.

 Instead of following Step 4 from the preceding example, you can use the behavior Play Movie X from the Navigation library included with Director. This is accessed with the Window, Library Palette menu. More information on assigned behaviors is in Chapter 7, "Using Behaviors," page 149.

Drag the behavior from the library to assign it to the script channel of the first frame of the movie. Type the name of the first movie in your project into the behavior property dialog box. Remember to leave off the filename extension to provide resiliency for Shockwave and protected movies. Figure 6.10 shows an example of this dialog box. Again, the @ symbol signifies that the destination movie is in the same folder as the current movie.

 The movies called "stub.dir" and "first.dir" on the CD-ROM are examples of how a stub movie works.

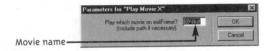

Movie name

Figure 6.10   The parameter dialog box for the Play Movie X behavior has one input box for the movie name.

You should keep the number of cast members and casts to a minimum in stub movies. For example, do not link to external shared casts. This will let the stub movie load and start playback as quickly as possible, thereby giving the end user immediate feedback that something is happening.

Organizing Multiple Movies

When you use multiple movies, you need to organize them effectively. One method is to put all the movies for a project in one folder, along with the projector. This has the advantage of simplicity, but can lead to confusion if other files are included. For example, if external casts specific to each movie are also used, then they should also be located in this folder. These additional files can make file management cumbersome.

A better solution is to keep only the global project files in the main folder. The rest of the movie files for each section should reside within specific subfolders. This method is advantageous because all the files associated with a movie are together, and there is no confusion about where they belong.

Examples of files that should remain in the main folder are as follows:

- The projector application or stub Shockwave movie
- External globally shared casts
- Settings or preference files

The folder hierarchy described in the previous two paragraphs consists of a main folder and a series of subfolders only one level deep. Figure 6.11 shows a visual representation of this hierarchy.

 This folder hierarchy is on the CD-ROM in the project folder inside the Chapter6 folder. Examine how the files are organized, and open each movie to look at the behavior that runs the next movie. Then, run either the projector or the stub Director movie to demonstrate that it works properly.

Scripts and behaviors that refer to movies in subfolders must include the subfolder in the full filename. For example, a movie called "page2.dir" in the page2 subfolder is referred to by the path and filename "@\page2\page2" in Windows and "@:page2:page2" in Macintosh. The drive or volume name is not required as long as the movie is in a subfolder.

Jumping from one movie in a subfolder to another movie in a different subfolder follows a similar convention. You use the path prefix . in Windows and : in Macintosh to signify moving the folder hierarchy up one level. Following the example from the preceding paragraph, a movie in the subfolder page1 refers to the movie "page2.dir" as "..\page2\page2" in Windows and ":page2:page2" in Macintosh.

Macromedia Director

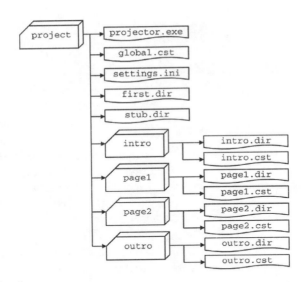

Figure 6.11   This is an example of a folder hierarchy for organizing multiple movies.

Note

An alternate method is to use @\\ or @:: on Windows and Macintosh, respectively.

If the entire project is intended to execute from a CD-ROM or Web site, then the external assets for each screen can be included in the movie folders as well. Being located in folders with the movies aids in organization. Again, global assets (shared casts or shared linked cast member files) should go in either the main project folder or in a global subfolder.

Tip

Create the folder hierarchy and template movies early in a project. Test all variations of navigation paths that your project will support. The navigation code is easiest to change before a lot of work is done on the movies.

Interactive Portfolio Project

In Chapter 5's project section, you created a movie for the introduction sequence and added some text and graphics with animation. With the portfolio project section in this chapter, you will create the rest of the movies required for the project. You won't finish the movies because there are still more chapters to cover additional topics. However, by the end of this chapter, you will have six more movies ready for your project.

Creating the Main Movie

Because the introduction movie (intro.dir) leads into the main movie, you need to start by creating this one first in this section.

The rest of the movies in the project will all have common features, such as a quit button and a border around the edge of the stage. They will also link to the four external casts created in the project section of Chapter 5, "Creating the Score." This is the perfect place to create a template movie that can be used as the basis for all the subsequent movies. This will save some time by avoiding the redundant work of creating six movies with the same settings.

The Movie Template

The template movie file needs to have three areas created to be useful as a template:

- The movie properties must be set to the desired values.
- The external casts must be linked to the movie file.
- Some of the images and text from the global casts must be placed in the score.

The following steps lead you through the creation of the template movie:

1. Create a folder called Chapter06 in the Portfolio_Project folder on your hard drive. This is where the files for this chapter will be stored.

2. Start Director, or create a new movie if Director is already open. Open the movie properties dialog box (by selecting Modify, Movie, Properties), and change the settings to match those in Figure 6.12. Use a stage size of 640×480 pixels, a stage color of pure black, RGB color selection, and 50 score channels. Close the properties dialog box when you are finished. In the Control Panel window, set the tempo of the movie to 30 frames per second.

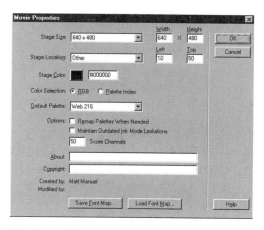

Figure 6.12   The settings for the template movie will be used by all the movies based on the template.

3. Copy the four external casts (`AnimatedFont.cst`, `StaticFont.cst`, `GlobalImages.cst`, and `GlobalCode.cst`) from the Chapter04 folder on your hard drive to the Chapter06 folder. This continues the version-control process by ensuring that working copies are kept safe while modifications are made. If you prefer, you may use the files from the Chapter04 folder inside the Portfolio_Project folder on the CD-ROM.

4. Save this movie as "template.dir" in the Chapter06 folder on your hard drive. This movie will not be distributed with your project. It is just used to create other movies.

5. Open the Movie Casts dialog box by selecting Modify, Movie, Casts. It shows only one cast associated with the current movie, the internal cast (see Figure 6.13).

Figure 6.13 All new movies are created with an internal cast, by default.

6. Use the Link button to repeatedly link to each of the global external casts. Use the copies in the Chapter06 folder on your hard drive (the same folder where the "template.dir" movie resides). The order of linking doesn't matter. Figure 6.14 shows the dialog box with all four external casts linked. Close the Movie Casts dialog box when you finish.

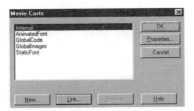

Figure 6.14 The four global external casts are now linked to the template movie. All movies based on the template movie now have access to these casts.

7. Switch to the `GlobalImages` cast window. Drag the border cast member to the score in channel 1. This sets it behind any other sprites on the stage. Set its begin frame to frame 1, and its end frame to frame 30. You should leave its ink effect on Copy so the white portion stays visible. This is also the most efficient ink effect for playback. Figure 6.15 shows this sprite in place.

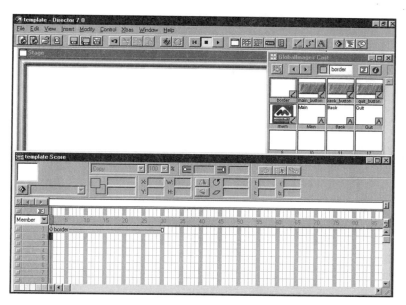

Figure 6.15   The border sprite is positioned in channel 1 of the score and can be seen centered on the stage. Because this cast member is 640×480 pixels in size, it fills the entire stage.

8. Drag the quit button cast member to channel 45 in the score. Position it onstage so it is in the lower-right corner, inside the border. Drag the quit text cast member to channel 46 in the score. Center it within the quit button sprite, and set its ink effect to Background Transparent. Set the begin and end frames of both sprites to 1 and 30, respectively.

9. Place the main button and back button cast members into channels 47 and 49. Position them onstage so the main button sprite is in the lower-left corner of the stage, and the back button sprite is centered at the bottom edge of the stage.

10. Place the main and back text members into channels 48 and 50. Position each text sprite within its corresponding button sprite. Set the text sprites' ink effects to Background Transparent, and make all four new sprite spans begin at frame 1 and end at frame 30. Figure 6.16 shows these sprites on the stage, and Figure 6.17 demonstrates the score layout.

11. Next, you will add one behavior to the last frame in the movie, frame 30. Switch to the GlobalCode cast. Drag the Go Loop behavior to the frame script channel (channel 0) of the score at frame 30. This behavior causes playback to jump back to the previous marker in the score. If there is no marker, as in this case, it jumps back to the beginning of the score. This causes the template movie to loop continuously.

Figure 6.16   All three buttons will not necessarily be used in every movie based on this template movie. It is easier to delete the sprites that are not required rather than add them in the correct positions.

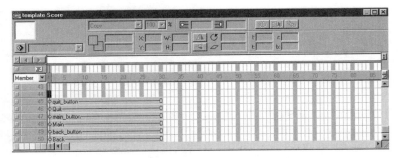

Figure 6.17   It is important that the text sprite for each button appears in a higher channel than the button image sprite. However, the channel ordering between buttons is irrelevant.

> **Note**
>
> By adding behaviors already, you are getting a little ahead of the material covered in the book so far. But the efficiency gained by adding them now warrants a little advanced work.

12. From the GlobalCode cast, drag the Play Done behavior to the main button and back button sprites. This may be easier in the score because you want to make sure that the behavior is attached to the image sprites, not to the text sprites. The behavior returns to the movie or frame where a play Lingo command was issued. You will learn more about this in the project section of Chapter 7, "Using Behaviors," page 149.

13. You also need to attach a behavior to the quit button sprite. Drag the Jump to Movie behavior onto the image for this button. A standard file location dialog box appears, asking you to locate the movie file to jump to when this behavior is activated. Because you have not yet created the credits Director movie (where you eventually want this button to take you), select the "template.dir" file in the Chapter06 folder on your hard drive. You will change this in a later section in this chapter.

14. The parameters dialog box for this behavior appears next. Set them with the values from Figure 6.18. The movie name should be "@\template.dir," as chosen in the previous step. Click OK to close the dialog box.

Figure 6.18   By assigning this behavior at this stage, you avoid a little extra work with each movie that is based on the template.

15. Save the template movie before moving on to the next section.

The template movie is now ready for use in preparing the other movies that actually make up the project. A finished version of this movie is named "template.dir" in the Chapter06 folder inside the Portfolio_Project folder on the CD-ROM. Next, you will create the main movie for the project.

The Main Movie

The main movie is like a menu for accessing different parts of the portfolio. It will have a title to identify to the user where they are the project. Links to the four areas (skills, accomplishments, employment, and education) will be presented with text sprites. Interesting ambient animations act as points to identify each area.

The following steps lead you through the creation of this movie:

1. If the template movie is still open in Director, use the File, Save As command to save it under the name "main.dir" in the Chapter06 folder on your hard drive. If it is not open, copy the "template.dir" file and rename it to "main.dir," and then open "main.dir" in Director. This step is important because you do not want to accidentally modify the template movie.

2. Create four text members by using an appropriate font and font size in the internal cast. Their contents are "Accomplishments," "Skills," "Employment History," and "Education." Use the same text for the name of each cast member.

3. Place each text cast member in the score in channels 20, 23, 26, and 29. Use Background Transparent ink, and set the sprite spans to frames 1 through 30. See Figure 6.19 for the score and cast at this step.

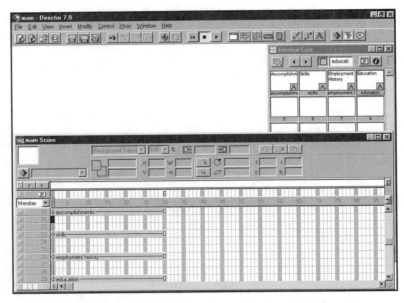

Figure 6.19 The four text members are in the score at the correct channels. Each cast name matches the contents of the cast member for clarity.

4. Position the sprites on the stage so they are left-aligned, about 100 pixels in from the left edge. Order them from top to bottom so they are roughly centered vertically with a natural space between them. Figure 6.20 shows an example of the layout on the stage.

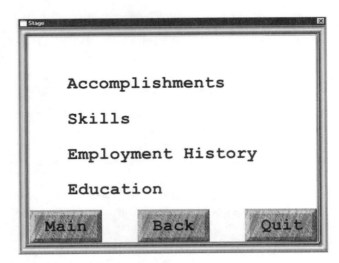

Figure 6.20 The order of the text sprites on the stage does not have to match that shown here. Consider placing your best point at the top of the list.

5. Select the internal cast window. Import all the Animated GIF files from the main images folder inside the Portfolio_Project\Chapter06 folder on the CD-ROM. Choose the Animated GIF format option for all four images.

6. Place these images in channels 21, 24, 27, and 30 in the score with the usual sprite span of frames 1 through 30. Move the image sprites on the stage, so one image is beside each line of text. Figure 6.21 shows a possible choice for the matching order. Animated GIF sprites ignore the ink settings, so you have to ensure that they do not overlap (and obscure) part of the border or text sprites.

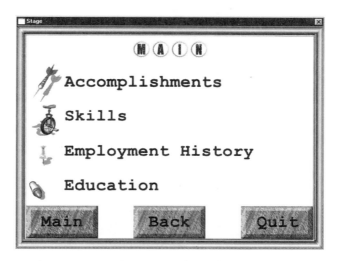

Figure 6.21 Because these are animated GIF images, they will act as idle animations while the movie plays.

7. With the bullet points complete, you can move on to creating the title text. You will use the special character images that were imported in Chapter 4's project section. Switch to the StaticFont cast; and drag the cast members M, A, I, and N to the score in channels 3 through 6. Set the usual sprite span of frames 1 through 30.

8. Position all four images near the top of the stage (a Y value of 50 works well). Spread them out so the word MAIN is spelled, as shown in Figure 6.22. You used the bitmap image versions of the characters in the score.

Note

In Chapter 8, "Understanding Scripts," page 183, you will learn how to create a script that switches each letter to the animated version whenever the user rolls over the letter.

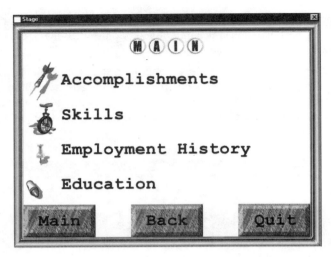

Figure 6.22 You may choose to group the letters close together like this, or you may want to spread them out so they cover the top of the stage.

9. Because this is the hub screen, you require neither the back button nor the main button. They were inherited from the template movie. Delete the four image and text sprites for these buttons from the stage or score.

10. Save the movie ("main.dir") to complete this section of the project for this chapter.

The main movie is not quite complete because you have not linked the text sprites to their respective movies yet. The next section shows you how to create these movies, and then you will return to this movie to finish the links.

Creating the Information Movies

All the information movies start with the template movie as their base. They have text members to describe key points in their subject areas. The title for each screen will also be spelled out with images from the imported font files.

Accomplishments Movie

The accomplishments movie serves to list all the outstanding achievements in your life. You might want to list projects you completed, awards you won, or anything else you are proud of. Creating this movie is similar to the main movie in that it will consist of lines of text, animated images, and a title across the top of the stage.

The following steps show how to create this movie:

1. Open the template movie ("template.dir") from the Chapter06 folder on your hard drive. Save it immediately as "accomplishments.dir" in the same location.

2. Create text members for each of your accomplishments. A suggestion is to list the item separately from the institution associated with it. For example, an author could list the

title of a book as an accomplishment and provide the name of the publisher, but in separate cast members. Use descriptive names for the cast members.

3. Place the text members in the score, starting in channel 20. Leave two blank channels between each item to allow for the image to be placed later in this section.

4. Position the text sprites on the stage in a manner similar to the main movie. Figure 6.23 shows an example of the stage at this step.

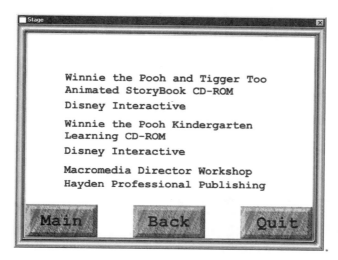

Figure 6.23 Depending on the amount of information you have to display, you may want to decrease the font size for the text sprites.

5. Import the files from the accomplishments images folder under the Portfolio_Project\ Chapter06 folder on the CD-ROM. Use the Animated GIF format option and put the files in the internal cast.

6. Place one of these images beside each accomplishment point on the stage, shown in Figure 6.24. Use the empty score channel below the text sprites for each point.

7. Switch to the StaticFont cast. Place cast members in the score to spell ACCOMPLISHMENTS, starting at channel 3. Position these sprites at the top of the stage, and spread them out as you did for the title in the main movie. See Figure 6.25 for an example.

8. The back button is not used in this movie. Delete both the image and text sprites from the score or stage.

9. Save the movie ("accomplishments.dir"); you are finished with it for this section.

When you link to this movie from the main movie, the back button will become functional. After you create the credits movie, you will come back to this movie and fix the link for the quit button.

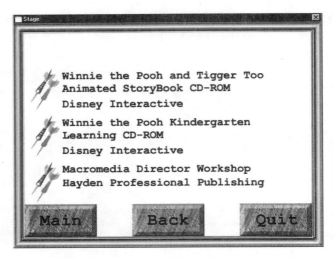

Figure 6.24 The images here relate to the theme of the images in the main movie—the accomplishments point in the main movie had a dart beside it, too.

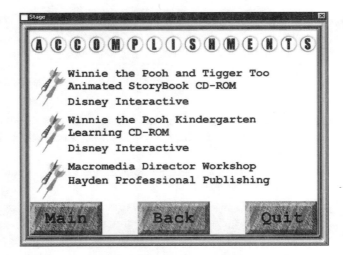

Figure 6.25 Because there are so many letters in the word ACCOMPLISHMENTS, it may be difficult to get them all onstage. Try to avoid overlapping them, if possible.

Skills Movie

The skills movie will be slightly different from the accomplishments movie. Because skills typically require a little more detail to explain, you will create multiple areas of the score for this movie. The first area will be very similar to the accomplishments movie you just completed in the previous section. The other areas will have more information about a specific skill identified in the first area. The final step is to link the sections together by using simple behaviors.

The following steps lead you through the process of creating this movie:

1. Build the main screen of this movie by following the first seven steps of the previous section, substituting information for skills instead of accomplishments. Start with the template and save it under a new name. Create and position the text. Import the images from the skills images folder and position them. Create the title SKILLS by using the StaticFont cast members. Figure 6.26 shows what your movie should look like after this step.

> **Note**
>
> There are two extra images in the skills images folder. Go ahead and import them. They are used in subsequent steps in this section.

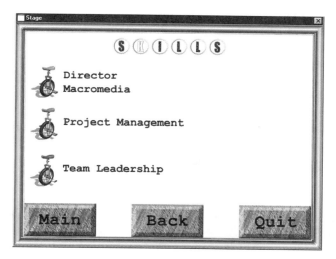

Figure 6.26   Because the steps are so similar for the first part of this movie, use the previous section as a guide. This is what the stage should look like when you are ready to proceed.

2. Create markers for each skill at intervals in the score. For example, create one called Director at frame 40, Project at frame 80, and Team at frame 120. These denote where the screens with the details will be located. Figure 6.27 shows the score with these markers added.

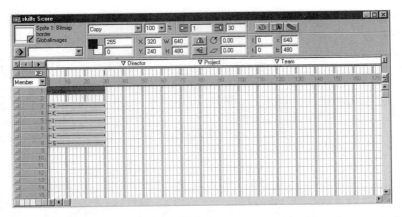

Figure 6.27   The score is scaled to 50% for this figure. You may want to also scale your score window if all the frames cannot fit onscreen at the same time.

3. Expand the spans of some of the sprites out to frame 150. Do this for the border, quit button, quit, back button, and back and title character sprites. Change the start frame for the back button and back sprites to frame 40, corresponding with the Director marker. Now, the main sprites extend across the entire movie, and the back button appears only in the detail screen areas.

4. Copy the text sprites from the main screen to their respective areas in the score. For example, copy the director sprite so it starts at frame 40, where the Director marker is located. These text sprites will serve double-duty as subtitles for each of the different areas. Move them up to just underneath the SKILLS title and center them onstage.

5. Create new text members with the detailed information about each skill. Use a smaller font size so you can fit more information on each screen.

6. Place these cast members in the score in a channel just below the subtitle for each screen. Position them on stage to your liking.

7. Open the GlobalImages cast window. Place the MWM cast member (the Made with Macromedia logo) in the Director area of the score, below the detail text sprite. Position it on stage below the same sprite. Figure 6.28 shows the stage at this section of the score.

8. Place the Earth and ball toy cast members in the score in the Project and Team areas, respectively. Position them onstage like the MWM sprite. These images may not fit the skills areas that you have included in your portfolio. Try substituting other images that are more suitable if this is the case. Figures 6.29 and 6.30 show these two screens with all their pieces on the stage.

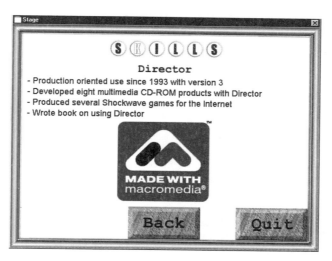

Figure 6.28   The Director section has a subtitle, detailed text, and an image to reinforce the content.

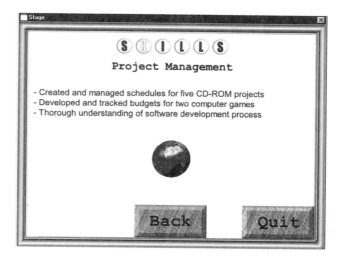

Figure 6.29   The project management screen is similar to the Director screen. The image of the Earth rotates when the movie plays.

Working with Movies

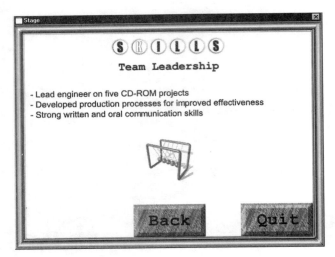

Figure 6.30   Following the pattern of consistency, the team leadership screen is similar to the other two screens. If your skills are unrelated or extremely different, you may want to have each subscreen appear different as well.

9. The Go Loop behavior on frame 30 will not work as you expect any longer. It defaults to moving the playback head to the first marker it finds. If there is no marker in the score, it returns to the beginning of the movie. Because you added markers, it now jumps to the Director marker. Place a marker named Skills at frame 1 in the score to fix this.

10. Now, you have areas of the score devoted to each skill to present detailed information. There is still no way for the user to view this information while the movie is playing. You will add behaviors to the text members on the first screen that jump to different markers in the score. Open the GlobalCode cast window to continue.

11. Place the Go Loop behavior at frames 70, 110, and 150 in the frame script channel of the score. These frame numbers are the end of the sprite spans for each subsection of the score. This will loop the playback head back to the previous marker, keeping the current screen displayed.

12. Drag the Play Frame X behavior to the Director text sprite in the Skills section of the score. Enter frame 40 (corresponding to the Director marker) in the parameters dialog box, shown in Figure 6.31. Although it is better to use a marker name than a frame number, this behavior accepts only numbers.

> **Note**
>
> If you change the layout of the score (moving markers, for example), you will have to update this behavior for it to continue to work as expected.

Figure 6.31 Following the pattern of consistency, the team leadership screen is similar to the other two screens.

13. Attach the Play Frame X behavior to the remaining skill text sprites (Project Management and Team Leadership) in the Skills area of the score. Enter the frame number for the corresponding marker in the behavior parameters dialog box.

14. Play the movie and experiment with the navigation. Click the skill text on the first screen to jump to the details screen for that skill. The back button causes playback to return to the first screen when it is clicked. The Play Done behavior that was attached to this sprite in the template movie causes this effect.

The skills movie is almost complete for this chapter. After the credits movie is created, the quit button will have to be linked to it instead of to the template movie. The next section shows how to build the next two movies.

Employment and Education History Movies

The employment and education movies are essentially the same format as the accomplishment movies, but with different information, of course. Rather than duplicate the steps to create them here, this will be left as an exercise.

The image files required to complete these movies are in the employment images and education images folders inside the Portfolio_Project\Chapter06 folder on the CD-ROM. You may import these and use them as idle animations for the main points in each movie.

Figures 6.32 and 6.33 show the stage for completed versions of these movies. If you get stuck while creating them, you may refer to the finished movies "employment.dir" and "education.dir" in the Chapter06 folder in the project area of the CD-ROM.

The initial versions of all the movies in the portfolio are complete, except for the credits movie. In the next section, you will make this movie and enter your contact information.

Creating the Credits Movie

The credits movie will play whenever the user of the portfolio clicks the quit button. The purpose of this movie is to provide contact information, so the portfolio user knows who created it. The movie will pause on the contact information and wait for a mouse click. The Macromedia logo will be displayed for a few seconds, and then the project will halt.

Follow these steps to create the final movie.

1. The credits movie is also based on the template movie. Open the template movie file, "template.dir," to start. Save it immediately with the new name "credits.dir."

2. Delete all three button sprites and their text sprites from the movie. Because the user has already pressed the quit button, there is no way to get back to the other movies.

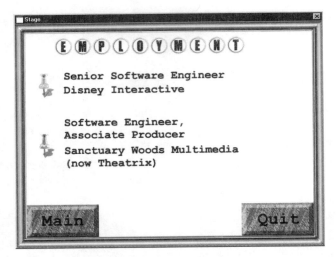

Figure 6.32 The employment screen in this figure has two previous positions and employers. There is one more pushpin icon available if you want to include three items here.

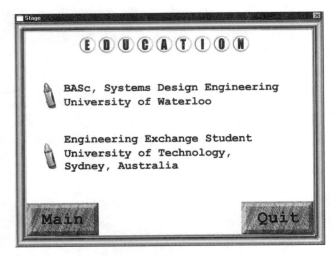

Figure 6.33 The education screen is very similar to the employment screen. Another crayon icon is also available for you to use.

3. Create a new text cast member in the internal cast that contains your contact information. Include at least your name and phone number or email address, but more is better here.

4. Place the text member in channel 3 in the score. Use the usual start and end frames of 1 and 30. Center the sprite horizontally and move it to the top half of the stage.

5. Create another text member with the contents `click to continue`. Place it in channel 4, centered horizontally and in the bottom half of the stage. Figure 6.34 shows both text members in position.

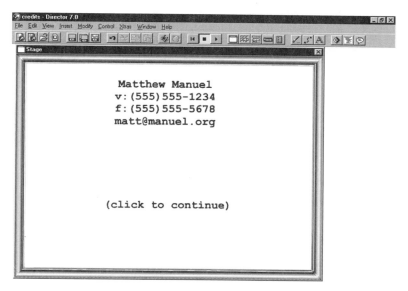

Figure 6.34 The phone numbers in this figure are obviously invalid. Make sure that you use the correct information in your portfolio.

6. Contract the click to continue sprite span so its end frame is at frame 15. Open the `GlobalImages` cast and drag the MWM member to channel 4, starting at frame 16. Truncate this new sprite span at frame 30. Figure 6.35 shows the score at this point.

7. Move the Macromedia logo sprite (MWM) downstage so it doesn't overlap the contact information. A sample configuration is shown in Figure 6.36.

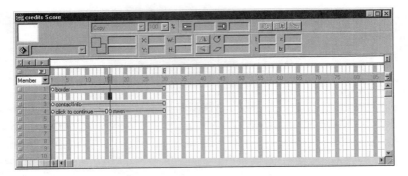

Figure 6.35 This movie is divided into two portions: the contact information with the click to continue instruction and the contact information with the Macromedia logo.

Figure 6.36 Macromedia requires the use of its logo on any commercial product made with Director. Refer to the files in the Made with Macromedia folder inside the Director installation folder on your hard drive for more information.

8. If not already shown, expand the score so the effects channels are visible. You're going to set the tempo channel to wait for a mouse click and pause for a few seconds. Double-click in the tempo channel (the top channel) at frame 15 to open the Frame Properties: Tempo dialog box. Activate the Wait for <u>M</u>ouse Click of Key Press option button (see Figure 6.37). Click OK to continue.

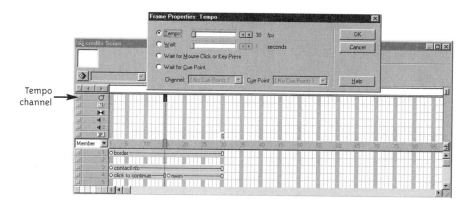

Figure 6.37   The tempo channel provides a simple way to pause the movie or change the tempo.

9. Double-click on the tempo channel in the last frame of the movie. Select the <u>W</u>ait option button and set the slider to four seconds. This will pause the movie for four seconds and then continue.

10. Because this is the last movie to play in the project, you do not require the Go Loop behavior on the last frame anymore. Delete the behavior from this frame. If you do not have Director set to loop the movie, it will stop playback after playing this movie once. A projector will quit when it reaches the end of this movie.

11. Play the movie to see the effects of the tempo channels settings. Director automatically changes the cursor when it is set to wait for a mouse click. Click the stage to finish the movie.

All the movies for the project have been created now. The next section shows you how to link them together to form navigation paths between them.

Linking the Movies

Now that Director files exist for all the movies, you can proceed to link them together by using simple Lingo and Behaviors. In this section, you will link the introduction movie to the main movie, the main movie to all four information movies, and the quit button to the credits movie.

The following steps provide the details on how to accomplish this:

1. Copy the previous version of the "intro.dir" movie file from the Chapter05 folder on your hard drive to the Chapter06 folder. Open the movie from the Chapter06 folder.

2. Go to the last frame of the movie, frame 150, and select the frame in the script channel. Type the letter g; the script window opens with an exitFrame handler already started. This is exactly what you need. Finish this handler by entering the script go to movie "main" (you already started with the g earlier in this step). See Figure 6.38 to see the way this handler should appear.

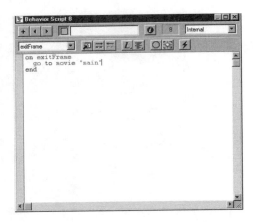

Figure 6.38 When you start typing with a frame in the script channel selected, Director assumes that you want to create an exit frame handler.

3. Close the script window and save the movie. Rewind and play the movie. After the score animation finishes, you'll see that it automatically opens the movie "main.dir."

4. Open the GlobalCode cast window. Attach the behavior Play Movie X to the Accomplishments text sprite. The parameter dialog box shown in Figure 6.39 appears. Type @\accomplishments into the field, and click OK. This behavior uses the Lingo command play instead of go. The play command remembers where it was executed. When Director encounters the play done command, it returns to this point in the project.

Figure 6.39 The @ sign before the movie name tells Director to look in the current folder for the movie being referenced.

5. Attach this same behavior to the other three text sprites. Use the movie names skills, employment, and education as parameters for the behavior. You have now created links from the main movie to the four information movies.

6. Click on the quit_button sprite and open the Behavior Inspector window (Window, Inspectors, Behavior) shown in Figure 6.40.

7. Click the behavior parameters button (the blue diamond icon) to open the parameters dialog box for this behavior. The file selection dialog box opens to select a movie, just like when you first assigned this behavior to the quit button sprite while making the template movie. This time, select the file "credits.dir." Leave the other settings in the parameters dialog box the same as before. Click the OK button to continue.

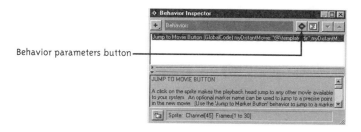

Behavior parameters button

Figure 6.40 The Behavior Inspector window allows you to see what behaviors are attached to a sprite. You will learn more about this topic in Chapter 7, "Using Behaviors."

8. Now, the quit button is linked to the credits movie. Whenever the user clicks this button, the project will change to the credits movie with the contact information, and then quit.

9. Open each of the four information movies ("skills.dir," "accomplishments.dir," "employment.dir," and "education.dir"), and repeat Steps 7 and 8 with the quit button sprites. Each time, select the file "credits.dir."

All of the movies are now linked. The main movie plays each of the information movies. These movies, in turn, return to the main movie. The quit button causes playback to go to the credits movie. When the credits movie finishes, the portfolio stops playing.

Wrap-up

This was a fairly involved project section because so many movies were created. Each movie displays some information about the specific area of the portfolio. The skills movie even has subscreens for more detailed information on specific skills.

Several behaviors were introduced that provide navigation options within and between movies. This lets you link all the movies together so you can navigate between them for the first time. Finished versions of all the movies and casts from this chapter are in the Chapter06 in the Portfolio_Project folder on the CD-ROM.

The next chapter goes into more detail on the use and creation of behaviors. You will create a few behaviors that add even more interactivity to the portfolio project.

Using Behaviors

Behaviors, which are Director's scripting macros, are some of the most valuable and versatile features of Director. They give programmers and nonprogrammers alike easy access to Director's infinite possibilities, and they can be as powerful as any Lingo script.

Starting to use behaviors is fairly easy; fully understanding them involves a paradigm shift that can be difficult. But once mastered, behaviors are incredibly useful.

They are not a panacea for all interactivity in Director, though. Overall program control and complex data-oriented scripting is still best done with normal Lingo coding. Chapter 8, "Understanding Scripts," covers general scripting in detail.

This chapter introduces behaviors and shows how to use them and even how to create them. Behaviors by their nature encourage good programming practices, so they're a great introduction to creating complex interactivity. They encourage you to think in object-oriented and user-centered paradigms.

What Is a Behavior?

There are two ways to look at behaviors: from the perspective of the person using a behavior that is already made and from the behavior script author's perspective. From the first perspective, a behavior is like a personality to apply to a sprite. It controls how the sprite reacts to events and how it behaves over time. From the second perspective, a behavior is a specialized form of Lingo scripting.

> **Note**
>
> Behaviors can also be attached to frames, rather than to sprites, in the Frame Script channel. Frame-based behaviors use a subset of events that sprite-based behaviors use. This chapter concentrates on sprite-based behaviors.

In essence, a behavior receives events (called *handlers* in Director) and responds with actions. Director transmits an event (such as a mouse click) to a behavior, and the behavior performs some predetermined action (such as playing a sound) according to its handlers.

A metaphor for behaviors is the biological notion of stimulus and response in organisms. The environment (Director) produces stimuli that cause responses in organisms (behaviors). Using behaviors with sprites in Director is akin to adding personalities to objects (see Table 7.1).

Table 7.1 Examples of stimuli and responses.

	Stimulus	*Response*
Organisms	Tickle	Twitch
	Excessive heat	Movement away from heat
Sprites	Mouse click	Play a sound
	Frame advance	Move to the next step on a path

To a script author, a behavior is simply a special type of Lingo script that allows the author access to the attached sprite's properties. Behaviors also receive a standard set of events automatically; that is, behaviors have certain reserved handler names that are automatically called by Director when certain conditions are met.

A behavior is perfect for reuse within a movie and between multiple movies or projects because they deal with sprites directly. Multiple movies may need to have a sprite act in a similar manner to a behavior that already exists so they just use the same behavior. Because behaviors have a somewhat constrained structure, they are also an excellent introduction to general Lingo. (See the sections "Creating Your Own Behaviors" and "Creating Behaviors Using Lingo," later in this chapter, which deal with modifying behaviors and writing new behaviors for more details.)

Benefits of Behaviors

The greatest benefit of behaviors is that they allow nonprogrammers to create interactive experiences without writing Lingo scripts. Behaviors are a fabulous feature of Director that enables people to create movies that are more engaging and responsive. It still takes planning and work, but it is far easier than starting with a blank Script window.

As shown by the behaviors included with Director and in collections on the Internet, behaviors are reusable. People create libraries of general-purpose behaviors and share them for all to use. This is actually one of the hallmarks of good programming practice: code reuse. Why invent the wheel again and again when a good solution already exists? Director makes reusing behaviors easy and accessible.

The Parameter dialog box is an excellent way to see inside a behavior. It allows the user to modify a behavior's parameters in an easy-to-understand, visual way. Remember that different sprites can use the same behavior differently if you modify the behavior's properties.

If written properly (using a `GetBehaviorDescription` handler), behaviors can be self-documenting, although it's up to the author of the behavior to include this information. When present, this description is easy to see and travels with the behavior, which means that the user never has to locate a separate file to understand how to use a behavior.

More than one behavior can be attached to a sprite. Complex actions can be built by combining the simple building blocks of individual behaviors. For example, a scale Behavior and a Rotate behavior can operate simultaneously with no modifications, and can therefore take the place of a more complex behavior. As noted earlier, not all behaviors can coexist on one sprite because some conflict with others.

Behaviors are intimately tied to the events of the movie. Behaviors operate at the same tempo as the movie, so they automatically stay synchronized. Behaviors are entirely aware of the global movie parameters, so they act in concert. Director broadcasts a standard set of events to all behaviors in every frame.

How Are Behaviors Used?

The main purpose of behaviors is to have a sprite respond to events. Often, a behavior already exists that has the desired event–response (stimulus-response from biology) relationship you need. In this case, the behavior is attached to a sprite, which should respond in a predetermined manner.

Attaching a behavior to a sprite or a frame is straightforward. The following steps show how to use a preexisting behavior with a sprite:

Note

You can follow along using the movie "use_behavior_start.dir" in the Chapter07 folder. Try playing this sample movie before starting these steps. You'll confirm that the ellipse doesn't do anything yet.

1. Open the library that contains the behavior you want to use (see Figure 7.1). In this case, use a behavior from the Animation, Automatic library that comes with Director. You can access different behavior libraries from the Library palette in the Window menu, and you can switch libraries by using the button in the upper-left corner of the Library palette. To open the Library palette, select Window, Library Palette.

Library select button →

Figure 7.1   The behavior is ready to be attached to a sprite.

2. Drag the behavior from the cast or library onto the sprite on either the stage or the score. (It doesn't matter whether you choose the stage or the score—the actions have the same effect—it's just a matter of preference.) For this example, drag the Random Movement and Rotation behavior onto the ellipse.

3. The Parameters dialog box (if the behavior has one) now appears. Fill in the properties you want to use with this instance of the behavior. It's important to note that the values of the properties you choose here apply to this behavior on this sprite only. You can use different values for different sprites.

   Leave the defaults for the behavior in this example (see Figure 7.2). Click OK to close the dialog box. Clicking the Cancel button will not attach the behavior.

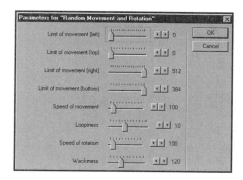

Figure 7.2   The Parameters dialog box for the sample behavior.

4. Select the sprite on the stage, and open up the Behavior Inspector window by clicking
   the diamond-in-a-box icon in the sprite info overlay (see Figure 7.3). The sprite info overlay is the translucent box that appears below a sprite and contains information about the
   sprite.

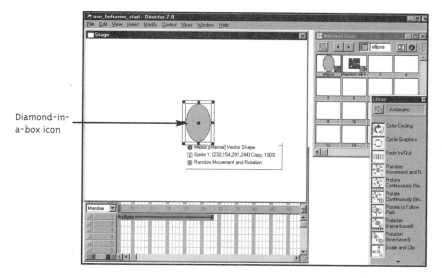

Diamond-in-
a-box icon

Figure 7.3   The Ellipse sprite is selected onstage, showing the sprite info overlay.

The behaviors attached to the selected sprite are listed in the window. There is only one
attached so far in this example (see Figure 7.4). The diamond icon near the upper right of
the Behavior Inspector window opens the Parameter dialog box for the selected behavior.
Modify the properties if you want.

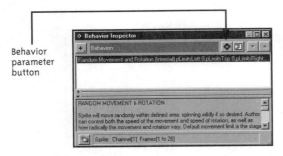

Behavior parameter button

Figure 7.4   The Behavior Inspector window, showing information for the Ellipse sprite.

Tip

Pay careful attention to the behavior description section of the Behavior Inspector window. If written into the behavior, this area will show valuable information on how to use the behavior, including any of its limitations. Not all behaviors have information here—the behavior's author can decide whether to include it. However, each of the behaviors that come with Director has a description.

5. Close the Behavior Inspector window (or make the stage the front window). Notice that a copy of the Random Movement and Rotation behavior is in the Internal cast of the movie (see Figure 7.4). This happens when you drag the behavior from the library onto the sprite. The behavior must remain with the movie to stay associated with the sprite. This also ensures that the original behavior in the library remains unchanged, even if you modify the copy.

6. Advance the playback head to the last frame of the movie, where the Ellipse sprite ends. Attach the Go Loop behavior from the Navigation behavior library to the stage. Drag the behavior to an empty spot on the stage or to the Frame Script channel in frame 28 in the score (see Figure 7.5). This frame script will loop back to the previous marker or to the beginning of the score, if there is no marker (as in this case).

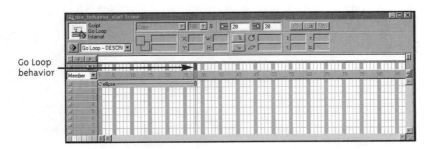

Go Loop behavior

Figure 7.5   The Go Loop behavior is attached to frame 28.

7. Now, play the movie. The Ellipse sprite moves randomly around the stage. It also rotates as it moves. Notice that it never moves off the stage.

 Try modifying the properties of the behavior to get a feel for how modifying properties changes the way a behavior operates (see Figure 7.6). If you change only one or two property values at a time, the effect will be more evident.

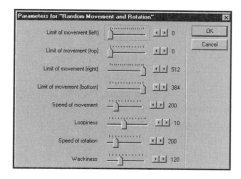

Figure 7.6 The Speed of movement and Speed of rotation behaviors are now 200.

To add more behaviors, follow the same steps as outlined previously. Note, however, that not all behaviors work together; they may conflict with each other. Also, not all behaviors work on all cast member types. A member type must have the properties available for the behavior to modify.

 Refer to the Director movie "use_behavior_finish.dir" for an example of a completed version of this movie.

Behavior Libraries

A collection of behaviors can be made into a *behavior library*, which is essentially an external cast that contains only behavior members. Libraries are a good place to collect similar or often-used behaviors for quick access.

Anyone can make custom behavior libraries. First, you create a new external cast, and then you copy or create the desired behaviors. Custom libraries can even appear in the Library Palette window in Director, similar to the built-in libraries. Simply place the library (external cast file) in the Libs subdirectory of the Director installation directory. Quit and restart Director if the library doesn't appear right away.

A Quick Tour of Available Behaviors

Director comes with several built-in behavior libraries for specific uses. As mentioned previously, you access behavior libraries through the Library Palette window. You can switch libraries by using the icon in the upper-left corner of the window.

The following sections describe the behaviors available from the libraries. Be sure to check the libraries before creating your own behavior; a suitable behavior may already exist.

Automatic Animation Behaviors

The Automatic library contains behaviors that continuously vary a sprite's properties over time. They also don't require user input to work. You can use them as a quick way to add interesting animations to the sprites in your movies.

Interactive Animation Behaviors

Interactive behaviors cause sprites to react in some way to user input. Mouse clicks, rollovers (when the mouse cursor rolls over the screen space where a sprite is displayed), and mouse drags can all be used to change a sprite's properties. Exciting interactivity is fairly easy to achieve by mixing these behaviors. Note that some behaviors require other behaviors in order to work properly, such as the Drag and Toss behavior and Vector Motion behavior pair.

Controls

Controls allow sprites to graphically represent underlying data, such as the time or text, on the stage. They are also used to associate sprites with some movie navigation actions.

 As an exercise, use the Analog Clock behavior to build a movie that displays the current time (see Figure 7.7). Refer to the behavior's description for specific instructions. The movie "analog_clock.dir_" contains a completed version.

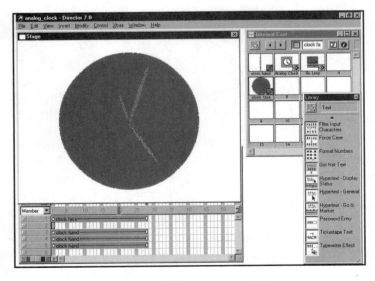

Figure 7.7 An analog clock, which was created by using no scripting.

Internet Form Behaviors

Form behaviors are advanced behaviors that send information from a Shockwave movie to a server over the Internet.

Multiuser Internet Behaviors

One of Director's advanced features is its capability to connect to multiuser servers by using special Lingo commands. You can use Multiuser Internet behaviors (that harness these Lingo commands) as a starting point for a multiuser Shockwave application.

Streaming Internet Behaviors

Because the Internet is a much slower medium than CD-ROM or hard drives, cast members are loaded gradually over time. You can use streaming Internet behaviors to control a movie while waiting for cast members to load. It is always a good idea to display a progress bar for any load that takes longer than a few seconds.

Java Behaviors

Another advanced feature of Director is its capability to save a movie as a Java applet. However, not all of Director's capabilities can be translated directly to Java. The Java Behaviors library contains behaviors written specifically to convert to Java.

Flash, QuickTime, and Sound Media Behaviors

The Flash, QuickTime, and Sound libraries have behaviors that allow nonprogrammers to effectively use specialized media. For example, one behavior will play a sound whenever a sprite is clicked. Another behavior sets the properties of a Flash cast member.

Navigation Behaviors

Complex navigation (such as movement between frames, markers, and movies) can be accomplished with Navigation behaviors. Some must be used in the Frame channel, others on sprites, and still others on either. These behaviors can be used to create good score organization.

Text Behaviors

The Text library is very useful when dealing with text in any form. It contains a set of utility behaviors that display text in different ways. Some are also useful for formatting text as input. A fun example is the Typewriter Effect behavior that plays a sound whenever a key is pressed, simulating a typewriter.

Behaviors from the World Wide Web

The Behaviors.com Web site (http://www.behaviors.com) offers a collection of behaviors in libraries for download. This site promotes sharing and use of behaviors by anyone. The behaviors on this site were submitted by other users and might help you solve a problem in your Director project.

A Sample Game Created with Built-In Behaviors

So that you can see how easy it is to add interactivity to your movies, this section shows how to create a little game using only behaviors that come with Director and no Lingo scripting.

To save a bit of time, start with a movie that already has sprites:

1. Open the movie "ballgame_start.dir_." Play the movie, and note that nothing happens (see Figure 7.8). (The last frame already has the Go Loop behavior attached to it, so the movie will loop forever.)

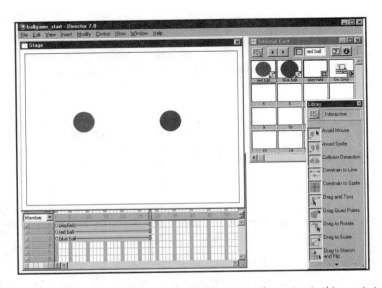

Figure 7.8   You will be attaching behaviors from the libraries to the sprites in this movie to create a simple ball game.

2. From the Library palette, locate the Animation, Interactive section. Attach the Constrain to Sprite behavior to each of the red and blue balls. Choose sprite channel 1 for the constraint channel and uncheck the Draggable option (see Figure 7.9). This behavior will ensure that the two balls never go outside the playfield sprite.

Figure 7.9   The Parameters dialog box of the Constrain to Sprite behavior allows you to set the channel of the sprite that this behavior references.

3. Attach the Avoid Mouse behavior to the blue ball. Choose a value of 25 for the distance parameter because this matches the radius of the ball. All others can remain at their default values (see Figure 7.10). Now, the blue ball will move away from the mouse cursor whenever the cursor is near.

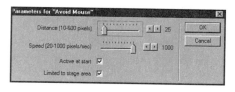

Figure 7.10 Parameters of the Avoid Mouse behavior include the minimum distance the mouse can approach the sprite before the sprite moves away. The speed to avoid the mouse can also be set here.

4. Play the movie and see how the behaviors you attached to it so far affect the sprites. The blue ball will now move out of the way of the mouse cursor.

5. Attach the Drag and Toss behavior to the red ball sprite. Leave the Sensitive Period property at the default value. Make sure that the Sprite Jumps to Mouse on mouseDown property box is not checked (see Figure 7.11).

Figure 7.11 By leaving Sprite Jumps to Mouse on mouseDown box unchecked, you ensure that the user has to click on this ball to toss it.

6. Attach the Vector Motion behavior to the red ball sprite. It is located at the bottom of the Animation, Interactive behavior library. The Drag and Toss behavior requires this behavior. Look in the behavior description of Drag and Toss for this information. Leave the default values unchanged in the Parameters dialog box (as shown in Figure 7.12).

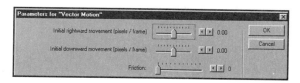

Figure 7.12 The default values for the property dialog box of the Vector Motion behavior are o in all three areas. After you have this game working, experiment further by changing some of these values and noting their effects.

7. Play the movie again, and try dragging the red ball and releasing the mouse button while it is moving. It should continue on its path, even off the stage. The red ball didn't stay within the playfield as expected. Why?

8. The red ball sprite doesn't seem to be paying attention to the Constrain to Sprite behavior that was attached. This is because the order in which you attach behaviors to a sprite determines the precedence. Right now, the Drag and Toss behavior is taking precedence over the Constrain to Sprite behavior.

9. Correct the order by opening the Behavior Inspector window for the red ball sprite. Now, select the Constrain to Sprite behavior in the list and click the down arrow (in the upper-right corner) until it reaches the bottom of the list (see Figure 7.13). Play the movie, and notice that the red ball now does not leave the area of the playfield sprite.

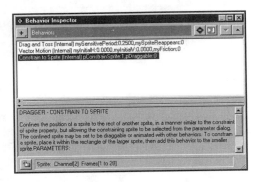

Figure 7.13   The Behavior Inspector window shows the new order of the behaviors for the red ball sprite.

10. The game would be better if the red ball were to push the blue ball around. Attach the Avoid Sprite behavior to the blue ball. Choose channel 2 as the channel of sprite to avoid (the channel of the red ball), and set the distance to 50 pixels, which is the diameter of one ball (see Figure 7.14).

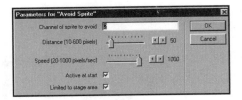

Figure 7.14   By setting the speed to its maximum value of 1000, you ensure that the blue ball avoids the red ball as quickly as possible, reducing the possibility of overlap.

Now, play the movie and throw the red ball around. No matter how fast you throw it or in which direction, the blue ball will always avoid it. If the blue ball gets caught in a corner, remember that you can coax it out with the mouse.

Other ways to enhance the movie are to add more ball sprites and attach the same group of throw or avoid behaviors to them. Keep in mind that you might have to add multiple copies of the Avoid Sprite behavior to each ball that you want to dodge another ball.

Try adding friction to the red ball by modifying the friction property in the Parameters dialog box of the Vector Motion behavior. Now, it will slow down over time.

You can also try adding the Random Movement and Rotation behavior from the first example to some of the blue balls. You might have to play with the order of the behaviors to get the effect you want. Try putting the Random Movement and Rotation behavior second in the list for each Blue Ball sprite. Now, they wiggle around the playfield as you throw the other balls at them.

 Open the movie "ballgame_finished.dir" to see an example of a multiball game (see Figure 7.15).

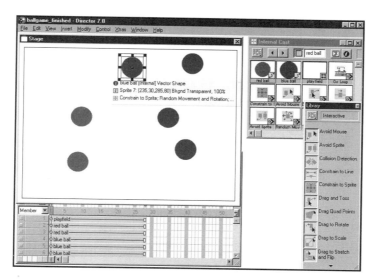

Figure 7.15 The ball game has been enhanced by adding more balls to each side. All the blue balls will avoid each of the red balls, creating a chaotic playfield.

Save-as-Java Techniques

Director has the capability to save movies as Java applets. This is similar to saving a movie as a Shockwave movie, but there are still significant differences. This chapter covers Save-as-Java techniques that are specific to using behaviors.

The main advantage of converting a movie to Java is compatibility. Shockwave movies can play only on Windows or Macintosh platforms. Java is much more widespread—almost any modern operating system can run a Java applet. By sharing your movies this way, you can reach a broader audience.

Director cannot convert every available feature into a Java applet. The Save-as-Java command converts only a subset of Director's capabilities. For this reason, it is often useful to pull behaviors from the Java Behaviors library included with Director. These behaviors are specially written by Macromedia to contain only functions that will convert to Java. If you know you want to distribute a movie as a Java applet, you should use this library.

Creating Your Own Behaviors

Remember that just like anything good in life, using behaviors properly doesn't come without effort. Even though you don't need to know Lingo, you still need an understanding of the terminology and paradigms of interactivity.

Still, it takes a special mindset to create effective and efficient interactivity. Take some time to do up-front planning for exactly what you're trying to accomplish. Frame your thoughts in terms of events and actions, stimuli and responses.

Even if you don't have very much programming experience, creating your own behaviors is not too difficult. Don't be intimidated—the framework that Director provides makes it easy to start.

Getting Started

There are two methods of creating your own behaviors. The best way to start is to use the Behavior Inspector. You can build a behavior step-by-step by using supplied events and actions. The second method is to start with a blank Lingo script and write exactly what you need. However, this requires a good knowledge of Lingo.

Building interesting and useful behaviors with the Behavior Inspector is possible. You might be constrained by the events and responses available for building them, but it's a good way to learn. You still won't have to write Lingo code, but you'll become familiar with some of its terminology.

Standard Events

To understand the capabilities of behaviors, you need to understand what events are available and what they represent. Table 7.2 lists the events presented by the Behavior Inspector to construct a new behavior.

Table 7.2 Default events for behaviors.

Event	Description
mouseUp	A mouse button is released inside a sprite.
mouseDown	A mouse button is pressed inside a sprite.
mouseEnter	The cursor enters the area of a sprite.
mouseWithin	The cursor is within the area of a sprite; repeated if the cursor is left inside.
mouseLeave	The cursor leaves the area of a sprite.
keyUp	A key is released.
keyDown	A key is pressed.
rightMouseUp	The alternate mouse button (mouse button+Ctrl on a Macintosh) is released.
rightMouseDown	The alternate mouse button (mouse button+Ctrl on a Macintosh) is pressed.
prepareFrame	The stage is about to be updated with all the sprites' positions, once per frame.
exitFrame	The playback head is about to leave a frame, once per frame.

Creating Behaviors by Using the Behavior Inspector

The following steps illustrate the process of creating a new behavior by using the Behavior Inspector:

1. Open the movie "build_behavior_start.dir." A sprite is already onstage, and the Go Loop navigation behavior is attached to the last frame of the sprite span (see Figure 7.16).

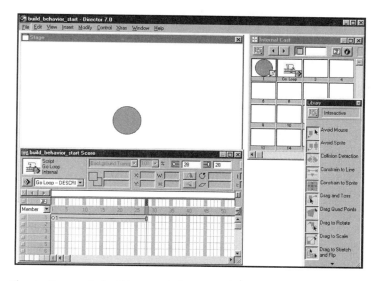

Figure 7.16 The starting movie for this example has a simple circular sprite and a loop behavior on the last frame.

2. Select the sprite and open the Behavior Inspector window. Just below the list of behaviors (which is still empty) is a line with a small arrow on the left side. If the arrow is not already pointing down, click it to open the Events and Actions areas of the window.

3. Create a new empty behavior by selecting New Behavior from the plus sign icon in the top left of the Behavior Inspector window. Call it `myFirst` or something similar. Notice that a new cast member is created, containing the new behavior (see Figure 7.17).

4. From the Events area, choose Mouse Up from the drop-down menu on the plus sign icon. To make it easier to read, the menu has spaces between the words of the events and capitalizes each word (for example, `Mouse Up`). Notice that the event name in the Events list doesn't have spaces (for example, `mouseUp`): This is the Lingo equivalent of the event. Lingo keywords can't contain spaces.

5. Now, choose the Sound, Beep action from the drop-down menu you get when you click the plus sign icon in the Actions area (see Figure 7.18). Play the movie and click on the sprite. You should hear a system beep whenever you release the mouse button over the sprite.

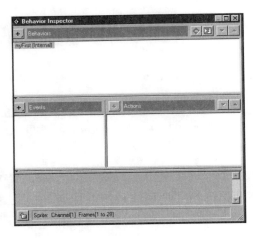

Figure 7.17 The new behavior is now visible in the Behavior Inspector window and the Cast window.

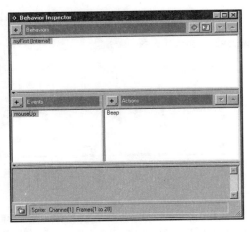

Figure 7.18 The new behavior now has a Beep action associated with the mouseUp event.

6. Add a mouseEnter event, and associate it with the Cursor, Change Cursor action. Select the Finger cursor from the dialog box (see Figure 7.19).

7. Add a mouseLeave event, and associate it with the Cursor, Restore Cursor action. Play the movie, and watch how the cursor changes over the sprite. It should change into a finger when it's over the sprite and back into the default cursor when it's not on the sprite.

Figure 7.19 The Specify Cursor action has a list of cursors to choose from. A few of the choices are a hand, a watch, a finger, a crosshair, a pencil, and an eraser.

Events can have multiple actions associated with them in the same behavior. For variation, try adding a Change Cursor action to the mouseDown event with the Hand cursor. Also, add a mouseUp event with the Change Cursor action with the Finger cursor.

Add a Beep action to the mouseEnter and mouseLeave events. Now, the movie is noisy and the cursor is active. Refer to the movie "build_behavior_finished.dir" for an example of this step (see Figure 7.20).

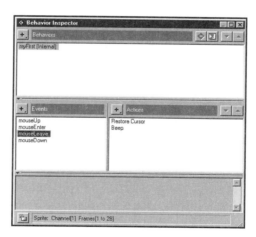

Figure 7.20 Now, the behavior has many events and actions defined.

Creating Behaviors by Using Lingo

Situations may arise in which no available behavior provides the feature you want in your movie. If you can't build the behavior step-by-step by using the Behavior Inspector methods, as discussed previously in the "Creating Behaviors by Using the Behavior Inspector" section, you will have to write it in Lingo.

Because Chapter 8, "Understanding Scripts," has specific details on writing code with Lingo, this section mainly introduces Lingo concepts that deal with behaviors. It is possible to use only a small subset of Lingo code and still write interesting and useful behaviors.

Remember that a behavior receives events and produces actions according to how it is defined. As you have learned, another name for events in Director is *handlers*. The Lingo that defines a behavior is a collection of handlers with specific names, corresponding to the events that Director sends to sprites.

Handlers are similar to functions or procedures in other programming languages (such as C, C++, or Pascal) and subroutines in BASIC. A handler is a collection of Lingo lines, like sentences, wrapped on each end by the handler definition. Listing 7.1 shows an example of a basic handler.

Listing 7.1 An example of a simple behavior.

```
on beginSprite me
    set piSpriteNum = the spriteNum of me
    set the loc of sprite piSpriteNum = point(100,100)
end beginSprite
```

The name of this behavior is beginSprite. It corresponds to the name of the event Director sends to all the behaviors on a sprite when the playback head first encounters the sprite span in the score. The first and last lines define the scope of the Lingo in the behavior.

The first line tells Director to start executing Lingo in this handler when a beginSprite event is generated. The word me following the name is a parameter for the handler. In the case of behaviors, all handlers must have the me parameter first, and it is often the only parameter. For more details on parameters, see Chapter 8, "Understanding Scripts," page 183.

Similarly, the last line of Listing 7.1 tells Director to stop executing Lingo for this particular handler. Notice that the end line doesn't have parameters. Even though the end line is optional, it is always a good idea to include it because it makes the code easier for people to read.

The two Lingo lines in the body of the handler contain Lingo keywords and operators that perform some simple tasks. The most complex handlers are still made from simple individual lines of Lingo.

In this case, the first line sets the variable piSpriteNum equal to the value the spriteNum of me. The channel of the sprite that this behavior is attached to is referred to as the spriteNum of me. This just makes it easier to refer to piSpriteNum rather than the spriteNum of me all the time.

The second line sets the position (location, or loc) of the sprite to a point defined by x-axis and y-axis values 100. When the playback head first encounters this sprite, Director positions the sprite so that its registration point is located at position (100,100) on the stage. For reference, position (0,0) is the top left of the stage.

As you can see, Lingo is a fairly friendly language to learn. It reads much like simple English. However, you still need to know the specific words to use, and that knowledge will come with study and time. Refer to the Lingo-specific help file, accessed with the <u>W</u>indow, <u>L</u>ingo Dictionary command, for details on all the commands available.

Structure of Handlers in a Behavior

Behaviors are most frequently written to affect the properties of the sprites they're attached to. A typical behavior follows a standard structure, defined by simple handlers. Listing 7.2 shows the skeleton of a typical behavior.

> **Note**
>
> Anytime two dashes (--) appear in Lingo, Director ignores the rest of the line. These are areas used for comments about the code, which make it easier for people reading the code to understand. It is a good practice to include the name of the behavior in a comment on the first line of the script. It will then show up in the cast window and make locating the behavior easier. Follow the name comment with a brief comment describing the behavior.

Listing 7.2 *The basic structure of a behavior.*

```
-- behavior name

-- a short description of what this behavior does plus
-- any special requirements should go in comments
-- at the top

on beginSprite me
  -- place Lingo here that gets executed once when the sprite
  -- is first encountered in the score
end beginSprite

on prepareFrame me
  -- place Lingo here that gets executed every time the
  -- playback head moves on to a frame with this sprite
  -- remember this occurs before the stage is updated
end prepareFrame

on exitFrame me
  -- contains Lingo for just before the playback head leaves
  -- the frame
end exitFrame

on mouseUp me
  -- put Lingo code here that gets executed whenever the user
  -- releases the mouse button while over this sprite
end mouseUp
```

```
on endSprite me
   -- Lingo code to clean up whatever has been done by this
   -- behavior should go here. It gets executed just before
   -- the playback head leaves the sprite span
end endSprite
```

The `beginSprite` handler is the same as the sample behavior from the last section (see Listing 7.1). This is where any setup Lingo code should be written.

Handlers for `prepareFrame` and `exitFrame` events get called every time the frame changes in a movie, even if the movie is looping. Typically, `prepareFrame` has code to calculate a few items and then update sprite properties before the stage is updated. Likewise, `exitFrame` might determine a few items based on new sprite properties. In practice, `prepareFrame` is used more often for complex behaviors. The `exitFrame` handler is a good place to put movie navigation code.

The `mouseUp` handler should look familiar from the section "Creating Behaviors by Using the Behavior Inspector." This event is passed to any behavior on a sprite when the user releases the mouse button while the cursor is over the sprite. Lingo that changes properties of a sprite based on user actions would go here. Other handlers like this are `mouseDown`, `mouseEnter`, and `mouseLeave`.

Finally, for this skeleton code, the `endSprite` handler is called when the playback head leaves a sprite span (the area of the score containing a sprite). Use this handler for cleaning up anything the behavior may have changed about the sprite or the movie in general.

All the handlers of a behavior are optional. If the behavior doesn't need to respond to a particular event, there is no need to include a handler for that event. If Director doesn't find a handler that corresponds to an event, nothing happens.

Properties of Behaviors

A property in a behavior is like a container that stores an item between handlers. Sometimes, a `prepareFrame` handler needs to know something that a `beginSprite` handler calculates. Normally, handlers are independent and don't know anything about each other. Properties allow handlers to communicate with each other and store state information about the behavior. Contrast this with parameters that are passed to a handler; these are accessible only within the specific handler.

For example, the `piSpriteNum` item in Listing 7.1 would be a good choice for a property. All the handlers in a behavior might want to refer to the sprite channel where the behavior is running. Lingo allows for this with the `property` keyword. Anything that is defined as a property of a behavior is accessible by any handler in the behavior. Listing 7.3 shows an example of this.

Listing 7.3 A behavior that demonstrates the use of properties.

```
-- property example behavior

-- this behavior demonstrates the use of properties

property piSpriteNum  -- the sprite channel
```

```
property psMyName        -- the name of this behavior


on beginSprite me
  set piSpriteNum = the spriteNum of me
  set psMyName = "property example"
end beginSprite


on mouseUp me
  if piSpriteNum = 10 then
    put "My name is " & psMyName
  end if
end mouseUp
```

Two properties are defined at the beginning of the behavior, with the `property` keyword. Property names must not have any spaces in them (for example, `piSpriteNum`). It is a good idea to use just letters and numbers, with no special characters. For this book, all property names begin with p and are followed with a letter that corresponds to the type of data stored in the property. In this case, `piSpriteNum` stores an integer number that represents the sprite channel. Also, `psMyName` stores a string representing the name of the behavior. This convention is completely optional, but may make your Lingo code easier to understand.

The `beginSprite` handler sets the values of the two properties. Then, the `mouseUp` handler refers to the properties. First, it checks to see whether the behavior is on a sprite in channel 10. If it is, it puts a note into the Message window with the name of the behavior.

You can watch this behavior work in the movie "property_behavior.dir." Make sure that you have the Message window open so you can see the output. Every time you click on the red sprite, a note appears in the message window. Clicking on the blue sprite doesn't do anything because it's not in channel 10. Figure 7.21 shows an example of this movie.

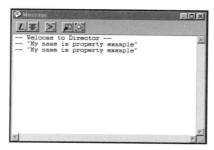

Figure 7.21 Notice that the note appears in the message window only when the red sprite is clicked.

Putting It All Together to Create a Behavior

Now that you know the basics of the Lingo needed to write your own behaviors, it is time to build a useful one from scratch. In this section, you'll make your own behavior that causes a sprite to react to a mouse click.

Start with the movie "lingo_behavior_start.dir." For simplicity, the movie is already set up with two sprites and a loop behavior on the last frame. No other behaviors are in the movie.

You're going to make a behavior that causes a sprite to jump to a new location onstage whenever it is clicked on:

1. Select a blank cast member, and open the Script window. Name the cast member Random Jump. Type the code in Listing 7.4 to start your behavior. Refer to Figure 7.22 for details.

Listing 7.4 The two properties and the beginSprite handler of the Random Jump behavior.

```
-- Random Jump

-- this behavior will cause a sprite to jump to a new
-- location on the stage whenever it is clicked

property piSpriteNum  -- the sprite channel
property ppStartPoint -- original location

on beginSprite me
  set piSpriteNum = the spriteNum of me
  set ppStartPoint = the loc of sprite piSpriteNum

  -- start the sprite in a random location
  set stageRect = the rect of the stage
  set newX = random(the width of stageRect)
  set newY = random(the height of stageRect)

  set the loc of sprite piSpriteNum = point(newX, newY)
end beginSprite
```

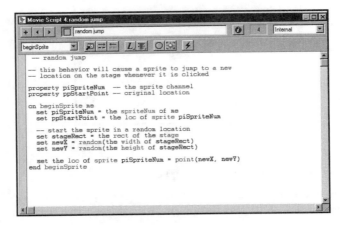

Figure 7.22 The Script window, showing the start of this behavior script.

> **Note**
>
> Notice that in the beginSprite handler, you are careful to ensure that the sprite stays on the stage. The reference the rect of the stage gives us the size of the stage. Then, you use the width and height of this rectangle to generate a new random position. Finally, you update the sprite location with this position.

2. Close the script window and make sure that the new script cast member is still selected. Open the Script Cast Member Properties dialog box by clicking on the blue circle with the letter i in it. Change the type of the cast member from Movie to Behavior. This tells Director that it is a behavior script and not a movie script. Only behavior scripts can be attached to sprites. Figure 7.23 shows this dialog box.

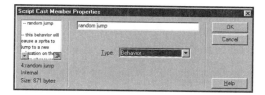

Figure 7.23   The Script Cast Member Properties dialog box for the behavior script.

3. Attach the behavior to each sprite by dragging it from the cast to the sprite. Try playing the movie several times, and notice that each sprite moves to a random location whenever the movie is started. The sprite still doesn't react to a mouse click.

4. Select the behavior cast member again, and open the Script window. (The icon beside the info icon is a shortcut to the Script window for a script cast member.) Add the code from Listing 7.5 to the bottom of the script for this behavior. Close the script window again.

Listing 7.5   The mouseUp handler to be added to the Random Jump behavior.

```
on mouseUp me
  -- move the sprite to a new random location
  set stageRect = the rect of the stage
  set newX = random(the width of stageRect)
  set newY = random(the height of stageRect)

  set the loc of sprite piSpriteNum = point(newX, newY)
end mouseUp
```

> **Note**
>
> You're reusing the Lingo from the beginSprite handler in this handler by simply copying it within the script.

Macromedia Director

5. Play the movie and click on each sprite several times. They should jump around the stage, to a new random location with every mouse click.

Note

An interesting thing to note here is that you didn't have to reattach the behavior to the sprites. After a behavior is attached, you can modify that behavior's Lingo and it will automatically update with each sprite.

Refer to the movie "lingo_behavior_finish.dir" to see it in action.

Creating a Subroutine Handler

Because the Lingo to move the sprite to a new location is duplicated in two handlers, it would be better to make a new handler that does only this task. This will be a custom handler that doesn't correspond to a standard Director event. The only way to execute the Lingo in this handler is by calling it from other handlers.

To see this implemented, replace the entire behavior script with the code in Listing 7.6.

Listing 7.6 The revised Random Jump behavior has the jump Lingo code isolated in a new handler.

```
-- random jump

-- this behavior will cause a sprite to jump to a new
-- location on the stage whenever it is clicked

property piSpriteNum  -- the sprite channel
property ppStartPoint -- original location

on beginSprite me
  set piSpriteNum = the spriteNum of me
  set ppStartPoint = the loc of sprite piSpriteNum

  -- start the sprite in a random location
  jump me
end beginSprite

on mouseUp me
  -- move the sprite to a new random location
  jump me
end mouseUp

on jump me
  set stageRect = the rect of the stage
  set newX = random(the width of stageRect)
```

```
  set newY = random(the height of stageRect)

  set the loc of sprite piSpriteNum = point(newX, newY)
end jump
```

The Lingo that causes the sprite to jump to a new location is now contained in handler called `jump`. Because Director doesn't have any predefined event called `jump`, the only way this handler will be executed is by other handlers. Where the jump Lingo used to be in the `beginSprite` and `mouseUp` handlers, there is now a single line with the code `jump me`.

Whenever the normal Director events occur, the Lingo in those handlers is executed. When Director gets to the `jump me` line, the Lingo in that handler is called just as if it were in the main handlers. This is called a *subroutine*.

Subroutines are useful programming constructs. They allow code to be reused throughout a behavior, which makes the behavior smaller and easier to follow. Another benefit is that an error in a subroutine needs to be fixed in only one place. If the same code were copied to different handlers, it would have to be fixed in each location.

 The movie "lingo_behavior_finish2.dir" shows this change in the Random Jump behavior.

Advanced Behavior Concepts

Some of the concepts for writing behaviors in Lingo are beyond the scope of this chapter. By following the previous examples and making small changes, you should have a basic understanding of what it means to write a behavior in Lingo. This section introduces a few common techniques, such as self-documenting behaviors, that make behaviors even more useful. For more information, refer to the online help on these topics.

The `GetBehaviorDescription` handler is useful for documenting your behaviors. What you include in this handler is what appears in the description area of the Behavior Inspector window when the behavior is selected. It is a good idea to use this handler and keep the information up-to-date.

The `GetPropertyDescriptionList` handler is extremely useful for writing generic behaviors. This handler controls the property dialog box that appears when you first drag a behavior onto a sprite. The user selects the values of the properties that the behavior will use.

Sometimes, it is necessary to communicate between behaviors or between a movie script and a behavior. You can use the Lingo keywords `sendsprite` and `sendallsprites` for this purpose. These Lingo commands execute handlers in the target sprite's behaviors, just as if an event of the same name were received.

Remember that behaviors should be collected into external casts to become Libraries. This makes them more accessible and thus more likely to be used often. Reusing behaviors can result in significant timesavings.

Interactive Portfolio Project

In this chapter, you learned more formally about behaviors. They are special Lingo scripts that are attached to sprites. Events are received by a behavior in the form of handlers. Each handler performs an action according to how it is programmed.

At this stage of the Portfolio Project, you should have a working version of your project with complete navigation between the component movies. In this chapter, you will add some behaviors to the project to give it more life and interactivity.

Some of the information in the portfolio will be linked to Internet Web sites with a built-in behavior. You will use the behavior inspector to create a behavior that changes the cursor over active areas. Two behaviors will be written from scratch to provide feedback to users as they click on information sprites.

Applying Standard Behaviors

In the previous chapter, you attached a few standard behaviors to sprites. This provided navigation functions to the sprites so the end user could interactively decide which portions of the portfolio to look at. In this section, you will apply another standard behavior that opens the default Web browser and loads a specified URL. This provides more information about specific points in the portfolio, such as companies and educational institutions.

1. Start by copying all the Director movie and cast files (except "template.dir_") from the Chapter06 folder on your hard drive into a new Chapter07 folder. This is the familiar version control step. These files are also on the CD-ROM in the Portfolio_Project\Chapter06 folder.

2. Open the movie "accomplishments.dir" in Director. Switch to the GlobalCode cast window.

3. The first accomplishment in the sample movie is an animated storybook CD-ROM product. Attach the Go to URL behavior to this text sprite. The parameter dialog box shown in Figure 7.24 appears. This is where the full URL is entered.

4. Enter the URL http://disney.go.com/DisneyInteractive/Pooh/wtpttasb/index.html in the dialog box. (Use your own URL if you have an accomplishment you want to link to.) Click OK to continue.

5. Attach the Go to URL behavior to the Disney Interactive line of text in the first accomplishment point. Making this a separate sprite in the previous chapter allows you to attach different behaviors to the same general point. This time, enter http://www.disneyinteractive.com/ as the URL for linking.

6. Connect to the Internet manually if you are not already connected. Play the movie, and click either of the sprites with the Go to URL behavior. Your default Web browser will open and automatically start loading the specified Internet link.

7. Attach the Go to URL behavior to the other sprites in this movie, using URLs for each sprite according to Table 7.3.

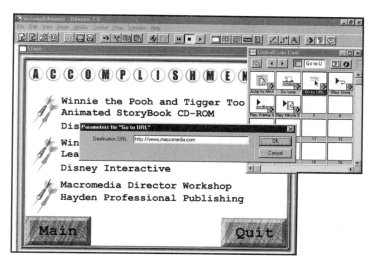

Figure 7.24   The Go to URL behavior takes a URL as its only parameter. Notice that the default parameter is a self-promotion link for Macromedia.

Table 7.3   Sprites and associated URLs for the Go to URL behavior in the "accomplishments.dir" movie.

Sprite	URL
Pooh Kindergarten	http://disney.go.com/DisneyInteractive/pooh/ poohlearningseries/kindergarten.html
Disney Interactive	http://www.disneyinteractive.com/
Director Workshop	http://www.mcp.com/
Hayden	http://www.mcp.com/

Note

At the time of this writing, there was no separate link available for this book. The publisher's Web site is used here instead.

8. Modify each of the remaining three information movies: "skills.dir," "employment.dir," and "education.dir" by attaching links to the appropriate sprites. Table 7.4 lists the sprites with their URLs.

Table 7.4 Sprites and associated URLs for the Go to URL behavior in the remaining movies.

Sprite	URL
"skills.dir"	
Macromedia	http://www.macromedia.com/
"employment.dir"	
Disney Interactive	http://www.disneyinteractive.com/
Sanctuary Woods	http://www.theatrix.com/
"education.dir"	
Systems Design	http://sydewww.uwaterloo.ca/
University of Waterloo	http://www.uwaterloo.ca/
University of Technology, Sydney	http://www.uts.edu.au/

With all the appropriate text cast members linked to an Internet site, the portfolio end user can easily get more information about a specific item. At this stage, there is no feedback to let the end user know that these links exist. In the next section, you will learn how to create a behavior that does this.

Creating a Simple Behavior by Using Events and Actions

In the section, "Creating Behaviors by Using the Behavior Inspector," you learned how to create a behavior without any Lingo scripting. You will create another behavior in this section by using the same method.

This behavior provides feedback to the end user. It changes the cursor from the default cursor to a finger cursor. This is a signal to end users that something will happen if they click on a sprite with this behavior attached.

1. Open the movie "main.dir" in Director. Switch to the GlobalCode cast window. This behavior will be used in most of the movies, so it should be included in the global external cast.

2. Select the first empty cast member in the GlobalCode cast. This ensures that the new behavior is created at this position.

3. Select the Accomplishments sprite and open the Behavior Inspector window (choose Window, Inspectors, Behavior). Expand the window so the Events and Action sections are visible, as shown in Figure 7.25.

4. Create a new behavior with the New Behavior option on the Behaviors selection button (the top plus sign button). Name the behavior finger cursor to signify what it will do.

5. Select the mouseEnter event from the Events plus sign button. You want to change the cursor whenever the cursor enters the sprite.

6. Select the Cursor, Change Cursor action from the Actions plus sign button. Choose the finger cursor from the list presented in the dialog box. The results are shown in Figure 7.26.

Behavior
selection
button

Figure 7.25 The Behavior Inspector window shows the behaviors attached to the current sprite—in this case, the Play Movie X behavior.

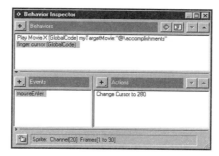

Figure 7.26 Director represents cursors internally with an integer number. That is why the finger cursor you chose appears in the dialog box as cursor 280.

7. Add the mouseLeave event to the Events list. Select the Cursor, Restore Cursor action for this event. This action sets the cursor back to the state it was in before it entered the sprite.

8. Close the Behavior Inspector window and play the movie. Now, as you roll the cursor over the Accomplishments sprite, the cursor changes into a finger cursor. It resets back to your default cursor when you roll off the sprite.

9. Attach this behavior to all the sprites that are appropriate in all the movies. For example, the Quit, Back, and Main buttons should have this behavior. (Be careful to attach it to the image sprite, not the text sprite for the buttons.) All the text sprites that navigate within or between movies, or link to URLs should also have this behavior.

Now, you added feedback for the end users. They will know which areas of the screen lead to more information on a particular topic. In the next section, you will create two behaviors that provide even more feedback.

Creating Behaviors with Lingo

The previous section demonstrated how to create a custom behavior by using events and actions. In this section, you will create two behaviors using Lingo directly.

You have not used any of the animated GIF images from the `AnimatedFont` cast yet in the project. All the section titles at the top of the stage in each movie are made from the character images in the `StaticFont` cast. The first behavior in this section swaps the static image for the animated image whenever the mouse cursor rolls over a letter.

The second behavior will be used on the images for the button sprites. To provide feedback that the button sprite received the end user's mouse press, you will make it look like the button is indented. Flipping the button image over its vertical and horizontal axes can simulate this. Because the button appears to have beveled edges with shadows, the flip effect provides the illusion that the button is pushed into the screen rather than extending out from it.

1. Open the movie "main.dir" in Director. Switch to the `GlobalCode` cast. These behaviors will be used in most of the movies, so they should be in the global external cast.

2. Select the next empty cast member. Open the script window (choose Window, Script). Enter the Lingo code from Listing 7.7 into the window.

Listing 7.7   The letter swap behavior uses properties to store the cast member name and the names of the two casts with the letter images.

```
-- letter swap

-- this behavior swaps an animated letter image in place of a static
-- one when the user rolls over the sprite

property pMemberName
property pStaticCastName
property pAnimCastName

on beginSprite me
   -- store the name of the member
   pMemberName = sprite(me.spriteNum).member.name

   -- store the names of the two casts
   -- this cast has the static letters in it
   pStaticCastName = "StaticFont"
   -- this cast has the animated letters in it
   pAnimCastName = "AnimatedFont"
```

```
end beginSprite

on mouseEnter me
  -- switch the the animated image
  sprite(me.spriteNum).member = member(pMemberName,pAnimCastName)
end mouseEnter

on mouseLeave me
  -- switch back to the static image
  sprite(me.spriteNum).member = member(pMemberName,pStaticCastName)
end mouseLeave
```

3. Name this cast member letter swap, as shown in Figure 7.27. Open the Script Cast Member Properties dialog box with the information button or the [Ctrl+I] (Cmd+I) shortcut key. Select Behavior from the type menu to tell Director to treat this script as a behavior. Close the dialog box and script window to continue.

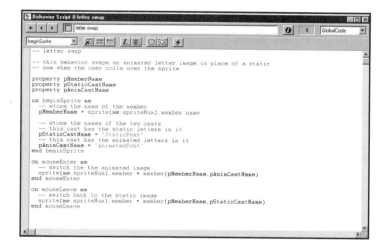

Figure 7.27   The script window shows the syntax of the Lingo code using colors. This is useful for quickly identifying different types of Lingo such as comments, keywords, and strings.

4. Attach this behavior to all the letter sprites that make up the title. You can do this quickly by selecting them in the score and attaching the behavior to the sprite spans. This assigns the same behavior to all the selected sprites.

5. Play the movie and test the new behavior. As you hold the cursor over each letter, it plays the animated version.

6. Select the next empty cast member in the GlobalCode cast. Open a new script window and enter the Lingo code from Listing 7.8.

Listing 7.8   The Button Flip behavior uses custom subroutine handlers such as the Random Jump behavior in Listing 7.6.

```
-- button flip

-- this behavior flips the associated sprite on mouseDown
-- it then unflips it for other events

on mouseDown me
  flip(me)
end mouseDown

on mouseLeave me
  unFlip(me)
end mouseLeave

on mouseUp me
  unFlip(me)
end mouseUp

on mouseEnter me
  if (the mouseDown) then
    flip(me)
  end if
end mouseEnter

on flip me
  sprite(me.spriteNum).flipV = TRUE
  sprite(me.spriteNum).flipH = TRUE
end flip

on unFlip me
  sprite(me.spriteNum).flipV = FALSE
  sprite(me.spriteNum).flipH = FALSE
end unFlip
```

Note

This behavior uses four mouse events to achieve the proper effect. The mouseDown event is expected because that is the intent of the behavior: to flip the button image on mouseDown. The mouseUp event resets the image, also as expected. Recognizing the mouseLeave event is a little more advanced. You want the behavior to reset the image if the user moves off the sprite. The mouseEnter event is even more interesting. You use the mouseDown event to determine whether the mouse button is pressed when you get the mouseEnter event. If it is, you flip the image; if not, you ignore the event.

7. Name this cast member `button flip` and set its type to `Behavior`, also. Close the script window when complete.

8. Attach this behavior to the quit button image sprite. (Do not attach it to the quit text sprite.) Save the movie before continuing.

9. Play the movie and experiment with the quit button. Press the mouse button on it, and move off the sprite before you release the button. Press the mouse button down while off the sprite and move onto it. Verify that the sprite still functions correctly by releasing the mouse button. Director should open the "credits.dir" movie.

10. Attach the letter swap behavior to all the sprites that make the titles in the other four information movies. Also, attach the button flip behavior to all the button image sprites in the same movies.

Now, you have created feedback and interactivity for the end user. The portfolio project is looking more professional and interesting with every step.

Wrap-up

The Portfolio Project gained another feature in this chapter: the capability to display information from an Internet Web site by opening the end user's default browser. The Go to URL behavior does not have to be used on text sprites. Try adding a hidden link to an image sprite by using this behavior.

Feedback for the end user was provided by two new behaviors. The first, created by using the Behavior Inspector, changes the cursor when it is over sprites that link to other areas of the project or to Internet sites. A behavior that makes the button images visually respond to mouse clicks was created in Lingo. Another behavior, used to swap the static character images in the title with animated versions, was also written.

Final versions of the movies for this chapter are in the Portfolio_Project\Chapter07 folder on the CD-ROM.

In the project section of the next chapter, you will create two more behaviors that are slightly more advanced. They will provide even more feedback capabilities.

Understanding Scripts

Lingo provides the most capabilities for interactivity in Director movies. It is virtually required to create unique and ambitious titles. Understanding various aspects of Lingo will lead to better movies overall, even if you do not create any scripts from scratch.

The different types of scripts are covered in this chapter, along with their suggested uses. Basic scripting for controlling the flow of a movie and interacting with an end user is introduced.

Although this chapter can't teach everything about scripting, it shows a few intermediate and advanced concepts. Shockwave Lingo limitations are touched on, and various debugging techniques and tools are presented.

Types of Scripts

Director is a very powerful and flexible environment for scripting. However, scripting can be confusing, especially for inexperienced users.

All scripts share some common features. For example, they are all made up of *handlers*, which are akin to functions or procedures from other programming languages such as C or Pascal. A handler is composed of one or more lines of Lingo code that accomplishes some task.

You can call (or *invoke*) handlers from other handlers by using the handler name in a line of Lingo. Parameters can be passed to handlers, and handlers can return values to the code that called them. One way of understanding handlers is to realize that they extend the Lingo language by providing a simple method of executing a section of Lingo.

The different script types have various capabilities, advantages, and disadvantages. Movie scripts, the default script type, contain handlers that are available to every other script in the movie. Cast scripts belong to one cast member only. Frame scripts usually control movie flow. Parent scripts are used to extend the Lingo language. Behaviors are special scripts that are attached to sprites. The following sections outline the particulars of each type.

Movie Scripts

A movie script is the most accessible type of script. It is the default type for scripts created in a blank cast member space. The handlers in a movie script are accessible to any other scripts in the current movie.

To create a movie script, open a script window with an empty cast member selected. Select the Window, Script menu. See Figure 8.1 for an example of an empty movie script.

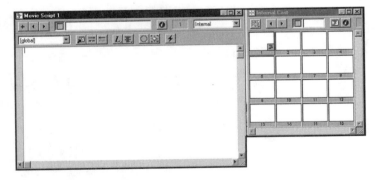

Figure 8.1 An empty movie script cast member, created by opening a script window.

For organizational purposes, it is a generally a good idea to name all movie scripts. The cast member name is used for the movie script name. Director does not require this name, however.

Follow these steps to create and test a simple movie script:

1. Select an empty cast member, and open a new script window.

2. Type Listing 8.1 into the script window. Figure 8.2 shows how the finished script appears in the window. Notice that Director applies colors automatically to the script according to its syntax.

Listing 8.1   A sample movie script that plays the system beep noise twice when executed.

```
-- beep twice when called
on beeptwice
    beep (2)
end beeptwice
```

Note
Lines in Lingo that start with two dashes (--) denote comments in the script. Comments are for reference by script authors only; Director does not attempt to execute commented lines. Therefore, comments do not need to conform to Lingo syntax structures. Comments should be used liberally, even in code that is not distributed beyond the project team, because often the meaning of Lingo code becomes unclear after time—even to the original author.

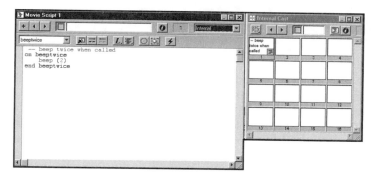

Figure 8.2   The script from Listing 8.1 in the movie script window.

3. Name the script sample movie script, and close the window.

4. Open the Message window from the Window menu.

5. Type the name of the handler, beeptwice, into the Message window and press Enter (see Figure 8.3). The handler in the movie script runs, and two system beeps are played. Refer to the file "beeptwice.dir" from this book's CD-ROM for a Director movie that contains the finished version of this example.

Note
On Windows computers, the beeps play very quickly. Two beeps may sound like only one, but they are actually both playing.

Understanding Scripts

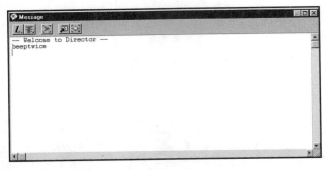

Figure 8.3 The Message window, showing the handler name from the movie script. Pressing Enter tells Director to execute the handler independently of a running movie.

The Message window is an invaluable tool when developing scripts. It can be used to call handlers in movie scripts, as in this example. Any type of script can also output information to the Message window as it is executed.

Movie scripts are useful for containing handlers that need to be globally accessible by any other scripts in the movie, including from the Message window. Any number of movie script cast members can exist concurrently in a movie, including members of external casts. Director searches through all the movie scripts to find the correct handler. Duplicate handlers result in the handler in the movie script with the lowest cast number and cast member number being called. Others are ignored.

Director sends three messages (or *events*) relating to movie progress that can be captured by movie scripts: prepareMovie, startMovie, and stopMovie. Each event is sent to an identically named handler in a movie script. These handlers need not exist in a movie at all. No error messages are generated if Director does not find them.

The prepareMovie handler is called before Director plays frame 1 of the movie. This is analogous to the Before Frame One setting in the cast preload parameter outlined in Chapter 4, "Working with Casts."

The startMovie handler is called just before Director plays frame 1 of the movie. This is a useful location to start an ambient sound playing, for example. Any other setup code should be placed in this handler as well.

As the movie ends, either before going to another movie or as the application quits, the stopMovie handler is called. The Lingo contained within the handler is the last code to execute during the running of the current movie. Cleanup code and any preparation for the next movie should be in this handler.

Listing 8.2 shows an example of a movie script containing these three handlers.

Listing 8.2 **A movie script containing handlers automatically called by Director during movie playback.**

```
-- movie script
on prepareMovie
    -- explicitly load the background sound here
    put "prepareMovie"
end prepareMovie

on startMovie
    -- start playing the background sound
    put "startMovie"
end startMovie

on stopMovie
    -- stop playing the background sound
    put "stopMovie"
end stopMovie
```

Note

The comments in this listing do not describe the actual Lingo in this case; they are merely suggestions for Lingo that is applicable to these handlers.

The fact that movie script handlers are accessible from every other script in a movie can also be a disadvantage. Sometimes, it is desirable to have handlers of the same name perform different functions at different points during playback of a movie. Other types of scripts, such as frame scripts and behaviors, allow this flexibility.

Cast Scripts

Scripts assigned to cast members are still supported in Director, but they have been all but replaced by behavior scripts. The main advantage to a cast script is that it is carried with the cast member wherever it is used in the score. Each sprite that uses the cast member has the cast script associated with it. This is useful for consistency. However, this same property is also the cast script's major drawback. Cast scripts reduce the flexibility of scripting in Director because there is no choice involved. As described in Chapter 7, "Using Behaviors," page 149, behaviors are assigned to sprites in the score and thus provide greater flexibility.

An additional limitation is that each cast member can have only one cast script associated with it. Behaviors solve this by allowing multiple scripts to be assigned to a sprite.

Because of these limitations, the use of cast scripts is not recommended. However, in some cases cast scripts are useful, and they are easy to create. The process is similar to creating a movie script, except a nonempty cast member is selected before starting the script.

Instead of opening an empty script window using a menu command or keyboard shortcut, you must click the script button in the cast window. This opens a new Script window, with the default handler `mouseUp` already started in the script. Figures 8.4 and 8.5 show examples. Because the `mouseUp` handler is used so often in these types of scripts, Director includes it by default.

Script button →

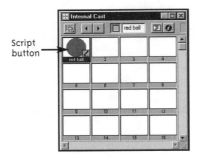

Figure 8.4 The cast member red ball is selected, and the script button in the cast window is enabled.

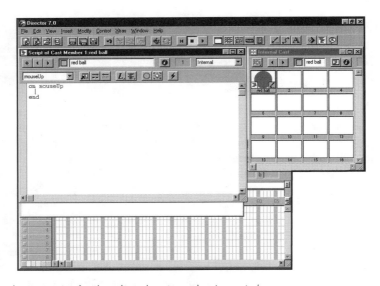

Figure 8.5 The cast script for the selected cast member is created.

Consider the alternative script types seriously before using a cast script. Most often, a behavior script is a better choice because it is so much more flexible. It can be applied to sprites independently of their cast members.

Frame Scripts

Frame scripts are similar to movie scripts, except that they are limited in scope to the frames where they exist in the score. Unlike movie script handlers, frame script handlers are accessible only to other scripts in the same frame.

Because of this limitation, frame scripts are not often used to hold custom handlers. Rather, they are used to respond to events that Director generates automatically. This is similar to the movie event handlers described previously in the chapter, in the section called "Movie Scripts."

Using Frame Script Event Handlers

Common Director events that correspond to handlers in a frame script are prepareFrame, enterFrame, idle, and exitFrame. Each handler is called in succession as Director plays back a frame of the movie. Listing 8.3 shows an example of a movie script that contains all four frame event handlers.

> **Note** As in Listing 8.2, the comments do not apply to actual Lingo in these handlers.

Listing 8.3 A frame script containing handlers automatically called by Director at specific points in a frame during movie playback.

```
-- frame script

on prepareFrame
    -- this code is executed before the automatic 'updatestage'
    put "prepareFrame"
end prepareFrame

on enterFrame
    -- this code is executed after 'updatestage'
    put "enterFrame"
end enterFrame

on idle
    -- this handler may be called multiple times within one frame
    put "idle"
end idle

on exitFrame
    -- this code is executed just before the playback head
    -- moves to another frame
    put "exitFrame"
end exitFrame
```

> **Note**
>
> The put Lingo command is used in this script to send the string in quotes to the Message window. When each handler runs, the corresponding text appears in the Message window.

Director generates each of the four events as the playback head moves into a new frame. The order of the events is as shown in Listing 8.3.

The prepareFrame handler is called as the playback head enters the frame. The stage has not been updated at this time with any new sprites or changes in sprites in the score; it still shows the images from the previous frame.

Director executes an automatic updateStage function call between the prepareFrame event and the enterFrame event. The updateStage call makes the required changes to the stage to reflect any new sprites in the score, sprites that are no longer in the score, and any changes to sprites' properties in the score. After this updateStage event, Director calls the enterFrame handler, if it exists in the frame script.

The idle handler is called between the enterFrame and exitFrame handlers. It is unique in that it may be called multiple times by Director during the same frame. As its name implies, it is called whenever Director is idle during the frame. This idle period changes, depending on the speed of the computer and the frame rate of the movie. The movie author cannot depend on this handler being called a specific number of times, only that it will be called at least once per frame.

Finally, the exitFrame handler is called. This is the last of these four handlers to be executed before the playback head leaves the frame for the next frame. This is a common place to put go to frame or go to movie Lingo code.

Creating a Frame Script

A frame script is created from scratch in exactly the same way as a behavior script. (Refer to the section called "Behavior Scripts" or to Chapter 7, "Using Behaviors," page 149, for more details.) Both are the same types of script to Director. The difference is how they are applied. A frame script is like a behavior that is assigned to a frame (or series of frames) in the script channel of the score.

Another way to create a frame script is to enter it directly into the score. Follow these steps to create two frames scripts by using this method:

1. Click on the script channel in frame 1 of the score. The script channel is directly above sprite channel 1.

2. Start typing the contents of Listing 8.3. As you type the first character (the letter *O* in Figure 8.6), a new script window is opened.

> **Note**
>
> The `exitFrame` handler is shown because it is the most common handler for this type of script. If this were the only handler for this script, you could just type the Lingo for the handler directly into the Script window.

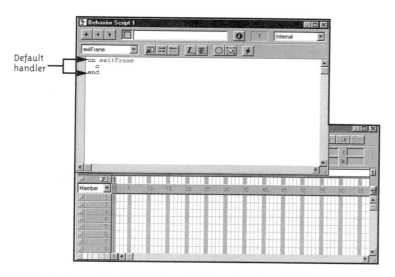

Figure 8.6   When you type the first key with the script channel selected in a frame, this default handler is displayed in a new script window.

3. Because a script already exists from Listing 8.3, select the default script and delete it. Finish entering the script from Listing 8.3. Name this script `frame one script`. Figure 8.7 shows the finished script.

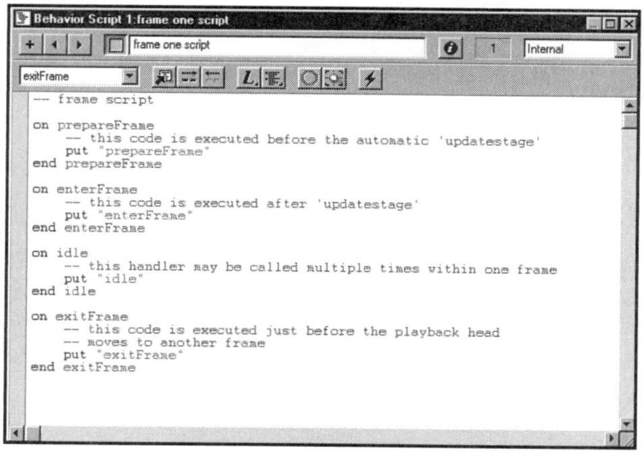

Figure 8.7   The contents of Listing 8.3, shown in the new Script window, whose two scrollbars are active because this script is too big for the current Script window.

4. Select frame 2 of the script channel. Type the contents of Listing 8.4 into the Script window that appears automatically. Because the `exitFrame` handler appears by default, there is no need to type that portion of the listing. Name this script `loop to frame one` (see Figure 8.8).

Listing 8.4 A frame script that creates a loop.

```
-- loop back to frame one of the current movie
on exitFrame
    -- this command tells Director to play frame
    -- one after this one
    go to frame 1
end exitFrame
```

> **Note**
>
> This frame script causes Director to play frame 1 of the movie after the current frame is finished. This effectively loops the movie forever. Because the command is in the `exitFrame` handler, it will execute when the current frame is finished.

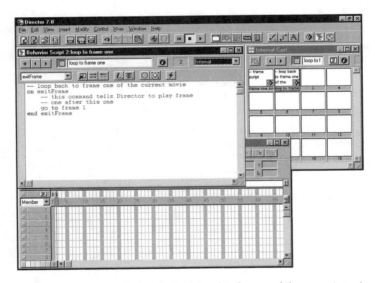

Figure 8.8 A simple script that sends the playback head to frame 1 of the current movie.

5. Open the Message window, and rewind and run the movie. The text from each handler is output to the Message window as the handler is executed. Notice that the order of the handlers never changes. The number of idle messages may be different on different computers. Figure 8.9 shows the Message window after the movie runs for a few seconds.

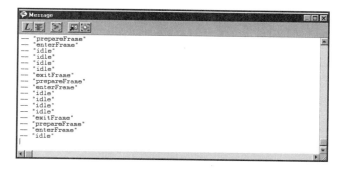

Figure 8.9 The Message window, which is full of text that corresponds to the handlers being executed by Director.

Note

Often, the Message window information appears too quickly during playback to be useful. It is valuable information that is accessible after a movie stops.

The file "framescript.dir" on this book's CD-ROM is a finished version of the movie from this example.

Parent Scripts

Parent scripts are a more advanced concept than the previously discussed types of scripts. They extend Lingo into the area of object-oriented programming. In traditional programming parlance, parent scripts are called *classes*. Objects are instantiated (created) from these classes when the movie is played.

A parent script is not associated with any part of the score or with another cast member. Objects created from parent scripts exist in memory and are accessible from other scripts in the movie at the discretion of the movie author. Just like strings, integers, and characters, an object is another basic variable type in Lingo.

All parent scripts must have a special handler called new, which takes a construct called me as its first parameter. (Other parameters may follow.) The new handler must return the value of me when the handler finishes.

The keyword me in Lingo has special significance. In the case of parent scripts, it represents the object in memory where the parent script resides at runtime. When the new handler returns me, it is actually telling the handler that called new where in memory it exists. This allows the calling handler to keep track of the object.

Parent scripts are used for a wide variety of tasks in Lingo. They can be used to control sprites on the stage, but behaviors are generally better-suited to this task. More often, a parent script controls a more abstract concept. For example, the logic of a game can be contained in a parent script. Or a parent script can be used to provide specialized functions to other handlers, such as a sound or timer object. This allows a set of complex code to be simplified into a few handlers within the object. Other scripts that use the object benefit from its features, but it is simple to use.

More information on parent scripts, including creating one, is contained in the "Advanced Scripting" section, later in this chapter.

Behavior Scripts

Behaviors are a specialized form of parent scripts. They are always attached to sprites in the score. Usually, they control some aspect of the sprite, but they are not limited to this.

Director extends the concept of parent scripts with behavior scripts, which are much more user-friendly. Because behavior scripts have special handlers, you can interact with them by using a visual interface. In the section "How Are Behaviors Used?" on page 151 of Chapter 7, "Using Behaviors," this has already been shown, with the properties dialog boxes that appear when a behavior is attached to a sprite.

You can create behavior scripts interactively by using the Behavior Inspector window. You can also create them in Lingo directly as script cast members.

Three special handlers can be used to provide this visual interface to a behavior:

- `getBehaviorTooltip`
- `getBehaviorDescription`
- `getPropertyDescriptionList`

These handlers are discussed in the following sections.

The `getBehaviorTooltip` Handler

The `getBehaviorTooltip` handler returns the string that appears when the cursor hovers over a behavior in a library. The tooltip provides a short description of what the behavior does. Figure 8.10 shows an example, and Listing 8.5 shows the Lingo used in this handler.

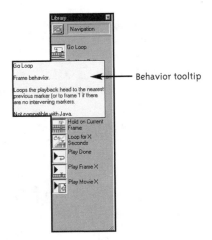

Figure 8.10 The box contains a short string that defines what a behavior can be used for, which is useful when you're scanning behaviors in a library before assigning one to a sprite.

A `getBehaviorTooltip` handler consists of a simple return statement with the string to be used for the tooltip. The RETURN words in the string signify a carriage return and create the blank lines in the tooltip.

Listing 8.5 **The** `getBehaviorTooltip` **handler.**

```
on getBehaviorTooltip me
  return "¬
    Frame behavior."&RETURN&RETURN&"¬
    Loops the playback head to the nearest"&RETURN&"¬
    previous marker (or to frame 1 if there"&RETURN&"¬
    are no intervening markers."&RETURN&RETURN&"¬
    Not compatible with Java."
end getBehaviorTooltip
```

> **Tip**
>
> The character ¬ at the end of the lines in listings in this chapter is used to allow one Lingo statement to extend over several lines of the script. It is used for readability. Use [Alt+Enter] (Option-Return) to insert this character.

The `getBehaviorDescription` **Handler**

The `getBehaviorDescription` handler also returns a string with information on how to use a behavior. This string appears automatically in the Behavior Inspector window when the behavior is selected. Typically, more detailed information on the uses and caveats of a behavior is presented here. Figure 8.11 shows a sample description, and Listing 8.6 contains the Lingo used in this handler.

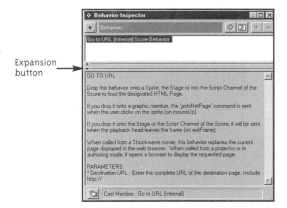

Expansion button

Figure 8.11 The behavior description is available in the bottom panel of the Behavior Inspector windows. It can be hidden and shown with the expansion button.

Understanding Scripts

Macromedia Director

This `getBehaviorDescription` handler also returns a string that defines what appears in the description section of the Behavior Inspector window.

Listing 8.6 The `getBehaviorDescription` **handler.**

```
on getBehaviorDescription me
  return "¬
    GO TO URL"&RETURN&RETURN&"¬
    Drop this behavior onto a Sprite, the Stage or into the Script Channel of ¬
    the Score to load the designated HTML Page."&¬
RETURN&RETURN&"¬
    If you drop it onto a graphic member, the 'gotoNetPage' command ¬
    is sent when the user clicks on the sprite (on mouseUp)."&RETURN&RETURN&"¬
    If you drop it onto the Stage or the Script Channel of the Score, ¬
    it will be sent when the playback head leaves the frame (on exitFrame)."&¬
    RETURN&RETURN&"¬
    When called from a Shockwave movie, this behavior replaces the current page ¬
    displayed in the Web browser.  When called from a projector or in authoring ¬
  mode, it opens a browser to display the requested page."&RETURN&RETURN&"¬
    PARAMETERS:"&RETURN&"¬
    * Destination URL - Enter the complete URL of the destination page. Include http://"
end getBehaviorDescription
```

The `getPropertyDescriptionList` Handler

The `getPropertyDescriptionList` handler is a relatively complicated handler to create. It defines the properties that appear in the properties dialog box for the behavior. The formats and definitions of the properties are also defined in this handler. This is what makes behaviors so powerful: You can modify their properties very simply. Figure 8.12 shows an example of a Parameter dialog box, and Listing 8.7 shows the handler that creates this dialog box.

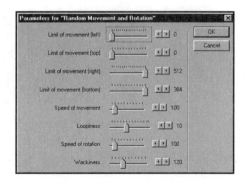

Figure 8.12   The chosen parameters for a behavior are presented to the user when it is first assigned to a sprite.

> **Note**
>
> The behavior parameters can be modified from the Behavior Inspector window. Note that slider bars are used to limit the input range for the properties and provide the user with a visual guide when making adjustments.

The Lingo script for a `getPropertyDescriptionList` handler is more complex than the previous two special handlers. Typically, some calculations or determinations are performed first. Then, a property list is created with all the properties for the dialog box. The keywords `#comment`, `#format`, `#default`, and `#range` determine how the property input appears.

Listing 8.7 The `getPropertyDescriptionList` **handler.**

```
on getPropertyDescriptionList me
  if not the currentSpriteNum then
    -- behavior has been attached to script channel
    exit
  end if
  vRect = the stage.rect
  vMemberType = sprite (the currentSpriteNum).member.type
  case vMemberType of
    #text, #picture: vRotateSpeed = 0
    otherwise
      vRotateSpeed = 100
  end case
  vPDList = [:]
  setaProp vPDList, #pLimitsLeft, [#comment: "Limit of movement (left)", ¬
    #format: #integer, #default: 0, #range: [#min: 0, #max: vRect.width]]
  setaProp vPDList, #pLimitsTop, [#comment: "Limit of movement (top)", ¬
    #format: #integer, #default: 0, #range: [#min: 0, #max: vRect.height]]
  setaProp vPDList, #pLimitsRight, [#comment: "Limit of movement (right)", ¬
    #format: #integer, #default: vRect.width, #range: [#min: 0, #max: vRect.width]]
  setaProp vPDList, #pLimitsBottom, [#comment: "Limit of movement (bottom)", ¬
    #format: #integer, #default: vRect.height, ¬
    #range: [#min: 0, #max: the stage.rect.height]]
  setaProp vPDList, #pSpeed, [#comment: "Speed of movement", ¬
    #format: #integer, #default: 100, #range: [#min: 0, #max: 1000]]
  setaProp vPDList, #pLoopiness, [#comment: "Loopiness", ¬
    #format: #integer, #default: 10, #range: [#min: 0, #max: 25]]
  setaProp vPDList, #pRotationSpeed, [#comment: "Speed of rotation", ¬
    #format: #integer, #default: vRotateSpeed, #range: [#min: 0, #max: 1000]]
  setaProp vPDList, #pWackiness, [#comment: "Wackiness", ¬
    #format: #integer, #default: 120, #range: [#min: 0, #max: 360]]
  return vPDList
end getPropertyDescriptionList
```

Basic Scripting

A good way to get started with Lingo scripting is to write some scripts that perform relatively simple yet useful tasks. This helps you get comfortable with the notion of writing scripts and with the various processes that Director requires. This section shows how to write Lingo scripts to control the flow of a movie and to switch the cast members associated with a sprite.

Controlling Movie Flow

Interactivity consists of controlling the playback of a movie based on user input. You can use Lingo to provide a unique experience to the end users by letting them choose the path they take through a project. There are two main aspects to controlling the playback of a movie: jumping between frames in the same movie and jumping to a new movie.

Moving Between Frames

The Lingo statement `go to frame` is used to tell Director to play a specific frame next. Normally, Director plays the next highest number frame. Frame 4 plays after frame 3, for example. Using the script bypasses the normal playback and plays the specified frame. Frame 10 can play after frame 3 if the script is written that way.

Although the code can be used in any script, the jump may not be carried out immediately. Director must still finish the normal course of events associated with a frame before going to a new frame. For example, if the `go to frame` script is in an `enterFrame` handler, Director will still execute all the scripts in the `idle` and `exitFrame` handlers associated with the current frame. Then, it will go to the new frame and start with its `prepareFrame` handler.

In Listing 8.8, the script could be a component handler of an interface behavior. It tells Director to jump to different marked frames, depending on the value of `the ticks`.

Listing 8.8   Using `go to frame` in a script.

```
-- jump to "too late" if the ticks is greater than 1000
-- otherwise jump to "early"

on mouseUp me
  if (the ticks > 1000) then
    go to frame "too late"
  else
    go to frame "early"
  end if
end mouseUp
```

> **Note**
>
> A `tick` in Director is the equivalent of one sixtieth of a second. The Lingo phrase the `ticks` signifies the number of ticks that have passed since the computer was turned on. You can divide the number of ticks by 60 to get seconds, and divide again by 60 to get minutes.

Listing 8.8 also contains a conditional statement. The Lingo keywords `if`, `then`, `else`, and `end if` are used to execute different code, depending on the result of a test condition. In this case, the `if` statement tests the value of `the ticks` against the value 1000. If `the ticks` is greater than 1000, the next line is executed. If it is not—that is, `else`—the line after the `else` statement is executed. This has the effect of jumping to the frame represented by different markers, depending on the condition of (that is, the value of) `the ticks`.

Another Lingo command that is useful within the `go to frame` syntax is `the frame`. The current frame of the movie is always accessible by using `the frame`. By using calculations within the `go to frame` command, you can decide where to jump to, based on the current frame. Listings 8.9 and 8.10 show examples of using `the frame`.

The script in Listing 8.9 unconditionally jumps to the previous frame on the `mouseUp` event. The parentheses around `the frame - 1` are optional, but serve to make the algebraic expression clear to movie authors.

Listing 8.9 A script using `the frame`.

```
-- jump to the previous frame


on mouseUp me
  go to frame (the frame - 1)
end mouseUp
```

Tip

You should use parentheses in any mathematical expression, even if it does not require them. Director obeys the standard order of operations for algebra, but extra parentheses are useful for clarity. They do not slow down execution, and may help eliminate hard-to-find problems before they appear.

Based on the current frame number of the movie, the script in Listing 8.10 jumps to either marker `outro` or `intro`. The script in Listing 8.10 provides different outcomes, depending on where it is used in the movie. If the sprite span that this behavior is attached to crosses frame 100, its outcome can be different, even within the same sprite span.

Listing 8.10 The script to jump to `outro` or `intro`.

```
-- jump to a new marker based on the current frame


on mouseUp me
  if (the frame > 100) then
    go to frame "outro"
  else
    go to frame "intro"
  end if
end mouseUp
```

> **Note**
>
> Listings 8.8 through 8.10 use the `mouseUp` event exclusively. The `go to frame` command is not dependent on the `mouseUp` event. Any event or other handler can use the `go to frame` script. For example, a frame script could use the `exitFrame` event to determine what frame to jump to next.

Moving Between Movies

The `go to movie` command is similar to the `go to frame` command, except it jumps to a different movie. The movie name is always contained in quotes. If the extension is left off the filename, Director assumes one of the standard movie extensions. As discussed in Chapter 5, "Creating the Score," page xxx, this is good scripting practice because the extension of a movie's filename depends on whether it is normal (`dir`), protected (`dxr`), or compressed (`dcr`). Scripts that have the extension included fail at a later point in the project if the extension changes.

Listing 8.11 shows the basic use of the `go to movie` command. This use of the `go to movie` command is typical in a frame script. When the current frame is about to end, Director sends the `exitFrame` event. The script in the `exitFrame` handler tells Director to close the current movie and open the specified new movie after this frame.

Listing 8.11   A script that uses the `go to movie` command.

```
-- go to a new movie after this frame is complete

on exitFrame me
  go to movie "page2"
end mouseUp
```

The `go to movie` command can also jump to a specific frame number or marker within the new movie. This is useful for bypassing introductions or other areas of the movie. The conditional statement in Listing 8.12 provides an example of this use.

Listing 8.12   A script for jumping to a specific frame of the new movie.

```
-- go to a new movie based on the cast member that
-- has been clicked on

on mouseUp me
  if (sprite(me.spriteNum).member.name = "intro button") then
    go to frame 1 of movie "page1"
  else
    go to frame "interactive" of movie "page1"
  end if
end mouseUp
```

This script needs to be in a behavior. It jumps to a specific frame of a new movie based on the name of the cast member of the sprite it is attached to. This script could be used on two different buttons, and its outcome depends on whether the button cast member is named `intro button`.

The interesting conditional expression from Listing 8.12 deserves some comment. The phrase `me.spriteNum` simply returns the sprite channel of the sprite that the behavior is attached to. The sprite object itself is referred to by `sprite(me.spriteNum)`. The first property of the sprite object is denoted by the `.member` postfix. A further property of the `member` property, the member's name, is defined by `.name`. So, this expression returns the name of the cast member of the sprite in the current sprite channel, exactly what is needed.

Similar to the `go to frame` command, the `go to movie` command does not stop the current movie immediately. It actually requests that Director go to the new movie at the earliest possible time. Other frame scripts (on the current frame only) and behaviors may still execute before the current movie is stopped. Additionally, the `stopMovie` event is still generated, so any code in the `stopMovie` handler is also executed first.

You should consider using any one of the built-in navigation behaviors before writing one from scratch. If one of the supplied behaviors from the library included with Director will accomplish the desired result, you should use it. Two behaviors from the Controls library are particularly useful: `Jump to Marker Button` and `Jump to Movie Button`.

Switching Cast Members

Changing the cast member of a sprite in response to user input is a very common script technique. It provides feedback to the user that the input has registered with the program. Menu selections can also highlight on mouse rollover by using the same method. This section shows several scripts that provide this type of user interface.

Behaviors are the best type of scripts to use for switching cast members. Because behaviors are attached to sprites, they have direct information about the sprite and control over its attributes. Follow the steps in the example that follows to create an interactive menu that responds to rollovers and button actions:

1. Open the movie "switchcast.dir" from the Chapter8 folder on this book's CD-ROM. This movie contains the cast members required for this exercise. They are already laid out in the score.

2. Create a new behavior script in the cast. Select an empty cast member and open the script window. Click the cast member properties button and choose Behavior from the drop-down list. This tells Director that this is a behavior script. Name this script `menu action` (see Figure 8.13).

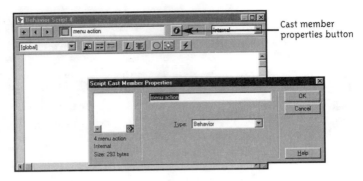

Cast member
properties button

Figure 8.13 Setting the script type to Behavior is critical for Director to allow the script to be assigned to a sprite.

3. Start with using the mouseEnter and mouseLeave events to create handlers that highlight the menu selections on mouse rollovers. Enter the script from Listing 8.13 into the script window for this behavior. (A text file containing this script, called listing8.13.txt, is on the book's CD-ROM in the Chapter08 folder.)

Listing 8.13 A script using mouseEnter and mouseLeave events.

```
-- behavior to give life to menu selections

property originalName

on beginSprite me
  -- store the current name of the cast member
  -- that is assigned to this sprite in the
  -- property originalName
  set originalName = sprite(me.spriteNum).member.name
end beginSprite

on mouseEnter me
  -- the cursor has entered the sprite's bounding box
  -- call the highlight handler
  highlight me
end mouseEnter

on mouseLeave me
  -- the cursor has left the sprite's bounding box
  -- call the unhighlight handler
  unhighlight me
end mouseLeave

on highlight me
```

```
-- change the cast member of the current sprite to
-- the original name plus the string " highlight"
  set the member of sprite (me.spriteNum) = member (originalName & " highlight")
end highlight

on unhighlight me
  -- change the cast member of this sprite back to
  -- the original one
  set the member of sprite (me.spriteNum) = member originalName
end unhighlight
```

For this behavior, the mouseEnter and mouseLeave handlers do not set the sprite's properties directly. Instead, they call other handlers within the behavior. This is not necessary if the code is used in only one place, but it will become handy in a later step.

> **Note**
>
> The handler beginSprite is used to capture the event generated by Director. This event occurs when the playback head first encounters a frame that contains the sprite span where this behavior is assigned. It is used for setting up properties that are referenced throughout the behavior. Director also generates a matching endSprite event, but it is not required for this behavior.

4. Assign the behavior to the three sprites in channels 3 through 5. Play the movie and watch the menu items highlight as you roll over them. Note that the cast member names were set up in the original movie to allow this sort of generic highlight behavior. Figure 8.14 shows the Main selection highlighted on the stage. In this case, the highlight cast member is exactly the same text, but in a different color. It could be any cast member, however.

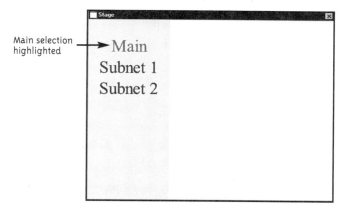

Main selection highlighted

Figure 8.14 A behavior that uses another cast member to show a menu selection highlighted.

5. Now add the handler for the `mouseDown` event. In this case the behavior moves the sprite down and to the right a few pixels to signify that the menu item is selected. Because most of the handlers are changed with this step, the entire script is duplicated in Listing 8.14, with the additions. Replace the script for the `menu action` behavior with this listing. (A text file containing this script, called listing8.14.txt, is on the book's CD-ROM in the Chapter08 folder.)

Listing 8.14 Adding a handler for the `mouseDown` event.

```
-- behavior to give life to menu selections

property originalName
property originalLoc

on beginSprite me
  -- store the current name of the cast member
  -- that is assigned to this sprite in the
  -- property originalName
  set originalName = sprite(me.spriteNum).member.name

  -- store the original location of the sprite
  set originalLoc = sprite(me.spriteNum).loc
end beginSprite

on mouseEnter me
  -- the cursor has entered the sprite's bounding box
  -- call the highlight handler
  highlight me
end mouseEnter

on mouseLeave me
  -- the cursor has left the sprite's bounding box
  -- call the unhighlight handler
  unhighlight me

  -- clean up from any mouseDown events
  resetOffset me
end mouseLeave

on mouseDown me
  offsetDown me
end mouseDown me

on highlight me
  -- change the cast member of the current sprite to
```

```
  -- the original name plus the string " highlight"
  set the member of sprite (me.spriteNum) = member (originalName & " highlight")
end highlight

on unhighlight me
  -- change the cast member of this sprite back to
  -- the original one
  set the member of sprite (me.spriteNum) = member originalName
end unhighlight

on offsetDown me
  -- change the location of the sprite on stage
  -- by 3 pixels right and 3 pixels down
  set the loc of sprite(me.spriteNum) = originalLoc + point(3,3)
end offsetDown

on resetOffset me
  -- restore the original position of the sprite on stage
  set the loc of sprite(me.spriteNum) = originalLoc
end resetOffset
```

Note

This version of the behavior script adds another property, originalLoc, which is used in beginSprite to store the original location of the sprite onstage. The mouseDown handler calls the offsetDown handler. This in turn changes to the location of the sprite onstage. To recover from this offset, the mouseLeave handler restores the sprite's original position by calling the resetOffset handler.

6. The behavior does not need to be reassigned to the sprites after the script is changed. Changes are automatically implemented. Play the movie again, and notice how the menu sprites move down and right slightly when the mouse button is pressed within their bounding boxes. Because there is no matching mouseUp behavior yet, the buttons stay selected until the offset is reset in the mouseLeave handler.

Note

Note that changing the properties of a sprite via Lingo does not permanently affect them. The sprite properties that are stored in the score, such as position and cast member, are kept the same. Lingo can affect a sprite only while the movie is running. Rewinding the movie resets all the properties back to their values from the score.

7. The last step in creating an interactive menu is to have the menu items react to a `mouseUp` event. Listing 8.15 contains the new handlers to add to the bottom of the existing `menu action` behavior. (A text file containing this script, called listing8.15.txt, is on the book's CD-ROM in the Chapter08 folder.)

Listing 8.15 Adding new handlers to the `menu action` behavior.

```
on mouseUp me
  -- flash the menu item to show the click registered
  flashHighlight me

  -- reset the offset in preparation for performing the action
  resetOffset me

  -- whatever action is desired on mouseUp goes here
end mouseUp

on flashHighlight me
  -- repeated unhighlight and highlight the sprite
  -- updatestage is needed here explicitly because
  -- the playback head is not moving, so no natural
  -- updatestage events are being generated by Director
  unhighlight me
  updatestage
  highlight me
  updatestage
  unhighlight me
  updatestage
  highlight me
  updatestage
  unhighlight me
  updatestage
  highlight me
  updatestage
end flashHighlight
```

The `mouseUp` handler calls a local handler, `flashHighlight`, to flash the sprite between its highlighted and unhighlighted states. It then resets the offset and performs the action that is desired. Because this is an example, no action is defined.

> **Tip**
>
> The `flashHighlight` handler could be scripted more efficiently by using loops. Loops are explained in the next section, "Advanced Scripting." Also, the speed of the highlight depends on the speed of the computer the movie is running on. Ideally, there would be a pause based on a length of time between the oscillations, but this is beyond the scope of this example.

8. Play the movie and try clicking on the menu options. They behave with interactivity that gives useful feedback to the user. A finished version of the movie from this example, "switchcast_finished.dir," is on the book's CD-ROM in the Chapter8 folder.

This example shows how to affect the properties of a sprite based on events from Director. A behavior is best for this task because it is closely coupled with the sprite it is to control. Custom handlers are included to show the benefits of code reuse within a handler. Several event handlers make use of the `highlight` and `unhighlight` handlers, for instance.

Advanced Scripting

The next several sections outline some more advanced scripting topics. When you become comfortable writing some basic scripts from scratch, it is worthwhile to move on to these topics.

These examples cover only a small portion of the capabilities of Lingo. Interested readers should follow this chapter with an exploration of the tutorial and help files included with Director. Numerous books are available to teach Lingo more completely.

Responding to User Input

The example in the "Basic Scripting" section demonstrates how to make interactive menu items that respond to mouse actions. The following list outlines the mouse events, along with suggestions on how to use them:

- **mouseEnter**—This event is sent to all behaviors on a sprite when the mouse cursor enters the bounding box of the sprite. Note that the matte ink effect can be used to generate the event when the cursor enters a nontransparent portion of the sprite instead. If multiple sprites are overlapping onstage, the sprite with the highest channel number gets the event message.

- **mouseLeave**—This is the corresponding event to `mouseEnter`. It is sent when the cursor leaves the area of a sprite (bounding box or nontransparent, depending on the ink). A sprite that is completely contained within another lower sprite onstage causes a `mouseLeave` event for the lower sprite when the cursor enters the smaller sprite. This occurs even though the cursor is technically still within the larger, lower sprite. According to Director, the cursor can be on only one sprite at a time, and the channel number takes precedence over sprite areas.

- **mouseWithin**—This event is generated once for every frame where the cursor is within the borders of the sprite. It is useful for scripts that need to run repeatedly while the cursor is over a sprite. Updating something that is dependent on the sprite (a text field, for example) is one example.

- **mouseDown**—Generated when the user depresses the main (usually left) mouse button on a sprite. There should be no way for a mouseDown event to occur without a corresponding mouseEnter event. You should not assume this, however, and should code in such a way that one event is not dependent on the other. Most user interfaces recognize a mouseDown event by changing the interface element in some way to signify that the press has been accepted. Usually, other actions are not performed on this event, however. This gives the user a chance to change his or her mind before releasing the button. An exception to this is an action game in which the mouse press should activate something right away without waiting for the mouseUp event.

- **mouseUp**—The match for the mouseDown event, this one is sent when the user releases a depressed mouse button over a sprite. As mentioned in the mouseDown description, the mouseUp event usually starts an action in the program, thus giving the user a chance to confirm the decision. This event usually causes the interface button to return to its preclicked state as well.

- **mouseUpOutside**—If the end user moves off a sprite with the mouse button still pressed and then releases the button, this event occurs. Note that the mouseUpOutside event is sent to the original sprite where the mouse button was first pressed. This event allows the behavior to realize that the user has decided not to follow the click with a button release. It is commonly used to reset a button or another element to its normal state.

In addition to the mouse events outlined previously, Director also generates events based on keyboard input. The main difference is that keyboard events are not tied to specific sprites. In fact, behaviors on most types of sprites cannot receive keyboard events. The best place to put keyboard event handlers is either in the movie script for global responses or in a frame script for localized responses. The following list outlines the various keyboard event messages and useful functions.

- **keyDown**—This event is analogous to the mouseDown event. It is generated when any standard key on the keyboard is pressed. Note that the event itself does not contain any information on what key was pressed. Contrary to the convention of mouseUp causing an action, keyDown usually starts an action based on a key. Thus, the action starts immediately when the key is pressed, but exceptions are possible.

- **keyUp**—The keyUp event is a match for the keyDown event. It is generated when any key is released after having been pressed previously. Again, no information about which key was released is contained in the event.

- **the key**—This is not an event but a Lingo keyword. It contains a string with the actual text of the key most recently pressed. You should use this within the keyDown or keyUp events to determine which key caused the event.

- **the keyCode**—This keyword also contains information about the last key that was pressed. Rather than a string, the keyCode contains a numeric value corresponding to the key on the keyboard. This is useful for recognizing keys such as function keys in a keyDown handler. Beware that key codes are not guaranteed to be the same on different computers, but this is not generally a problem.

- **the keyPressed**—This keyword can be used in two ways. The first is like the previous two keywords. You refer to the keyPressed in a keyDown handler to get a string containing the current key pressed. The second method is as a function. Use keypressed("a") to determine whether the A key is currently being pressed. If it is, the function returns TRUE, and if it is not, it returns FALSE. The is a useful feature for games because multiple keys can be pressed at the same time, and the function returns TRUE for all the queried keys currently pressed.

- **controlDown**—This keyword evaluates to TRUE or FALSE, depending on whether the Ctrl key is currently pressed. This works the same on Windows and Macintosh.

- **commandDown**—This keyword evaluates to TRUE or FALSE, depending on the state of the Ctrl key in Windows and the Command (Cmd) key on a Macintosh.

- **optionDown**—This keyword evaluates to TRUE or FALSE, depending on the state of the Alt key in Windows and the Option (Opt) key on a Macintosh. This keyword and the previous two can be difficult to use in the authoring environment because Director keyboard shortcuts take precedence over key input in the current movie. It is best to test any Lingo that depends on these modifier keys in a projector application or Shockwave movie in a browser.

- **shiftDown**—This keyword contains TRUE or FALSE, depending on the state of the Shift key.

Similar to the way the modifier keys do not always work as expected in Director, the Stage window usually has to be active and have focus for the keyboard events to be generated correctly. This is not a problem in a projector or Shockwave environment because the Stage window is the only window available.

Director provides a wide gamut of handlers and functions for dealing with end-user input. It's a good idea to explore their use and learn their limitations. Behaviors in the Interactive Animation library can also be used for ideas and reference.

Loops

As mentioned in the mouse input example (Listing 8.15), Lingo provides mechanisms for repeating code. These are called *loops*, and there are various types of loops for different uses. The listings in this section provide examples and explanations of their uses. Each of the listings can be inserted into a movie script, and the associated handler executed from the message window. Experiment with modifying and running the scripts to gain a full understanding of loops in Lingo. The "loops.dir" movie, found in the Chapter8 folder on this book's CD-ROM, contains individual movie scripts for each listing that are ready to run.

Loops Using `repeat with`

The basic repeat loop in Listing 8.16 uses the `repeat with` structure. Each `repeat` statement must have a corresponding `end repeat` statement to bracket the loop's contents. This example counts the variable n from 1 to 10. Each successive value of n is put to the Message window.

Listing 8.16   A script with a basic repeat loop.

```
-- basic repeat loop to count from 1 to 10 with n
on repeatWith
  repeat with n = 1 to 10
    put n
  end repeat
end repeatWith
```

Listing 8.17 shows a variation on the `repeat with` loop, and uses the `down` keyword to signify counting from a higher number down to a lower number. This script puts the numbers from 20 down to 10 into the Message window.

Listing 8.17   A variation on the `repeat with` loop.

```
-- repeat loop to count from 20 down to 10 with n
on repeatWithDown
  repeat with n = 20 down to 10
    put n
  end repeat
end repeatWithDown
```

Loops Using `repeat while`

A more advanced structure is the `repeat while` loop shown in Listing 8.18. This loop repeats as long as the condition in the `repeat` line is TRUE. Care must be taken to ensure that the loop will finish eventually, or an infinite loop will occur and the Director movie will essentially stop running. The example in Listing 8.18 stores the value of the ticks just before the loop starts. Then, the loop compares that stored value to the current ticks until 30 more ticks (half a second) have passed.

Listing 8.18   An advanced repeat structure.

```
-- repeat loop that waits for 30 ticks to pass
-- before continuing
on repeatWhile
  set startTicks = the ticks
  put "Start ticks = " & the ticks
  repeat while the ticks < (startTicks + 30)
    -- don't output to message window because
    -- there will be too many iterations of this loop
    nothing
  end repeat
  put "  End ticks = " & the ticks
end repeatWhile
```

The `nothing` keyword is used as a placeholder statement. No Lingo operation is performed, but the computer still does a finite amount of processing with a `nothing` statement. For absolute speed efficiency, you should comment out the `nothing` statement.

Loops Using `repeat with... in`

The `repeat with...in` structure is used to iterate over the values of a list, in order. Lists are Lingo containers with special properties. A list is denoted by a series of list items, separated by commas and surrounded by square brackets. This loop is useful because the loop variable—`listItem`, in this case—takes the value of each list item successively, as seen in Listing 8.19.

Listing 8.19   A script with the `repeat with...in` **structure.**

```
-- loop over the items in a list
on repeatWithIn
  repeat with listItem in ["Sun", "Mon", "Tues", "Wed", "Thr", "Fri", "Sat"]
    put listItem
  end repeat
end repeatWithIn
```

The `repeat with...in` structure is a useful aspect to Lingo. It provides a lot of control for very little effort. There is no need to increment a value or keep track of the number of items in the list. All this is done automatically by Director.

Creating Parent Scripts

Parent scripts are a complex aspect of Lingo. Their full use and understanding are beyond the scope of this chapter, but they are powerful tools well worth further exploration. This section provides an example of a basic parent script and how to use it. Refer to the Parent Scripts chapter in the Contents area of the Director help file for more information. As mentioned earlier in this chapter, a parent script is used for object-oriented programming in Lingo. The parent script defines a class that becomes an object in memory when it is instantiated. Instantiation is always accomplished by another script, and it has the effect of running the `new` handler in the parent script.

The following example creates a parent script that emulates the responses of a dog to commands and actions from its master. This is a somewhat contrived example, but is still useful for demonstrating the capabilities and use of a parent script.

1. Start by opening a new script window and setting the cast member type to `Parent`. Name the script cast member `dog` (see Figure 8.15).

Figure 8.15 A parent script is created similar to a movie script and behaviors, except for the script type.

2. The dog object will communicate with its master by using the message window. It will respond to commands by implementing handlers that put text back to the message window. Start with the one handler all parent scripts must have: the new handler. Enter the script from Listing 8.20 into the script window.

Listing 8.20 The new handler in the parent script.

```
-- dog parent script
-- responds to commands using handlers
-- all output appears in the message window

property dogState

on new me
   set dogState = #justBorn
   put "[dog was just created]"
   put "Bark!"
   -- this is required for the object in memory
   -- to be accessible to other scripts
   return me
end new
```

> Notice in Listing 8.20 that the dogState property is set to a new type of value. A series of letters and numbers prefixed with a pound sign (#) is called a *symbol*. (Symbols may not start with numbers, but may use them after the first character.) A symbol with a given name is unique within a Director session and is useful for storing things such as states or known values. More efficient than strings for comparison, symbols evaluate to unique integer values when Director runs the movie. Symbols are more readable than integers to movie authors because they tell something about what they represent.

Note

3. Open the Message window and type `set fido = new(script "dog")`, and then press Enter. Use another name for your dog by replacing `fido` with whatever name you choose. Remember to continue using your dog's name, instead of `fido`, for the rest of this example. Figure 8.16 shows the results of this step in the Message window.

Figure 8.16   A command that runs the new handler in the dog parent script and returns the resulting object in memory into the variable called `fido`. The variable `fido` representing the dog object is used to send commands to the virtual dog.

4. Add the script from Listing 8.21 to the dog parent script cast member. It contains a few more handlers that the dog object will respond to when ordered. (A text file containing this script, called listing8.21.txt, is on the book's CD-ROM in the Chapter08 folder.)

Listing 8.21   More handlers for the dog object.

```
on pat me
  set dogState = #happy
  put "[dog wags tail]"
end pat


on feed me
  set dogState = #full
  put "[dog gobbles food]"
end feed


on scratch me
  set dogState = #happy
  put "[dog's hind leg quivers]"
  put "Grunt"
end scratch me


on swat me
  set dogState = #scared
  put "[dog skampers out of reach]"
  put "Yip!"
end swat me
```

```
on whistle me
  set dogState = #happy
  put "[dog comes closer]"
end whistle
```

> **Note**
>
> If one of the new commands were given to the dog object at this point, Director would complain that the handler does not exist. Even though adding more handlers has modified the parent script, the object in memory is still composed of only the original new handler. This separation of the object from the script is a major difference between behaviors and parent scripts.

5. Before using the new handlers, you need to re-create the dog object from the new parent script. Reenter the text set fido = new(script "dog") into the Message window. The dog is created again, and it barks to its master. Now the dog knows its new commands.

6. Try out the new commands with the dog. A command is sent to an object by issuing the command name, followed by the variable name containing the object. Enter pat fido into the Message window, and the dog responds.

7. Use all the other commands and verify that they produce the expected responses. Enter feed fido, scratch fido, swat fido, and whistle fido one at a time, into the Message window. Figure 8.17 shows the responses.

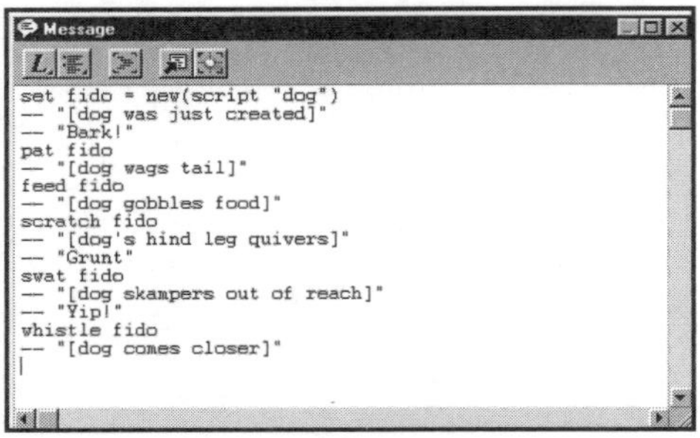

Figure 8.17   All of Fido's commands are exercised by calling handlers in the parent script, or sending events to the object.

This example also sets a property of the object called dogState with each command. This state is not visible to the master commanding the dog. Properties are local to each object and are stored internally to the object.

Each of the commands exists independently of the others. The outcome is not based on any previous commands, only on the current one. The dogState property could be used to tailor the responses based on past actions. For example, the dog's state might be only nonchalant if the whistle command is sent immediately after a swat command. This is left as an optional extension to the example.

The movie "dogObject.dir," found in the Chapter8 folder on this book's CD-ROM, contains a version of the dog object as implemented in this example.

Parent scripts are useful for implementing object-oriented programming techniques in Director. When an object is created by calling the new handler and assigning the result to a variable, all the handlers within the object are accessible. Handlers are executed by sending events to the object. The object then responds according to its internal Lingo code.

> **Note**
>
> Because they are not associated directly with a sprite, parent scripts are used most often to control more abstract concepts. There is no reason why a parent script could not control sprite properties as well, however.

Limitations of Shockwave

Shockwave movies have certain limitations because they support playback on the Internet. These limitations exist for two reasons: Functions are not available in the Shockwave browser plug-in, or they would violate security of the end user's machine.

The following list outlines some of the main differences between Shockwave movies and projector applications; most of the differences concern advanced features:

- The colorDepth command cannot be used to change the bit-depth of the user's monitor.
- For security reasons, applications cannot be started by using the open command.
- The restart and shutdown commands do not function.
- General file functions do not work. Shockwave movies are not allowed to look at the end user's hard drive.
- External files, including additional movies, must be downloaded before they are referenced in the current movie. You can download files into the Shockwave cache by using the preLoadNetThing command.
- The setprefs and getprefs functions work differently. Rather than saving files in the application directory, the preferences files are saved in the plug-in cache directory. These commands are used to store a variable's contents in a text file on the user's hard drive. By limiting the location where the file is stored, security is maintained.
- Advanced Lingo such as Movie in a Window and custom menus is not supported.

For more information, refer to the section called "Using Lingo in Different Internet Environments" in Director's help file.

In practice, a movie intended for Shockwave distribution on the Internet should be planned slightly differently from a projector application. Limitations must be accounted for before implementation starts. Fortunately, the vast majority of Director features are available in Shockwave movies.

Overview of Debugging Techniques

When a computer program has an error or unexpected condition, it is said to have a *bug*. The practice of playing a movie in development mode for the purpose of finding and eliminating bugs is called *debugging*. Several tools are available to assist in this process. The following sections give overviews of each method, along with some suggestions for their use.

> **Note**
>
> One explanation for the origin of the term *bug* refers to Admiral Grace Hopper, one of the first modern computer programmers, finding an actual moth inside a computer. The moth adversely affected programs on the machine, and the term was born.

There are four tools available to help you debug your Director movies. Scripts can use the Message window to display information while they execute. The Watcher window lets you see and modify variables. A detailed view of a script is available in the Debug window. Comments should not be overlooked for debugging; they provide valuable information to the movie author.

Debugging in Director is relatively simple because all these tools are available. A projector or Shockwave movie is harder to debug because none of the tools are accessible. The alert command can be useful for debugging problems that happen only in a projector or Shockwave movie.

The Message Window

The Message window has already been used extensively in the scripts in this chapter. The use of the Message window is threefold: It is used for viewing data output by a running script, sending events to scripts, and viewing movie state data.

The put command followed by a string causes the string to appear in the Message window when the code is executed. Strings can be made up of text surrounded by quotes, and variable and property values. The ampersand (&) is used to concatenate strings for output on the same line. (Refer to Listing 8.17 for an example of this.)

There are two disadvantages to debugging using put statements. First, too much information from them makes the Message window confusing and virtually unusable. Second, they are tedious to remove completely when they are no longer needed.

> **Tip**
>
> Each put statement takes some processing time, even in a projector application or Shockwave movie. For maximum efficiency, they should be removed, or at least commented out, before the movie is released for use.

The Message window is a powerful interactive development tool. As shown in the parent script example in this chapter, it is possible to run scripts and interact with objects from it. This makes experimentation and exploration easy. Lingo syntax and structure can be perfected in the Message window with immediate results, before being implemented in scripts.

> **Note**
>
> The limitation of the Message window for interactive development is that loops and more complicated structures are not available. Each bit of Lingo used here must fit on one line. In practice, though, the Message window is a common debugging tool.

Global variables are available in the Message window. Their contents can be viewed by using the put statement at any time. Additionally, the showglobals command puts the names and contents of all the current global variables into the Message window. Any Director parameter or function can also be used here. Use put the colordepth, for example, to see what bit-depth the movie is currently running in. All this is available while a movie is running.

The Watcher Window

The Watcher window is another useful debugging tool. Accessible from the Window menu, it is used to give a constantly updated view of selected variables. Expressions can be added to the Watcher window, and their values are always displayed there.

Figure 8.18 shows an example of the use of the Watcher window. Try entering the dogState of fido in the Watcher window while issuing commands to the dog object. Now, whenever the state of the dog object changes, it is instantly reflected in the Watcher window. This is a good way of seeing the internal state of the object.

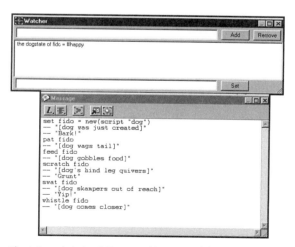

Figure 8.18   The internal state of the dog object is visible in the Watcher window. You use the syntax the [property] of [object variable] to view any object properties this way.

An especially nice feature of this tool is the capability to change values while the movie is running. This is useful for exploring hypothetical situations without having to change scripts.

> **Warning**
>
> Be careful when using this feature because it is easy to create error conditions within scripts by changing their properties externally.

It is occasionally difficult to get at the various parameters of the scripts you're interested in. For example, the properties of a behavior are hard to view in the Watcher window. Another drawback is that the contents of the window are not stored between authoring sessions. All the expressions must be reentered when Director is started.

Nevertheless, practice using the Watcher window because it is the best way to see the values of variables while a movie is running.

The Debug Window

When Director encounters an error in a script while the movie is running, it presents the option of opening the Debugger window. This window presents a snapshot of the offending script at the time the error occurred.

Figure 8.19 shows an example of the Debugger window open while the pat handler in the dog object is running.

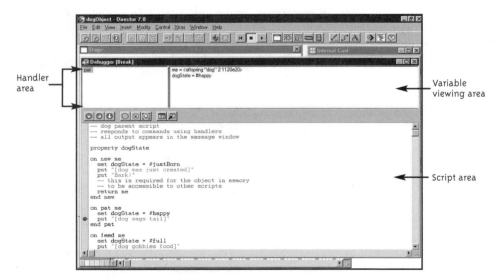

Figure 8.19   The Debugger window has three main panes of information.

In the upper right are the variables and properties Director decides are important to show. The bottom pane shows the script in question at the location where execution stopped. A list of handlers that ran to get to this point is show in the upper left.

The properties me and dogState are visible in the variable viewing area. Director decides automatically what to show here, based on the contents of the current line of code. It is similar in nature to the Watcher widow, except that the values cannot be modified.

Contents of the current script are shown in the script area. A green arrow indicates the current line. Scrollbars allow other portions of the script to be shown.

The handler area shows the list of handler calls that lead to the current line of code. In this case, only one handler, pat, was called so it is the only one shown. If another handler, praiseDog, for example, had called pat, praiseDog would be shown above pat in this area. The script for that handler could be viewed simply by clicking on the handler name. This is useful for tracing backward in code to determine the events that lead to the error condition.

Breakpoints can also be arbitrarily added to code. They are signified by red dots on the side of the script. Breakpoints automatically cause the Debugger window to appear, even if there is no error condition.

Breakpoints are useful for inspecting the inner workings of a section of code in great detail. You can add or remove a breakpoint by clicking the left margin of the script. After your inspection is complete, you can start the script again by choosing Command, Run Script menu or pressing the F5 key.

Comments

The use of comments in Lingo code cannot be overstated. Liberally adding comments, even when the code appears simple, can aid greatly in debugging. Properly written comments explain the intent of the code and what conditions are expected at that point in the script.

They serve as reminders to the original author and guideposts to any subsequent movie authors inspecting the scripts. Comments are also a great learning tool. A useful section of Lingo is more likely to be reused if it is commented well.

Creating Alerts

As shown in the preceding few sections, the Director authoring environment provides a useful array of debugging tools. While the movie is being created, you can peek and prod all over the scripts to make sure that they are running correctly. Unfortunately, this luxury is nonexistent for both projector applications and Shockwave movies. None of the tools outlined previously in this chapter are available when these movies are playing back. Normally, this should not matter because the performance of the movie in these modes should be exactly the same as in authoring mode. However, in practice, this is not always the case.

One minor additional debugging aid is available in a Projector or Shockwave movie, as well as the Director authoring environment. The alert command can be used synonymously with the put command. Text strings that would normally appear in the message window then appear as dialog boxes. The disadvantage is that these dialog boxes disrupt the normal flow of the movie, and it can be hard to re-create actual end-user conditions with dialog boxes appearing constantly.

A better methodology is to use the `alert` command only when something is about to go wrong. This involves constantly testing variables and properties against their expected range of values. Then, if they are ever outside this range, an alert dialog box is generated with the required information. The "Interactive Portfolio Project" section in this chapter demonstrates the use of the `alert` command to warn users they are running in the wrong color depth.

Going Further with Scripting

Lingo scripts are at the heart of interactivity in Director. It is easy to get started with scripts, and it seems like there is always something more to learn.

There are a variety of script types, which are all useful for different tasks. Movie scripts contain global handlers. Cast scripts are associated with only one cast member. Frame scripts are like behaviors that are attached to frames instead of sprites. Parent scripts can create abstract objects that extend the Lingo language. Sprites can have multiple behaviors attached to give them personality and distinctiveness.

Director provides a few tools to help movie authors perfect their scripts. The Message window, Watcher window, and Debug window all have different uses for finding bugs. Comments, `put` statements, and `alert` statements provide information about how scripts are running.

This chapter introduced the concepts of Lingo scripting. Interested readers are encouraged to read through the printed manuals and online help that come with Director for more information. Many of the Internet resources, such as mailing lists and Web sites, can also provide ideas and help.

Interactive Portfolio Project

Previous chapters have already used some scripts to create the interactive portfolio. You have assigned standard behaviors to sprites and frames to enable navigation between movies. In the project section of Chapter 7, "Using Behaviors," page 149, you created two behaviors using Lingo directly.

Three more scripts will be composed in the project section of this chapter. You will explore the use of the `alert` command in a movie script. Two more behaviors will be created to provide more feedback to the end user.

Adding a Movie Script

In the "Movie Scripts" section of this chapter, the concept of a global script repository was introduced. The handlers in a movie script can be called from any other script in the movie. A movie script can also contain handlers to receive events about the movie that are automatically generated by Director.

Because you are creating the portfolio to play back at 24-bit color depth, it would be nice to warn the user if their computer's display is not set to 24-bit. By using the prepareMovie handler and the alert command in a movie script, you can do just that.

Follow these steps to create a movie script that is the first script to run when the project is started:

1. Perform the usual version control step of creating a new folder, Chapter08, on your hard drive and copying the files from the Chapter07 folder.

2. Open the "intro.dir" movie file. Select the first empty cast member in the internal cast. This is where the movie script cast member will reside.

3. Open the script window by selecting Window, Script. Name this script cast member movie script. Director does not require this name but the script is easier to locate by movie authors.

4. Enter the contents of Listing 8.22 in the script window, as shown in Figure 8.20. Close the window when complete. (A text file containing this script, called listing8.22.txt, is on the book's CD-ROM in the Portfolio_Project\Chapter08 folder.)

Listing 8.22 The movie script checks the color depth in the prepareMovie handler.

```
-- movie script of introduction movie for the interactive portfolio

-- this project is intended to play at 24-bit color (millions of colors)

-- the Lingo in the prepareMovie handler presents a dialog box to the
-- user if their computer is not set for at least 24-bit color
-- if not at least 24-bit, the movie still plays after the warning

on prepareMovie
   -- this handler is run before anything appears on the stage

   -- check the color depth
   if the colorDepth < 24 then
     -- it's less than 24-bit, send an alert
     Alert("This portfolio looks best when your monitor is " & RETURN¬
           & "set to 24-bit color (millions of colors.)")
   end if
   -- continue with the movie
end prepareMovie
```

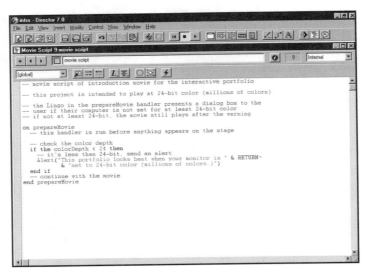

Figure 8.20 The **RETURN** keyword tells Director to start a new line with the second text string.

Note

If the color depth is not at least 24-bit, the movie will still continue playing. After the warning, you leave it up to the user to decide whether to quit and restart the movie. If you want the movie to stop if the color depth is incorrect, insert a `halt` command after the `alert` command.

5. Switch your monitor to 16-bit or 8-bit color, and run the movie. (You may have to restart your computer for the change to take effect.) The `alert` message appears with an OK button in the dialog box. Click OK and the movie continues to play. Save the movie before continuing.

The `alert` command takes any properly formatted Director string and creates a dialog box, with a single OK button, to display it. They are useful for getting the attention of the end user because the stop movie playback. Use them for warnings, as in this example, or error conditions.

Tip

In this script, you tested the value of the `colorDepth` in a conditional statement. You may also set the `colorDepth` to a proper bit-depth value. This changes the display color depth as the movie is running. Macintosh computers always support setting this value, but not all Windows computers do. If the computer does not support it, the color depth just does not change. Always check the `colorDepth` after setting it to ensure that the change took place, especially if you require a specific color depth.

Advanced Feedback Behaviors

In the project section of Chapter 7, "Using Behaviors," page 149, you made a behavior that provided feedback to the end user when a button was clicked. It flipped the image of the button to make it appear pressed. The first behavior you create in this section will provide the same sort of feedback for the text sprites in the movies by italicizing the text when the mouse button is pressed.

The Go to URL behavior that was assigned to many of the text sprites should have a specific feedback behavior.

Note

It is polite to signify to the end user that an external Web browser will open if the associated sprite is clicked.

The second behavior in this section is similar in nature to the behavior that swaps the static character images with the animated images, also created in the project section of Chapter 7. The previous behavior created an interesting effect when the cursor rolled over each letter in the titles. The behavior in this section underlines the text in a text sprite during cursor rollovers. You will attach this to the sprites that link to external Web sites.

The following steps demonstrate how to create each of these behaviors:

1. Open the "main.dir" movie file from the Chapter07 folder on your hard drive. Select the next empty cast member in the GlobalCode cast.

2. Open a new script window and name the script cast member italicize. The script you are about to create will change the style of the text in the attached sprite whenever the mouse button is pressed down on the sprite. It will restore the text when the button is released or moved off the sprite. This creates feedback that the button is working.

3. Switch the script type to Behavior in the Script Cast Member Properties dialog box. Enter the contents of Listing 8.23 into the script window. (A text file containing this script, called listing8.23.txt, is on the book's CD-ROM in the Portfolio_Project\Chapter08 folder.)

Listing 8.23 The Italicize behavior uses two custom subroutine handlers, such as the Random Jump behavior in Listing 7.6.

```
-- italicize text

-- this behavior italicizes text when the mouse is down
-- on the corresponding sprite

property pOrigMemberStyle

on beginSprite me
  -- store the original style of the member
  pOrigMemberStyle = sprite(me.spriteNum).member.fontstyle
end beginSprite
```

```
on mouseDown me
  italicize(me)
end mouseDown

on mouseLeave me
  unItalicize(me)
end mouseLeave

on mouseUp me
  unItalicize(me)
end mouseUp

on mouseEnter me
  if (the mouseDown) then
    italicize(me)
  end if
end mouseEnter

on endSprite me
  -- put it back to normal
  sprite(me.spriteNum).member.fontstyle = pOrigMemberStyle
end endSprite

on italicize me
  -- get the current font style list
  memberStyle = sprite(me.spriteNum).member.fontstyle
  -- add the italic style to the list
  add(memberStyle, #italic)
  -- assign the new style to the member
  sprite(me.spriteNum).member.fontStyle = memberStyle
end italicize

on unItalicize me
  -- get the current font style list
  memberStyle = sprite(me.spriteNum).member.fontstyle
  -- delete the italic style from the list
  deleteOne(memberStyle, #italic)
  -- assign the new style to the member
  sprite(me.spriteNum).member.fontStyle = memberStyle
end unItalicize
```

The contents of the italicize and unItalicize subroutine handlers are worth exploring. In each case, the current style of the sprite's cast member is stored in a local variable, memberStyle. Then, the symbol #italic, representing the italic style, is either added to (in italicize) or deleted from (in unItalicize) the memberStyle variable. Finally, the cast member's text style is set to this variable. This has the effect of selecting adding or deleting only the italic style while leaving any other styles on the cast member unchanged.

4. Close the script window and attach this new behavior to the Accomplishments text sprite. Play the movie, and press and hold the mouse button on the Accomplishments sprite. The text becomes italic while retaining its earlier bold style. If you move the mouse off the sprite without releasing the button, it returns to its original style. See Figure 8.21 for an example of what the text looks like with the italic style added.

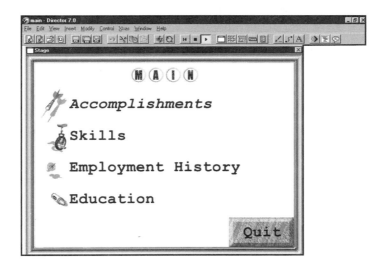

Figure 8.21   The Accomplishments text sprite is italicized because the mouse button is being held down over the sprite.

5. Attach this new behavior to the other three text sprites on this screen, and save the movie. Open each of the other movies in the project, and attach this behavior to any other text sprites that cause actions when clicked. Now, all the active text has feedback to let the end user know what is happening.

6. Open the "accomplishments.dir" movie file. This is the first movie that uses the Go to URL behavior to open an Internet Web site in the default browser. The next behavior you create will underline text as the cursor rolls over it to signify the Internet information.

7. Select the next empty cast member in the GlobalCode cast. Open the script window and name the cast member underline.

8. Enter the contents of Listing 8.24 into the script window. Change the script type to
   `Behavior`. Close the window when complete. (A text file containing this script, called list-
   ing8.24.txt, is on the book's CD-ROM in the Portfolio_Project\Chapter08 folder.)

Listing 8.24 The `underline` **behavior changes the style only with** `mouseEnter` **and** `mouseLeave`
   events.

```
-- underline text

-- this behavior underlines text when the mouse rolls over
-- on the corresponding sprite

-- use this on sprites with the Go to URL behavior

property pOrigMemberStyle

on beginSprite me
  -- store the original style of the member
  pOrigMemberStyle = sprite(me.spriteNum).member.fontstyle
end beginSprite

on mouseLeave me
  unUnderline(me)
end mouseLeave

on mouseEnter me
    underline(me)
end mouseEnter

on endSprite me
  -- put it back to normal
  sprite(me.spriteNum).member.fontstyle = pOrigMemberStyle
end endSprite

on underline me
  -- get the current font style list
  memberStyle = sprite(me.spriteNum).member.fontstyle
  -- add the underline style to the list
  add(memberStyle, #underline)
  -- assign the new style to the member
  sprite(me.spriteNum).member.fontStyle = memberStyle
end underline

on unUnderline me
  -- get the current font style list
```

```
memberStyle = sprite(me.spriteNum).member.fontstyle
-- delete the underline style from the list
deleteOne(memberStyle, #underline)
-- assign the new style to the member
sprite(me.spriteNum).member.fontStyle = memberStyle
end unUnderline
```

> **Note**
>
> This behavior responds to fewer events than the Italicize behavior. Because it works on rollover, it needs to worry about only the `mouseEnter` and `mouseLeave` events. The reason you are so careful about adding and deleting styles should be clear now. With both the Italicize and Underline behaviors on a sprite, they need to cooperate. If either behavior blindly set the text to its chosen style, it would erase the effect of the other behavior. Because you have implemented it, the styles can coexist where needed.

9. Attach the underline behavior to the first text sprite in the movie. Play the movie to watch its effect. As you roll the mouse over the sprite, the underline appears and disappears as you roll off it. Confirm that the Italicize behavior still works by holding the mouse button down on the sprite.

10. Attach this behavior to the other text sprites in this movie that use the Go to URL behavior to link to an Internet site. Save the movie when complete.

11. Open the remaining three information movies, and attach the underline behavior to all the applicable sprites in them as well.

With these two behaviors, you have added enough feedback to the project movies to make a user feel comfortable. It is important to be consistent with the feedback that you provide. It can be very frustrating for an end user to encounter different types of feedback (or missing feedback) at various points in a project.

Wrap-up

The project section of this chapter led you through the creation of three more scripts. The movie script had a `prepareMovie` handler that checks the color depth of the display just as the introduction movie starts. If the color depth will not provide optimal quality for the portfolio (24-bits), an alert is generated as a warning to the end user.

The two new behaviors continue adding interactivity to the project by providing more feedback. You first made a behavior that adds the italic style to text cast members when the associated sprites are clicked on. The second behavior added the underline style to text sprites with Internet links whenever the mouse rolls over them.

In the project section of the next chapter, you will import sound files to add an audio element to your portfolio.

Integrating Various Media Types into Director Projects

Director supports a wide variety of media types, which makes it a flexible tool that is capable of handling many assets. With this flexibility comes complexity, however. It is important to take advantage of the strengths of different types of media while minimizing their drawbacks.

This chapter covers many basic media types, such as audio, video, and text. Each section gives a brief overview of and suggests the best ways to use each media type when creating a multimedia project. Gauging which media type is applicable in different situations is an important skill, so this chapter also discusses their inherent limitations.

Using the right media leads to better overall presentation in terms of quality and effectiveness. Sound files, for example, are useful for creating an atmosphere, but would not be the best choice for conveying text reference information.

This chapter covers bitmap and vector images, text, sampled sound, digital video, as well as Flash movies. Each section describes the media type, along with the advantages and disadvantages of using it. Information on managing the various types is also presented.

Bitmaps

Bitmap cast members are a standard asset type for Director. Most Director movies use bitmap cast members extensively because they are versatile and easy to work with.

A bitmap, or *raster image*, is an image composed of a two-dimensional array of pixels. Each pixel has a horizontal and vertical location in the image, as well as a value that corresponds to a palette position for 8-bit images or an RGB tuple (a series of three numbers representing the red, green, and blue components of the color) for 16- or 24-bit images. A pixel can also have a transparency value, called its *alpha value*, in 32-bit images. A representation of a bitmap image with a palette is shown in Figure 9.1. An RGB image is shown in Figure 9.2.

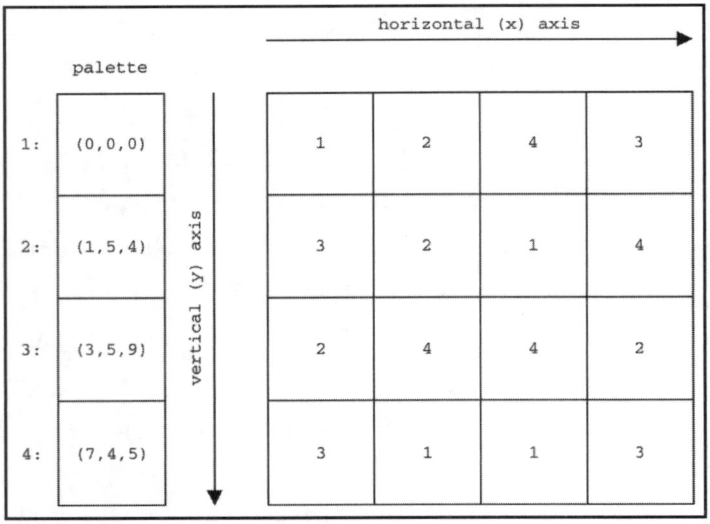

Figure 9.1   The pixels in this image have a value that corresponds to a palette position. The palette contains the RGB colors.

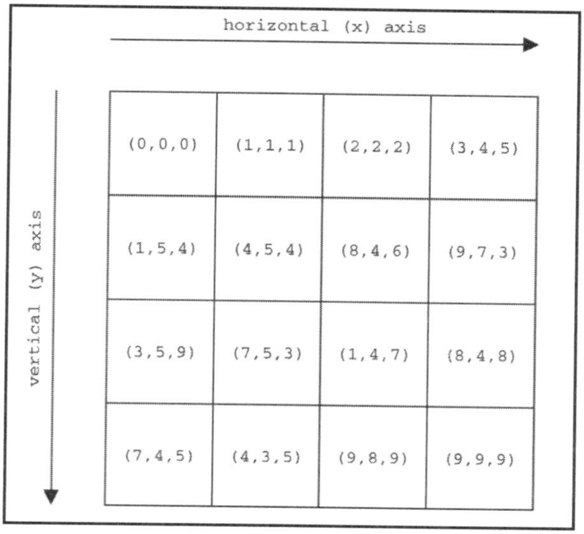

Figure 9.2   In this case, the pixels store the RGB values directly, eliminating the need for a palette but taking up more memory per pixel.

The arrangement of pixels in the image is referred to as a *map*. Each pixel has a certain number of bits, and that leads to the term *bitmap*. An uncompressed bitmap uses an amount of memory defined by its width multiplied by its height multiplied by the number of bytes per pixel. The image in Figure 9.1 is 4 pixels wide by 4 pixels tall, with one byte per pixel for a total of 16 bytes. The image in Figure 9.2 is the same dimension, but each pixel requires two bytes for a total of 32 bytes. Figure 9.3 contains a real-world example of a bitmap cast member.

> **Note**
>
> A pixel is the smallest unit of information in a bitmap image. The word *pixel* comes from a contraction of the phrase *picture element*.

Creating Bitmaps in Director

The Paint window contains basic tools to create bitmap cast members within Director. It can be used to create placeholder images or final art. Images that are imported can also be edited in the Paint window, making changes easy. The Paint window's integration with the Director authoring environment is tremendously useful. Figure 9.4 shows a sample image.

The Director help topic "Paint Window Basics" has information on all the tools available in the Paint window.

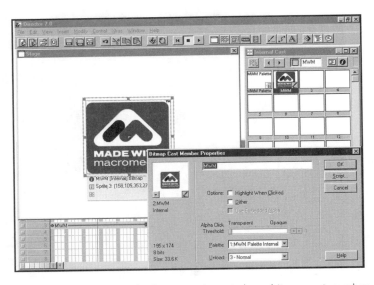

Figure 9.3   The Macromedia logo in this figure was imported as a bitmap cast member. Notice the dimensions and size of the image shown in the properties dialog box.

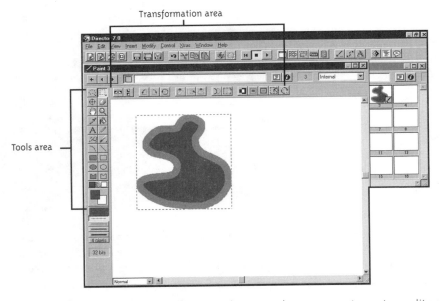

Figure 9.4   On the left side of the Paint window are tools you can use to create or edit an image.

The transformation buttons across the top become active when all or part of the image is selected. Using transformation tools, you can perform actions on the selected portion of an image such as adding perspective or rotating it.

Importing Bitmaps

You can also import images from external files to create bitmap cast members. Director supports a variety of file formats: Windows Bitmap (BMP), GIF, JPEG, Photoshop 3.0 or later, MacPaint, PNG, TIFF, PICT, and Targa (TGA). After such a file is imported as a nonlinked cast member, the original file format is discarded and the image is translated into Director's internal image format.

It is possible to import images from file formats not supported by Director's Import command. Open the image in another program and copy it to the Clipboard. Switch to Director, select an empty cast member, and paste the contents of the Clipboard. You can also paste the Clipboard directly into the Paint window.

Several types of multiple-image file formats can also be imported: FLC and FLI (Windows only), or PICS and Scrapbook (Macintosh only). When such a file is imported, each frame of the file creates a new separate cast member. A film loop representing the original file is also created. This is a quick way to import multiple images quickly.

Internal Versus Linked Bitmap Cast Members

Images, like most cast members, can be imported completely into the cast or imported with links to external files. Each method has advantages and disadvantages. Chapter 4, "Working with Casts," page 49, provides more information on linked assets.

Imported cast members are preconverted to Director's internal format so that no time is spent converting a file during movie playback. The image information is also stored with the movie (for internal casts) or with an external cast, which is advantageous when security of assets (imported images are not accessible outside of Director) or the number of files is a concern.

Linked bitmaps, in contrast to imported images, are easy to update to new versions. To update a bitmap image, you simply replace the file corresponding to the linked cast member with the new one rather than importing the image again to update it. After the image is updated, it is used the next time the movie runs.

This capability is especially useful for movies that use the Internet for linked images. The projector application or Shockwave movie does not need to be updated—just the files it links to need to be updated. This makes it easy to keep movies fresh and different.

> **Tip**
>
> Be careful to ensure that the updated images are the same dimensions and bit-depths as the ones they replace. Pad them with extra space, if necessary. Director reimports an image that is a different size, and the results may not be as you intended.

Compression Considerations

With any multimedia project, the file size of the assets is very important for load or download times, as well as memory usage. Compressed images can significantly reduce load or download times for their respective cast members. Certain file formats use image compression to help reduce file sizes. *Compression* is a process that discards certain information deemed not necessary in an image. Different types of compression methods are available, and each has distinct properties.

Lossless compression, using any algorithm for compression, uses a mathematical formula to reduce the file size of an image. In this case, the reconstituted (that is, uncompressed) version of the image contains exactly the same information as the original image, so no quality is lost. The image is compressed by organizing the information in the image in a more efficient format.

> **Note**
>
> *Lossless compression* gets its name from the fact that no information is lost during the compression process. The information is merely rearranged. In contrast, *lossy compression* throws away (loses) information during compression. This can lead to smaller file sizes but also reduced quality.

Lossy compression reduces the file size by discarding some of the information in the image permanently. The uncompressed image is not exactly the same as the original image after it is compressed by using a lossy method. Typically, lossy compression attempts to throw away information not usually seen by the human eye. The perceived quality of the image does not suffer very much if the level of compression is kept to a minimum. For example, to most people a high-quality JPEG image with mild lossy compression may be indistinguishable from the original.

It's important not to compress an image too much, however. The JPEG image format, for example, tends to lose detail as compression is increased. Figure 9.5 shows an example of an original image and one that has been overly compressed. These two images are on this book's CD-ROM in the file "bridgeimages.jpg" found in the Chapter9 folder.

> **Note**
>
> Note that compression has an effect only with externally linked assets. Compressed images that are imported normally do not exhibit the load-time savings because Director stores them losslessly in the movie or cast. In this case, the images are lower-quality, without the compression benefits.

Original image

Compressed image

Figure 9.5   The original, uncompressed image maintains all the details of the original photo. The image saved with the JPEG format's maximum compression, also referred to as lowest-quality, has lost detail because of compression.

Using a lower bit-depth for an image is also a form of lossy compression. Reducing the bit-depth from 24-bit down to 16-bit or 8-bit creates an image with two-thirds or one-third the file size, respectively. The number of colors used to represent the image is also reduced, and this can cause a loss of quality.

If file size is a large concern and some quality loss is acceptable, you should experiment with different compression levels and methods. A little extra time spent processing the images can lead to a much better end-user experience.

Note   Director does not have the capability to compress images at different levels of loss for comparison. Tools such as Macromedia Fireworks and Equilibrium DeBabelizer are very useful for exploring these options.

Vectors

Vector cast members are a native image format in Director that's new with version 7. They are a natural outgrowth of Director's capability to work with Shockwave Flash movies, which are covered later in this chapter.

Vector images are very different from bitmap images. Whereas bitmaps are made up of pixels, vector images are composed of points and lines, as shown in Figure 9.6. Only the properties of the line (its start and end points) are stored for vector images. For example, a box needs to store only its four points for the lines that make up its edges, no matter how big it is onstage.

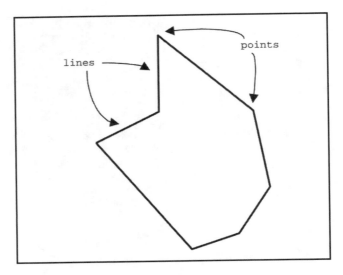

Figure 9.6 This simple vector shape has seven points and seven lines.

Vector images are created in the Vector Shape window, which is similar to the Paint window for bitmap images. The points that make up vector images remain editable after they are drawn. The vector in Figure 9.7 was drawn with the line tool.

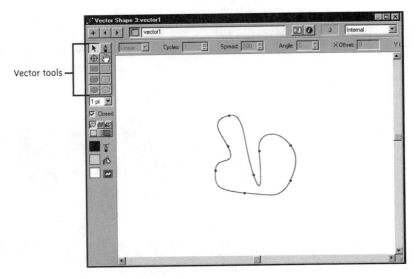

Figure 9.7 A curved shape formed by a series of lines and points.

Each point on a line has control handles that can be moved to change the shape of the line around the point. The points themselves can also be moved to change the shape of the object. Notice that the line is anti-aliased automatically as it is drawn.

Advantages of Vector Images

Because vector images store much less information than bitmap images, they use less memory. This helps reduce the load time of vector image cast members. Figure 9.8 shows a vector Cast Member Properties dialog box. The size of this vector image is much smaller than an equivalent bitmap image would be.

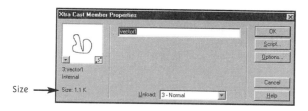

Size ——▶

Figure 9.8   The Cast Member Properties dialog box for vector images shows the heritage of vectors: They are called Xtra Cast Members.

Because vector images are stored as points and are mathematically rendered to the stage when required, other mathematical transforms work well with vector images. Vector cast members scale and rotate perfectly because the underlying shapes are scaled and rotated before the image is rendered. Bitmaps do not scale and rotate perfectly because their precision is limited to the pixels of the image.

Creating Vector Images in Director

You use the following steps to create a vector image cast member to compare its quality with a bitmap image:

1. Start with a new movie and open the Paint window with the Window, Paint command or [Ctrl+5] (Cmd-5). Create a rectangle of any color and moderate size. Figure 9.9 shows an example of this cast member. Name it *bitmap*.

2. Close the Paint window and open the Vector Shape window with the Window, Vector Shape command or [Ctrl+Shift+V] (Cmd-Shift-V). Choose a different color, and create a rectangle of a similar size. Figure 9.10 contains a sample vector shape. Name this cast member *vector*.

Note

Vector images in Director are composed of one continuous line. The end points of the line can be left apart for an open shape or the end points can be connected to form a closed shape.

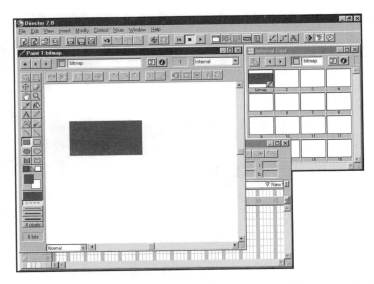

Figure 9.9   The exact size and color of the bitmap image do not matter for this example, but try to create the rectangle so it fits on the stage easily.

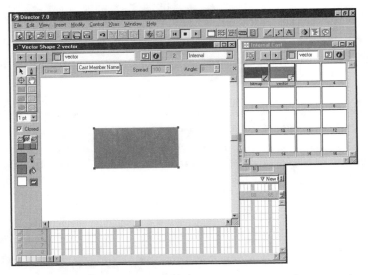

Figure 9.10   This vector image should be a different color from the bitmap cast member to make the sprites easy to identify onstage.

3. Close the Vector Shape window. Drag the bitmap cast member to the score in channel 1. Select the entire bitmap sprite span and change its X: and Y: location to (100,100). (Make sure that the entire sprite is onstage; move it if required.) Drag the vector cast member to the score in channel 2. Change its location to (350,150) or something similar so that it is entirely onstage (see Figure 9.11).

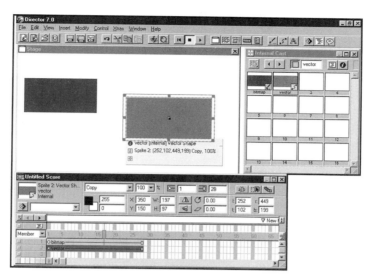

Figure 9.11   The vector and bitmap images are both displayed onstage, and the lines of the bitmap rectangle line up exactly with the horizontal and vertical sides of the stage.

4. Open the Navigation library and drag the Go Loop behavior onto the last frame of the sprite spans in the script channel. This creates an infinitely looping movie.

5. Switch to the Animation: Automatic library, and drag the Rotate Continuously (time-based) behavior onto the bitmap sprite. Set the behavior parameters according to Figure 9.12. This causes the bitmap rectangle to rotate once every 30 seconds.

Figure 9.12   The Rotate Continuously (time-based) behavior causes its sprite to rotate around its registration point for the duration of the sprite span, and because this movie loops to frame 1 at the end of the span, it will rotate forever.

6. Attach the Rotate Continuously (time-based) behavior to the vector sprite. Use the same parameters as in Step 4 to keep the comparison accurate.

7. Play the movie, and watch the edges of the rectangles as the sprites rotate. The vector image sprite has smoother edges than the bitmap image sprite. Figure 9.13 shows an example of both sprites partially rotated.

Macromedia Director

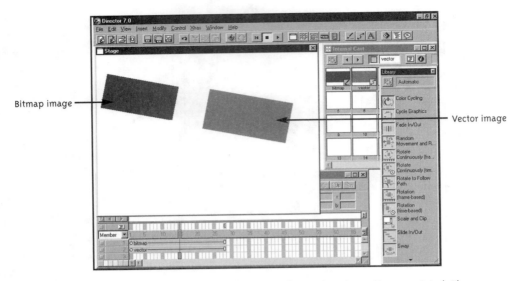

Bitmap image

Vector image

Figure 9.13 The quality advantage of vector images shows when the sprites are rotated: The bitmap image has edges that are jagged and stairstepped, whereas the vector image has smooth edges that look like straight lines at all angles of rotation.

Note

The phenomenon that creates these smooth edges on the vector images is referred to as *anti-aliasing*. It is accomplished by using intermediate colors between the solid colors of the rectangle and the stage. This fools the human eye into believing a straight edge exists, instead of a grid of pixels. The bitmap image edges are said to be *aliased* in comparison. The pixels change directly from the rectangle's color to the stage color with no intermediate colors. A vector image can be anti-aliased during playback because it is being rendered with each frame at the exact angle of rotation.

The points of a vector image are easy to modify even after the image is created. This creates flexibility because the image does not have to be created anew every time you want to change its shape.

Vector images are also bit-depth independent. Only the pure colors of the shapes are stored in the vector image data. The actual representation of those shapes is determined when the image is rendered during movie playback. The same vector image can work in movies with different palettes and in 24-bit movies.

Disadvantages of Vector Images

Director does not support importing vector images. Only cast members created in the Vector Shape window can be used. Shockwave Flash movies have many of the same benefits as vector images and can be imported, as you'll learn later in this chapter, in the section called "Using Shockwave Flash."

Rendering overhead can be a factor in how efficiently a movie plays back. Because each vector image must be drawn fresh for each frame, it can use a significant portion of the computer's processing power. Using many vector images, or a complex image consisting of many lines, slows the frame rate of the movie. So, you do have to pay a price for the quality of vector images.

Because each vector image can consist of only one line, closed or open, the style of artwork is limited. Simple shapes with uniform colors are best suited to vector images. Multiple vector images can be overlaid in multiple sprite channels to create more complex images, but this affects speed as well. It is therefore better to use bitmaps than vectors for photographs and other natural or complex images, despite the reduced quality.

Working with Text Media

Text is the main content of some Director projects, so Director provides a wide variety of tools for working with text. You should be able to have text appear exactly as you want it, in most cases, by using Director's features.

> **Note**
>
> In some cases, you might want to use bitmap cast members containing the text to get special effects, such as multicolored text or text on a curved path. Create these images in another tool such as Adobe Illustrator or Macromedia FreeHand. Then, they can be imported into a Director movie.

There are three types of text cast members in Director: fields, regular text, and bitmap text. Fields are the most limiting of these types, but they provide a few features not available with others. Regular text is most often used because it is very versatile. Bitmap text should be avoided whenever possible because of its larger size and noneditable nature. Each type is covered in more detail in the following sections.

Field Cast Members

Field cast members are used to display large amounts of text with relatively little formatting. The main advantages fields have over the other types of text cast members are speed and scrolling. They are also used for enabling the end user to type text while the movie is running.

Macromedia Director

Advantages of Using Field Cast Members

Because Director does not anti-alias field sprites, they tend to render more quickly to the stage for a given number of words. This also makes the contents easier to read at smaller font sizes (see Figure 9.14). Fields can use any font and font size, but they generally work best with simpler fonts and smaller sizes.

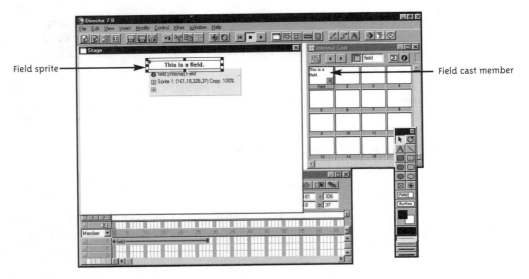

Field sprite

Field cast member

Figure 9.14 A field sprite onstage with its corresponding cast member.

If the number of words in a field cast member is too great to be displayed within the bounding box of the sprite, you can enable the scrollbars. Director automatically creates and handles these interface elements without any special scripting or behaviors. The end user can then scroll to display any portion of the field. Figure 9.15 shows an example of a field with a scrollbar.

Field Cast Member Properties

Several options in the Field Cast Member Properties dialog box are important to note. Figure 9.16 shows an example of this dialog box for the field in Figure 9.15.

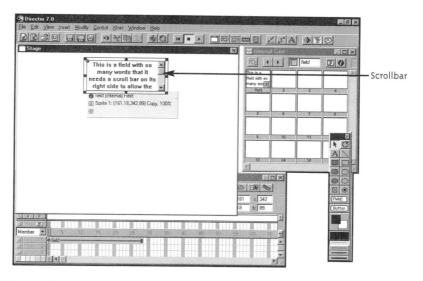

Figure 9.15 With scrollbars, you can lock down the size of a field sprite, regardless of its contents. As the number of words in the field grows or shrinks, Director automatically adjusts the scrollbars.

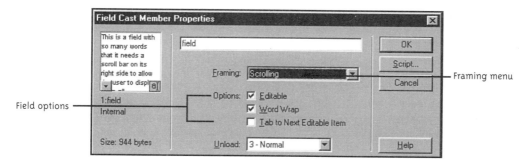

Figure 9.16 You can use the Field Cast Member Properties dialog box to control how a field sprite is presented onstage and find the amount of memory required to store the field.

The Framing drop-down menu contains four options: Adjust to Fit, Scrolling, Fixed, and Limit to Field Size. You use these options to control the bounding box, or frame, for the field:

- The Adjust to Fit option is common for fields that do not scroll. As you adjust one dimension of the field, the other dimension compensates to always show the entire contents. For a given height or width, the field always has the minimum required corresponding width or height.

- To turn on a scrollbar, select the Scrolling option. This places a scrollbar on the right side of the field. The scrollbar is always present, even if the contents of the field fit within the frame (in which case, it simply has no effect if moved).

- For ultimate control over the frame of a field, choose the Fixed option. With it, you can set both dimensions independently. If you choose this option, Director doesn't help you out by changing the frame size; you have to do it.

- The last Framing option, Limit to Field Size, is a variation on the Fixed option. If the field is set to Editable, Director does not accept more characters than will fit in the field. (The Fixed option, in contrast, accepts characters that do not show up in the field and stores them.)

The three Options available for field cast members are Editable, Word Wrap, and Tab to Next Editable Item, each of which controls a different aspect of the field:

- When a field is set to Editable, Director enables the end user to alter the contents of the field when the movie is running. This can include typing more text or erasing text already in the field. You use this option to gather information, such as a name, from the end user.

- The Word Wrap option controls the capability of a field to break lines between words. This allows more of the contents of the field to be shown within the frame. Without Word Wrap enabled, lines of words can extend beyond the borders of the frame. Leave this option enabled under most circumstances.

- When more than one editable field is onstage at a time, Director provides an interface convention for the end user to move between them. The end user can use the Tab key to move the input focus (the insertion cursor) to the editable field in the next highest channel. Users already typing into fields find this convenient because their hands do not have to leave the keyboard to move to the next field. You need to be sure to organize field sprites properly so that the tab order matches the users' expectations.

Regular Text Cast Members

Text cast members and sprites can be used for creating more complicated effects with words. They have many of the same properties as fields, but also have additional settings. If the desired effect does not require a text cast member, you should use a field instead because fields are more efficient for movie playback.

Advantages of Using Text Cast Members

Like vector images, Director automatically anti-aliases text sprites during movie playback. This is a major quality advantage over fields. However, the drawback is the additional processing time required. Anti-aliased text can significantly affect the playback speed of a movie. Figure 9.17 shows examples of anti-aliased and aliased text sprites.

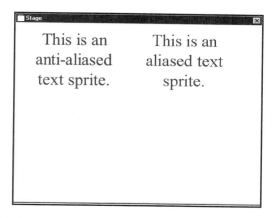

Figure 9.17   Notice that the edges of the letters in the anti-aliased sprite blend nicely into the background. The edges of the sprite that is not anti-aliased has letters that are more blocky.

Like bitmaps and vectors, text sprites can be rotated by arbitrary amounts. The quality of the text, even if anti-aliased, suffers somewhat when you use this technique. The flexibility of this option occasionally warrants the degradation in quality, however. Figure 9.18 shows an example of this, using a technique similar to that used in the section "Creating Vector Images in Director."

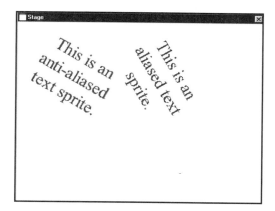

Figure 9.18   The sprites from Figure 9.17 are shown here, rotated. The left sprite is rotated 30 degrees clockwise, and the right sprite 60 degrees clockwise. Anti-aliased text again looks better than aliased text.

Text Cast Member Properties

You access the options for a text cast member by using the Options button in the Cast Member Properties dialog box. When you click this button, you get the Text Cast Member Properties dialog box shown in Figure 9.19. The properties in this dialog box are explained in the following paragraphs.

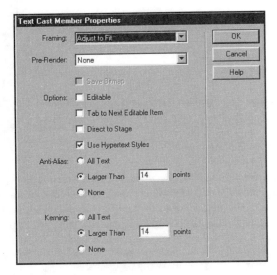

Figure 9.19   You use the Text Cast Member Properties dialog box to set various properties of text cast members.

The Framing drop-down menu operates exactly the same as with field cast members, however, the Limit to Field Size option is not available.

The Pre-Render drop-down menu provides options to increase the efficiency of text. The default choice, None, tells Director to render the text the first time it appears onstage. The other two options, Copy Ink and Other Ink, cause Director to render the text in memory immediately after it is loaded. Each choice is optimized for the type of ink used with the sprite. This trades off a little extra load time for less processing time during movie playback.

The first two Options, Editable and Tab to Next Editable Item, have the same effect as Field members. The Direct to Stage option increases the speed that text sprites are drawn onstage. The limitation is that the normal depth ordering is ignored and the text is always drawn in front of other sprites. Text members can have hot links embedded in them, and the Use Hypertext Styles option causes them to look like links in a Web browser.

The Anti-Alias options affect the entire contents of the cast member. If All Text is chosen, Director anti-aliases every character, regardless of size. The Larger Than option sets a threshold size. Director anti-aliases only words with a font size larger than that specified here. The final anti-alias option, None, causes Director to leave all the words aliased in the text member.

Font sizes of 12 points and below should not be anti-aliased. The process causes the letters to appear fuzzy and can make the text difficult to read.

Kerning options parallel the Anti-Alias options. Use them to selectively have Director automatically kern the contents of the text member.

Text cast members use more memory than field cast members with the same information. In general, the size of both types of cast members is so much smaller than that of images that the difference does not matter. Consider using fields exclusively if movie and cast size is paramount.

Bitmap Text Cast Members

For the greatest flexibility in visual representation of text, consider using a bitmap image instead of a text or field member. Many graphics programs provide a multitude of options for creating interesting text effects in bitmap images. For example, wavy text is not possible with a text member. Complicated shadow effects and multicolored letters are also best accomplished by using bitmaps.

The drawback of this method is that the text ceases to be editable, even by the movie author. After the bitmap is created, the text is frozen. This can create complications for international versions of a project because the bitmaps will have to be re-created for each language.

Several of the later versions of popular graphics programs enable text to be saved in an editable form within their custom file formats. Adobe Photoshop provides this feature, for example. Even though Director still sees the text as a bitmap image, these programs can make revisions easier. The bitmap simply needs to be reimported for revisions to take effect.

Note
Special care should be taken with text in compressed bitmaps. High levels of compression can adversely affect the quality of text before the rest of the image suffers. Test several levels of compression to reach a compromise in quality and file size. (See the section on "Compression Considerations," earlier in this chapter.)

For bitmap text creation within Director, consider using the Convert to Bitmap command from the Modify menu. This command is available only when a text or field member is selected. It irreversibly converts the current member to a bitmap image, based on how it would be rendered to the stage.

Adding Waveform Audio

Another name for *waveform* audio is sampled audio. This refers to the process of sampling an audio source at discrete intervals and storing the values as digital samples. This form of audio is very versatile because any kind of sound can be represented by it.

A waveform audio file consists of a series of samples that represent the amplitude (volume) of a sound at points in time. The computer reproduces the sound when these samples are played back in order at their original sample speed. Figure 9.20 is a visual representation of an audio file from the program Sound Forge XP by Sonic Foundry.

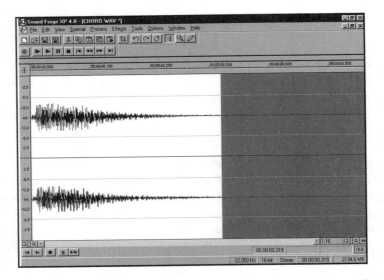

Figure 9.20   A stereo audio file is shown as a two-dimensional graph in Sound Forge. The two lines show this is a stereo file. Areas of higher volume are shown as wider sections in the line.

Some common file formats for waveform audio assets are AIFF, WAV, and MP3. Director can import sounds in any of these formats.

- AIFF files generally have the extension AIF; AIFF is an acronym for Audio Interchange File Format.
- WAV files are the native audio file type for Windows machines; WAV is short for waveform.
- MP3 files are becoming much more common as a way of storing music in highly compressed files at high quality; MP3 is a contraction of MPEG Layer 3.

Preloading Audio

A standard import of a sound file stores the entire contents of the file in the cast. When this sound file is played, the whole file is loaded and stored in memory before it starts. This is called *preloaded* audio.

For preloaded audio, the storage medium (CD-ROM, Internet) transfer speed affects only the load time, not the playback speed. Large preloaded sounds can take a long time to load, especially from the Internet. But after they are loaded subsequent times they are played, they start immediately.

The preloading technique is best used with small sounds that play more than once in a movie. The load time will be less and they will not consume too much memory. Preloaded sounds are also the best way to play more than one sound at once. Because they are already in memory, there is no contention for the storage device.

Streaming Audio

When a sound file is linked during an import, it plays back differently than if it is imported completely. Linked audio cast members are said to "stream" off the storage medium as they play. Rather than loading the entire sound into memory, only portions of *streaming* audio are loaded as it plays.

This uses less memory, especially for large sounds. The sections of the sound that have already played are discarded from memory immediately. It is the only way to play sounds that are too large to fit in memory.

The transfer rate of the medium in which the sound is streamed from affects the quality of sound that can be played. CD-ROM, with its relatively high bandwidth, is excellent at playing high-quality sound. The Internet, by contrast, typically has a much lower bandwidth and thus supports only lower-quality sounds.

Additionally, the access time of the medium affects when a streamed sound starts. The sound file must be accessed each time it is played, and this can lead to a noticeable delay between the time Director starts a sound and when sound is actually heard.

Streamed sounds are excellent for audio that will play only once in a movie. There is little benefit in preloading an entire sound, only to discard it after one use. By streaming a sound, the movie author can make better use of available memory and reduce movie load times.

Sound File Properties

Various properties of sound files affect their quality and size. In general, the bandwidth of an audio file (the number of bytes per second required to play it) is proportional to its quality. That is, higher-quality sounds have more information (bytes) per second of playback.

A simple formula for determining a sound's bandwidth is to multiply its bit-depth by its sample rate. The bit-depth of a sound refers to the size, in bits, of the individual samples in the file. Its sample rate is the number of these samples taken per second to represent the sound.

Compression in audio files is similar to bitmap-image compression. It reduces a file's size by selectively discarding information deemed redundant or not necessary. Many compression methods take advantage of the way the human ear perceives sound to remove information that is never perceived anyway.

Bit-Depth

The *bit-depth* of an audio file is the number of bits used to represent each sample. An 8-bit number can represent values between 0 and 255, and this determines the precision of each sample. Perfect quiet is stored as 0 and full amplitude as 255. Other levels fall between these values.

16-bit samples are most common now. They provide 256 times the precision of 8-bit samples so they more accurately reflect the actual audio represented by the sample. Compact disc audio is stored as 16-bit samples.

On the Internet, 8-bit samples are still used because of the smaller files that result. All other properties being equal, an 8-bit audio file is half the size of a 16-bit file, just like bitmap images.

> **Note**
>
> The Macintosh plays all sounds at 16-bit audio. It will upsample an 8-bit file to 16-bit as it is being played back. This does not provide higher quality but it can affect performance because of the extra computation. If playback performance on Macintosh computers is more important than file size, use 16-bit audio.

Sample Rate

The *sample rate* of an audio file defines how many individual values are stored per second to represent the sound. A higher sample rate will store a sound more accurately, but leads to larger file sizes and higher bandwidth requirements.

> **Tip**
>
> The sample rate is often referred to in units called *Hertz* or *kilohertz*. One Hertz is one sample per second. A kilohertz is one thousand samples per second. They are abbreviated as Hz and kHz, respectively.

The audio on a standard CD is stored at 44.1kHz (44.1 thousand samples per second). This number was chosen because of a concept known as Nyquist's Theorem. Nyquist, a scientist, discovered that a sound should be sampled at approximately twice the highest frequency of the sound. Because humans can hear sounds up to only about 20kHz, the sample rate of 44.1kHz can represent all the frequencies of human hearing.

This implies that as the sample rate is lowered, the frequencies that can be stored in the audio file are reduced. At the common sample rate of 22kHz (often used in multimedia), only the lower half of the range of human hearing can be represented. This is typically not a problem because most sounds have the most information in the lower frequencies.

In very bandwidth-constrained situations, a sample rate of 11kHz is still used. This can make audio files sound like telephone calls. More high-frequency information is lost and it is very noticeable. At this sample rate, deeper voices (often men's) are more understandable than higher voices (often women's).

Director can play back any common sample rate, but Macromedia recommends three standard values: 44.1kHz, 22kHz, and 11kHz.

Compression

Like bitmap images, audio files can be compressed using lossless or lossy methods. Lossy methods, especially more recent ones, can store amazing-quality sound in very low-bandwidth files. They work because human ears are more highly tuned to hear certain frequencies than others. Superfluous information is dropped where the human ear will not notice it missing.

File sizes (and therefore required bandwidth) can be reduced up to about one quarter their original sizes with good compression. Average listeners will not perceive a loss of quality without comparing the compressed and uncompressed files directly.

The current MP3 revolution is a good example of the power of audio compression. Music compressed as MP3 files typically requires about one-twelfth the bandwidth of compact disc audio, with little quality loss. This has enabled high-quality music to proliferate on the Internet.

Director supports MP3 audio directly and it should be considered as a primary format in any project. The one drawback is that the decompression process is fairly intensive. More of the computer's processing power must be used to play an MP3 than an uncompressed sound. This is ideal for Shockwave movies because bandwidth is more precious than computer power on the Internet.

Lingo for Audio Playback

Only two sound channels are provided in the score for audio playback. Director supports up to eight sound channels, but numbers three through eight are accessible only from Lingo. Two sets of Lingo commands are available: one for cast member sounds and one for playing sound files directly.

Cast member sounds can be played by using the puppetSound command. Use puppetSound with a channel number and cast member name to start the sound. Listing 9.1 outlines a behavior that plays a sound for the duration of a sprite.

Listing 9.1 Using puppetSound.

```
-- play a sound while the sprite is onstage

on beginSprite me
   -- start the sound in cast member "MP3" in
   -- sound channel 3
   puppetSound 3, "MP3"
end beginSprite

on endSprite me
   -- stop any sound playing in sound channel 3
   puppetSound 3, 0
end endSprite
```

Note
This behavior starts an audio cast member at the beginning of a sprite span and stops it at the end. It is simplified to show the use of puppetSound.

Use the Lingo command sound playfile to play an audio file directly from disk. It does not need to be imported as a cast member. Sounds played this way are automatically streamed. Listing 9.2 shows a similar behavior using this command. Rather than playing a cast member, this behavior plays a file directly. Again, it is simplified to show how to use the commands.

Listing 9.2 **Adding** sound playfile **Lingo.**

```
-- stream a sound while the sprite is onstage
on beginSprite me
  -- start the sound from the file "sound.mp3" in
  -- sound channel 3
  sound playfile 3, "sound.mp3"
end beginSprite

on endSprite me
  -- stop any sound playing in sound channel 3
  sound stop 3
end endSprite
```

Playing sounds using Lingo is straightforward. It provides much greater flexibility than just using the sound channels in the score. Explore the behaviors in the Sound behavior library for more ideas on how to use sounds.

Digital Video

Digital video practically launched the multimedia industry. When Apple's QuickTime was first released, people were amazed at seeing video play back on a computer screen. There was excitement, even though the video was postage-stamp-sized and very grainy.

CD-ROM transfer speeds (150kB/s nominal) and the required decompression effort limited early digital video. If the data rate of a video was too high, the video would start to skip frames and the audio would break up. If the computer's processor could not handle the decompression task, the video would not play smoothly.

Each of these limitations still exists today, but to much lesser degrees. CD-ROM and DVD-ROM drives can now keep pace with all but the highest-quality consumer digital video. Processors have advanced to the point where video decompression effort is minimal.

Video Formats

Two rival formats are commonly used. Video for Windows is officially supported only on the Windows platform. QuickTime is completely cross-platform.

Director is very capable of handling both formats, within the platform limitations. Digital video is handled as a normal cast member type. Like an audio file, it plays automatically when the playback head encounters its sprite span. Unlike audio, video is placed in a sprite channel like bitmap or vector images.

> **Note**
>
> Director does not have a way to edit video within the application; an external program must be used.

Video Compression Considerations

The eventual quality of a digital video file depends highly on the quality of the source. High-quality sources have little video and audio noise (errors or artifacts), and therefore compress better. This allows a lower bandwidth for a given quality or higher quality for a given bandwidth.

Almost all video compression schemes are lossy in nature. This is the only way of getting video to play back acceptably on computers. The effects of compression on video are cumulative. Compress video a minimum number of times while creating the final file. For example, the new digital video camcorders use a built-in compression scheme. Compression artifacts may appear when the video is edited and prepared for use in a Director movie.

Codecs are used to store and play back digital video. The term *codec* comes from the concatenation of compressor-decompressor. The original video source is initially compressed for storage using a codec. The decompression occurs on playback using the same codec.

An example of a codec is *Cinepak*. This compression method works well for real-world video content and is available on both formats. The compression process can take a long time, but the decompression occurs very quickly. This is called an *assymetrical* codec.

Other examples of a type of codec are the Animation (QuickTime) and Microsoft RLE (Video for Windows) codecs. They both use a lossless scheme at their highest-quality levels. The compression comes from noting where the same color pixel occurs repeatedly in rows. On compression, the color of the pixel is stored once along with the number of times it is repeated in the original frame.

This method is sometimes called Run Length Encoding, or RLE. It is best used for two-dimensional animation that contains large areas of the same color. RLE is not suitable for video recorded from a live source; the compressed video may actually be larger than the source.

As with bitmap image compression, covered previously in this chapter, video compression can result in quality loss. It is always a great challenge to reach a compromise between quality and data rate when preparing digital video. Figures 9.21, 9.22, and 9.23 show an original image and the results of compressing it with two different codecs. They have been doubled in size from their original size of 320×240 pixels to better show the results.

 Figure 9.21 This is the original image, a closeup of a polar bear's head. It contains all the detail available in the photograph. The file "uncompressed.avi" on the CD-ROM is available to view. Its size is approximately 302KB.

 Figure 9.22 The Indeo codec from Intel was used at a medium-quality setting to compress the original frame. The results are quite good, but some detail is lost, especially in the background and around the bear's head. This image is in the file "indeo.avi" on the CD-ROM. It is about 8KB in size.

Figure 9.23 An older codec called "Microsoft Video" at medium quality produced this frame. It is very blocky and much of the detail is gone. The resolution has effectively been reduced by the compression. The size of the resulting file, "video.avi," on the CD-ROM is actually larger than the Indeo file at 14KB.

Several utilities are available to interactively explore the effects of different codecs and settings on the quality and data rate of digital video. Media Cleaner Pro from Terran Interactive is one such tool. It can automatically compress video to a certain bandwidth while maintaining the highest quality possible. Serious video production is much more efficient with a tool like this.

An important distinction exists between the average and peak data rates of a digital video file. The average playback rate is calculated by dividing the file's size by its length. The peak data rate is more important for smooth playback: If the peak is too great, it will cause a skip or pause during playback, even if the average data rate is acceptable.

After working with digital video for a while, people develop an intuitive feel for which codec is correct for an application. The codec choice is not important in a Director movie because Director uses either QuickTime or Video for Windows to actually decompress as the movie plays. The only requirement is that the codec be available on the end user's computer for decompression.

Using Shockwave Flash

Flash by Macromedia is another interactive media creation tool. It is both a standalone asset creation tool and a companion product to Director. Flash works primarily with vector images and its primary market is Internet content creation.

The interface is somewhat similar to Director's, but many differences exist in the details. Director experience is not immediately transferable to Flash. Many new concepts must be learned and other concepts relearned. Figure 9.24 shows the basic interface for Flash.

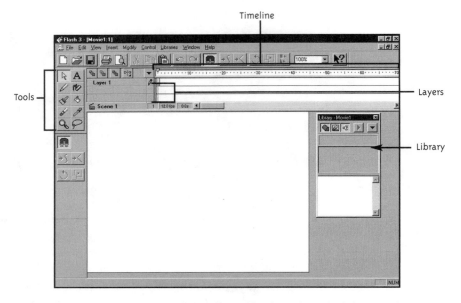

Figure 9.24 The Flash interface has parallels to Director's. The tools on the left are used to create vector images. Layers are like channels in Director. The timeline is analogous to the score. The Library window contains symbols like cast windows contain cast members.

Flash movies are very useful cast members within Director movies. They are imported like any other file and have the same general properties as vector images. Like vectors, Flash movies do not have specific palettes, but can be remapped at playback time to the current Director palette.

There are two main differences between Flash movies and vector images. The first is that Flash movies can have a virtually unlimited number of lines, in contrast to a vector's one line. This allows much more complex images. Secondly, Flash movies support multiple frames within one cast member. Animation effects are easy to create this way.

Preparing Flash Movies

This section is not intended to be a tutorial on how to use Flash. Rather, it contains a guideline for important aspects of Flash movies that will be used in Director projects.

Importing Assets

The best choices for importing assets into Flash are vector-based files. These take advantage of the unique qualities of vectors such as high-quality scaling and rotation. File formats such as Adobe Illustrator, AutoCAD DXF, and Windows Metafile are supported. Macromedia recommends FreeHand files because of FreeHand's understanding of Flash's capabilities.

For better playback speed, consider using the Optimization command on symbols in Flash. This reduces the number of points used in the lines while attempting to maintain their shapes as closely as possible. Having very few points leads to faster rendering times onstage.

Flash can also import audio files (WAV or AIFF format) for playback within Flash movies. The audio is included with the Flash movie when it is imported into Director. Audio that is tightly linked to a Flash movie should be used this way rather than imported separately into Director.

Creating Symbols Within Flash

The tools available in Flash are useful for creating symbols from scratch. (Symbols in Flash are analogous to cast members in Director.) Text, lines, and shapes are all easy to produce. They are more flexible and provide more features than the vector image drawing capabilities within Director.

Very interesting and useful effects can be created directly within Flash using these tools. The tutorials provided with the program are a good starting point for learning more about its features.

Exporting Flash Movies

Plain Flash movies are like normal Director movies. They are used to save movies with all their authoring features intact. Flash also provides a movie type called Shockwave Flash. They are similar to Director's Shockwave movies in that they are protected from modification and compressed in preparation for use on the Internet.

Use the Shockwave Flash export feature for creating Flash movies that will be used in Director. Save the regular Flash movies for revisions and archival storage.

Shockwave Flash in Director

Flash assets, like vector images, can be processor-intensive to render to the stage. The higher quality of vector-based assets involves more computation time each time the stage is drawn for a new frame. The size of the Flash movie has a large effect on this rendering speed. Keep the size as small as possible without sacrificing quality.

For this reason, it is best to use only a few Flash movies onstage at once. As more Flash is used, the frame rate of the Director movie will get slower. Use Flash only where the benefits of the vector format make sense.

A low-quality option is available for Flash cast members in Director. This forsakes anti-aliasing in favor of faster rendering speeds. Unfortunately, the quality suffers with this option to the point where many of the advantages of Flash are lost. Two examples of a Flash movie are shown in Figures 9.25 and 9.26.

Macromedia Director

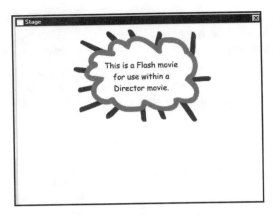

Figure 9.25 The Flash cast member in this figure is set to display at high quality. All the lines and text are anti-aliased to the background, providing smooth transitions.

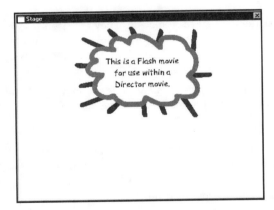

Figure 9.26 This figure shows the same Shockwave Flash movie imported as a new cast member and set to display at low quality. The lines are aliased and the quality of the text is reduced.

Flash assets have several unique properties not available with other cast members. As shown in the previous two figures, the quality of the rendering is controlled by the cast member properties. Other options are shown in Figure 9.27 and are explained in the following paragraphs.

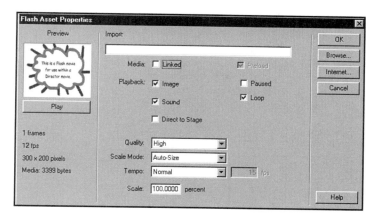

Figure 9.27   The different properties of Flash cast members are accessible from this dialog box. The dialog box is displayed using the Option button in the cast member information dialog box.

The preview thumbnail view is useful for playing the Flash movie within Director. Below the preview are the statistics about the asset, including the number of frames, the frame rate, the dimensions, and memory size of the movie. The frame rate of a Flash movie can be different from the frame rate of the Director movie it is used in.

The media section is used to specify whether the Flash asset is completely imported or linked to an external file. In the case shown earlier in Figure 9.27, the asset is imported so the Preload option is on by default and not available to change.

How the movie appears onstage is controlled by the playback options. The image and sound of the Flash asset can be individually enabled and disabled. The movie can start paused or already playing. It can loop automatically when complete or stop on the last frame. The Direct to Stage option makes the movie render faster, but it can no longer be layered with other sprites; it always appears on top.

The quality menu provides choices of High, Low, Auto-High, and Auto-Low. High and Low are self-explanatory and demonstrated previously in Figures 9.25 and 9.26. Auto-High starts the movie playing at high quality, but changes it to low if the Director movie's frame rate cannot be sustained. Auto-Low works in reverse, starting at low quality and automatically changing to high if the frame rate can be sustained.

The Scale Mode menu controls how the bounding box appears onstage and how the Flash movie appears within it. The most common choice is Auto-Size and works for the majority of movies. With this option, the movie scales within the bounding box if it is changed. Show All makes the entire Flash movie appear within the bounding box at its original aspect ratio. The Flash movie's aspect ratio is maintained with the No Border option but it may be cropped within the sprite. The bounding box determines the Flash movie's aspect ratio when Exact Fit is specified. Last, No Scale sets the movie to appear within the bounding box, cropped if necessary.

The Tempo menu has three options: Normal, Fixed, and Lock-Step. Normal uses the frame rate of the original Flash movie. Fixed lets the movie author specify a new frame rate for this asset. Lock-Step causes the Flash movie frames to play at the exact rate of the Director movie.

The Scale option sets the size of the movie onstage. It works in conjunction with the Scale Mode menu. For more details on all these options, with example images, refer to Director Help under the topic Using Flash Movies.

Flash assets are most useful for displaying high-quality, vector-based images. They scale and rotate smoothly and at high quality (if the corresponding option is set). Self-contained multi-frame animations can be stored as Flash movies, and they play back automatically as the Director movie plays.

Many of the behaviors from Director's built-in libraries work with Flash cast members. For example, the Automatic Animation behaviors provide very nice effects with Flash. The Flash-specific library contains three behaviors as well. They are used to set cast member options for individual sprites instead of with the cast members themselves.

Managing Media

This chapter has explored how to use different types of media within Director. It is also important to understand how to manage media within the broader scope of a multimedia project. Media (asset) management can determine the quality of the development experience. Closely controlled assets make the project more efficient and the end product better.

Experiment with the asset management process before a project enters production. It is not a good idea to wait until production starts to figure out how to handle all the media elements being created. A well-understood and closely followed process will avoid confusion among team members.

Track the production daily, at least to keep up-to-date on progress. It is easy to defer because it can sometimes seem like a burden. A small amount of work each day will pay off as the project continues.

Plan Ahead

As outlined in Chapter 3, "Planning Your Director Project," page 29, a functional specification is vital. Every asset to be created is referenced in this document along with how it is to be implemented. Keep the functional specification updated during the course of the project.

A good specification enables the asset creation team to know what to create. The Director authors will understand how to incorporate the assets into their movies. The project manager gauges progress by comparing what is complete to what remains.

Track Progress

As an additional tool to track the progress of a project, consider using an asset database. This concept was also introduced in Chapter 3. It is recommended for all but the smallest projects and practically mandatory for large ones.

All the assets exist as records in the database. Their fields will vary, depending on the processes and team makeup. Enough information should be kept to allow accurate tracking but not so much that the database becomes burdensome to the team.

A well-designed database lets team members know what they can work on next. There should never be confusion about what remains to be done. Statistics should be generated to allow the project manager to measure progress and identify any problems.

 Tip Translation to other languages is much easier with a good asset database. Not only do the general benefits apply to localization projects, but also the database can specifically identify assets that need to change for different languages.

Control Versions

The final component of media management is version control. It is vital that team members know when an asset is final and ready for implementation.

Good version control also allows revisions to be tracked closely. New versions are included easily in the movies. Without a version control process, there is a danger that nonfinal assets will be shipped with the title. Consider using a version control application, as mentioned in Chapter 3, to make sure this does not happen.

Being Productive with Media in Director

Director can use many different types of media. Choosing the best medium for a particular application is an important skill that is best learned with experimentation. The right medium helps spread the intended message.

Images can be either bitmap or vector formats. Bitmaps are more common and are excellent at representing details. Vectors are new to version 7 of Director. Their capability to be changed at any time makes them flexible, but they are best at representing abstract images.

Text in Director can be shown in any of three forms: fields, regular text, or bitmap text. Fields are fastest and allow the end user to enter information. Regular text looks good and is flexible because you can modify it at any time. Bitmap text is best as showing text effects such as multiple colors or irregular shapes.

Sound in Director can really bring a project alive. Sound can be either preloaded and played from memory, or streamed from a storage medium such as a CD-ROM. Preloaded memory plays immediately, whereas streaming sounds can take a fraction of a second to start. Streaming sounds do not use as much memory as preloaded sounds, however.

Digital video is a huge topic with many considerations. You must take care when capturing the video and pick a good compression method.

Shockwave Flash movies provide Director with many new capabilities. They are a vector-based format without the limitations of regular vector images.

Often, the success or failure of a project is dependent on how well the media are managed. It is important to understand all the production pathways that media go through on their way to your Director movies. Always keep track of the progress of media creation. Once behind, it is very hard to catch up.

Interactive Portfolio Project

In the previous chapter, you created more scripts to add feedback to your movies for the end user. The project section of this chapter shows you how to add sound to the portfolio.

The introduction movie will come to life with the addition of a short musical piece and two sound effects. (With the introduction of sound, you may notice a slight slowdown in the playing of the movie.) The interface of the main movies will become even more lively if you add a few button-click sounds. A smattering of applause is created for the credit movie.

You may want to work with other media types for your personal portfolio. Try adding some video, still images, or even a Flash movie. Anything you add will create a more personalized presentation.

Adding Sound to the Portfolio

You are going to use two methods for playing sound during the portfolio movies. The introduction and credit movies will use the two sound channels in the score for their sound. The main information movies rely on a behavior to play their sounds.

A new global external cast for storing the reused sounds will also be created. The information movies will use these sound cast members.

Introduction Movie Sound

The animation in the introduction movie is nice on its own, but could use something extra. By adding sound to the animation, you will be creating even more of an experience for the portfolio user.

Follow these steps to add some music and sound effects to the introduction:

1. Start by copying the movies from the Chapter08 folder to a new Chapter09 folder on your hard drive. Version control is still important as you near the end of the project.

2. Open the "intro.dir" movie in Director. Switch to the internal cast window and select the next unused cast member. You will import three sound files into this cast.

3. Start the import process. Navigate to the Portfolio_Project\Chapter09 folder on the CD-ROM. Open the intro_sounds folder.

4. Add all three sound files to the import list and complete the import. Three new sound cast members appear in the internal cast.

5. You can open the Sound Cast Member Properties dialog box by double-clicking a sound cast member. Figure 9.28 shows this dialog box for the lightning cast member.

Figure 9.28 The Sound Cast Properties dialog box lets you preview the sound with the Play button.

6. Expand the score to show the effect channels if they are not already displayed. Set the zoom factor so you can see the entire 150 frames of the score without scrolling.

7. Drag the music cast member to sound channel 1 at frame 1 in the score. Expand the sound in the score so it ends at frame 90, shown in Figure 9.29. This sound is just under three seconds long, so it lasts about 90 frames at your tempo of 60 frames per second.

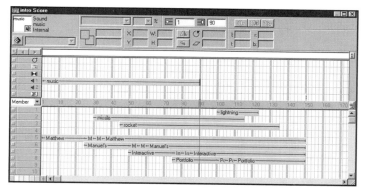

Figure 9.29 The music sound extends through the first three seconds of the movie.

8. Rewind and play the movie to hear the music play as the text slides onstage. (Choose to cancel when Director asks whether you want to save the movie before going to the next one. This restarts the current movie, and you can hit the stop button manually.)

9. Add the spaceship sound to sound channel 2 from frames 20 through 135. This sound is almost four seconds long.

10. Add the lightning sound to sound channel 1 from frames 100 through 130. It is just under a second long.

11. Save the movie, rewind it, and play it again. You should hear the music play, the space-ship sound starts before the music is finished, and then the lightning sound plays.

You have just added synchronized sound to the introduction movie animation. Feel free to move the sounds around to your liking or add your own sounds to make it distinct.

Next, you will add one sound to the credits movie by using a similar process.

Credit Movie Sound

In this section, you will add one sound to the first half of the credit movie. Again, it adds a bit of extra life to the project.

These steps outline how to add this sound:

1. Open the "credits.dir" movie from the Chapter09 folder on your hard drive. Select the next empty cast member in the internal cast.

2. Import the "applause.wav" file from the Portfolio_Project\Credits_sounds folder on this book's CD-ROM. Preview the sound if you like.

3. Drag the applause sound to the score in sound channel 1. Shorten the sound so its end frame is at frame 15, shown in Figure 9.30. This corresponds to the Wait for Mouse Click setting in the tempo channel.

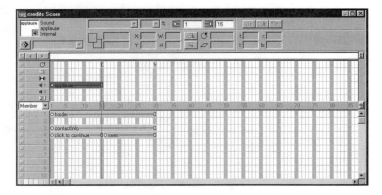

Figure 9.30 The applause sound ends when the user clicks the mouse because playback immediately jumps to an area of the score without the sound.

4. Play the movie and try two things: Wait until the sound is finished before clicking, and click before the sound is finished.

5. Save the movie when you are satisfied with the results.

This sound plays every time the user chooses to quit. It will stop as soon as they click to interrupt it.

Interface Sounds

Interface sounds are triggered by user actions, so they work well with behaviors. As sprites are clicked on, the associated sound will play.

As part of the continuing process of adding interactivity and feedback to the end user interface of the portfolio, you will add button-click sounds. There are several sounds to choose from in this section; you decide which ones you think are appropriate for the different actions.

Follow these steps to use a standard behavior to add button click sounds:

1. Open the "main.dir" movie file. Create a new external cast called GlobalSounds. Leave the Use in Current Movie box selected.

2. Switch to the GlobalSounds cast in preparation for importing WAV files. Save the new cast in the Chapter09 folder on your hard drive. (Remember to add the .cst extension to the filename.)

3. Import all six click sounds from the Portfolio_Project\Chapter09\global_sounds folder on this book's CD-ROM.

4. Open the Library window (Window, Library Palette) and select the Sound library in the Media section. Attach the behavior Play Sound Member to the Accomplishments text sprite. The dialog box shown in Figure 9.31 appears.

Figure 9.31 The properties dialog box for the Play Sound Member behavior.

5. Choose a sound cast member from the Play which sound? list. Leave the sound playing in channel 1, the default. (All the sounds for the interface are so short that you don't have to worry about them overlapping in sound channels.) Have the sound play on the mouseDown event. Click OK to continue.

6. Save the current movie. Rewind and play it. Click the Accomplishments sprite to hear the button-click sound you choose play.

7. Click the Main button to return to the "main.dir" movie.

8. Attach the same behavior to the other three text sprites, preferably using the same properties as the first one. If you use the same properties, it reinforces with the user that these buttons perform the same general function: to go to another screen in the project.

9. Use the same behavior on the quit_button sprite. This time, choose a different click sound, but leave the other properties the same. Now, you will hear another sound when the click button is pressed.

10. Go through the other four movies and link the global external cast GlobalSounds to each. This makes the sound cast members available in all the movies that need them.

11. Attach the same behavior to all other sprites (in the other movies) that have actions tied to them. You may want to differentiate the sprites that open the browser from those that navigate within the portfolio. Accomplish this by using a different click sound for the sprites with the Go to URL behavior.

12. As you modify each movie, add the same Play Sound Member behavior on the main_button and back_button sprites. Again, you may want to use a different click sound for each type of button.

13. Navigate through your portfolio, checking to see that all the active sprites have sounds attached to them now.

This section used a standard behavior to play a sound cast member when a sprite is clicked. A similar behavior, Play Sound File, can be used to play a file from disk that has not been imported. Play Sound File streams the sound while Play Sound Member plays preloaded sounds.

Wrap-up

The project in this chapter finally became audible. You added some synchronized sounds to the introduction animation using the score sound channels. Likewise, the credit movie has little sound effect on startup.

You further refined the interface feedback by adding sounds to all the sprites that perform actions. By using different sounds for different types of actions, you reinforce the end users' expectations, making them feel more comfortable.

The next chapter covers the use of Xtras in the portfolio.

Working with Xtras

Far from an esoteric topic, Xtras are vital to the success of any serious multimedia project undertaken in Director. An Xtra is a plug-in for Director that adds capabilities to the program. Vector, Flash, and text cast members rely on Xtras for their amazing capabilities, for example.

The five main types of Xtras extend Director's feature set by supporting additional file formats, adding new transitions, making new Lingo functions, and providing tools to movie authors. Third-party Xtras may come with an installation program or they may have to be installed manually.

There are two options for distributing Xtras with your projector. The first is by adding the Xtras to the projector as it is created. Movies that are added to a projector have a list of Xtras they require; this list is used to automatically determine which Xtras to include. Alternately, an Xtras folder can be included with your projector application. Put any required Xtra files in this folder, and the projector will find them.

Now that you have a basic understanding of Xtras, this chapter will go into more detail on how you can use them to enhance your Director projects. There are five main types of Xtras:

- Transition Xtras—Add transitions to Director's repertoire
- Cast Member Xtras—Increase the variety of cast members that Director supports
- Import Xtras—Enable Director to import files in additional file formats
- Script Xtras—Extend the Lingo language with new functions
- Tool Xtras—Help movie authors perform tasks in the Director authoring environment

This chapter will explain how you can use the Internet as a source for Xtras, and discuss the issues involved when creating and distributing Xtras with movies.

What Is an Xtra?

Xtras are used to extend Director's features and functions. An Xtra is a plug-in application that provides new capabilities to Director. By including the capability for Director to use Xtras, Macromedia has allowed Director to extend its abilities beyond the original application.

Several Xtras come with Director that are not apparent to the average movie author. These Xtras support built-in features such as importing and using Flash and QuickTime movie assets. Many other Xtras are available from third-party developers to perform a wide variety of tasks.

Because an Xtra is a small application, the same Xtra file does not work on both Macintosh and Windows platforms. When you create an Xtra to go with a cross-platform Director project, you must provide two versions of it—one for each platform.

Tip

You can tell from the file extension of an Xtra whether it is for Windows or Macintosh. A Windows Xtra has the extension of x32 or x16, whereas a Macintosh Xtra usually has no extension. x32 extensions exist on Xtras for 32-bit Windows versions (Windows 95, Windows 98, Windows NT, and Windows 2000). Director 7 does not support Windows 3.1, but Xtras with the x16 extension still exist for this operating system.

Sometimes, it is difficult to find an appropriate Xtra for cross-platform movies. This may be because the Xtra provides a feature found on only one operating system. Or, the demand might not warrant the additional development effort. Unfortunately, it is usually the Macintosh authors who miss out in this case, mainly because their market share is much lower than that of the Windows developers.

A Brief History of Xtras

The precursors of Xtras were XObjects, which provided similar functionality but were more limited than Xtras in scope. Macromedia replaced them with Xtras in Director version 5. XObjects are essentially obsolete now.

Most Xtras that were written for earlier versions of Director (5 or 6) will work with version 7. If an incompatibility exists, and the developer still supports it, the Xtra can be upgraded to work with the latest version. Some developers provide these upgrades for free, whereas others charge a nominal amount. Conversely, Xtras written specifically for version 7 do not work with earlier versions of Director.

Note

Developers who create Xtras conform to a specification called the Macromedia Open Architecture (MOA). This programming standard allows some types of Xtras to work in multiple Macromedia products. For example, a Transition Xtra is compatible with both Director and Authorware. The MOA enables Xtra developers to leverage their investment over several products, possibly resulting in an Xtra that would not otherwise be created.

Installing Xtras

You can install an Xtra in one of two ways: They can be distributed with an installation program or they can be installed manually.

If an Xtra comes in an installation program, the procedure is much like that for installing any other application. Simply run the installer and answer any dialog box questions about where to install the Xtra. Some installers require you to manually locate the Xtras folder inside the Director application folder.

More often, Xtras come in some sort of compressed archive file, either in zip or StuffIt format. In this case, installation must happen manually. These steps demonstrate how to install an Xtra manually:

1. Open the archive file and extract the included files to a new folder.
2. Copy the new folder to the Xtras folder in the Director application folder.
3. Quit and restart Director if it is running. The new Xtra is now available.

Note

Director can find Xtras in subfolders up to five layers deep within its own Xtras folder. Leaving the new Xtra inside a folder, rather than dropping it directly into the root folder, is a better way to organize the files. That way, any documentation or examples that came in the archive stay near the Xtra and are easy to locate later.

Exploring the Five Types of Xtras

Each of the five types of Xtras adds a different set of new capabilities to Director. The new features show up in various ways: new transitions to pick from in the transition score channel, new cast member types, new file formats to import, new Lingo functions, and new tools for building movies. The next five sections explain each of the different types of Xtras.

Transition Xtras

Transitions are special effects that occur between frames of a Director movie, and are placed in the Transition channel of the score (see Figure 10.1). Director comes with numerous built-in transitions, such as Checkerboard and Zoom Open.

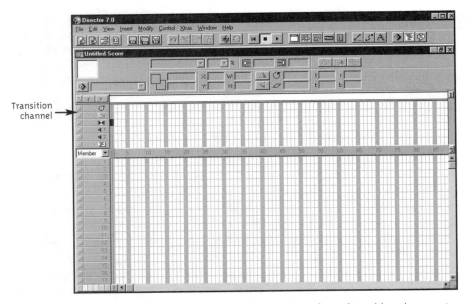

Transition
channel

Figure 10.1   You can double-click a frame in the Transition channel to add or change a transition.

The default transitions are accessible from the Transition dialog box. There are a fair number of them, but they are all rather simple. Figure 10.2 shows the Frame Properties: Transition dialog box with one transition (Center Out, Square) selected. This transition reveals the next frame contents by enlarging a square from the middle of the stage to the outside edges. As the square enlarges, more of the next frame appears until it is completely visible.

Transitions are difficult to describe with words. Experiment with the different transitions and their settings until you become more familiar with them. If you get stuck, refer to Director Help files for more details.

In the Transition dialog box, you can select a category and then select a specific transition to use. The options area allows you to set the duration, smoothness, and stage area of the transition. The duration corresponds to the number of seconds that the transition lasts. Smoothness is a general term that refers to how gradual the transition effect appears. Smooth transitions look the best, but also take more computational power. The Affects option can be set to either the entire stage or just the area that is different in the new frame.

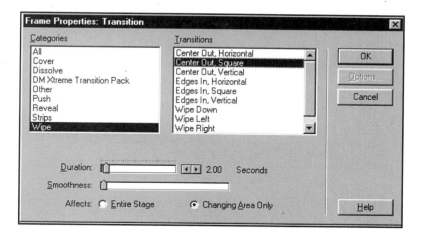

Figure 10.2 The Transition dialog box shows categories on the left and individual transitions on the right.

Transition Xtras expand the categories available and add new transitions to the available list. New transitions are typically more spectacular and more special-purpose than the ones that come with Director. The common effects, such as plain wipes and dissolves, are covered with the default transitions, so Xtras need to provide something beyond them.

> **Note**
> Special effects are easier to create with transitions than with Lingo or Score manipulation. They also do not require any extra assets, so the movie size is not affected.

One drawback is that transitions are generated as the movie plays. They require processing time, and thus may behave and look slightly different on different computers. It is best to check the quality of the transition on as many machines as possible before shipping a project.

Dedalomedia Interactive (http://www.dmtools.com) provides several Xtras with new and different transitions. They graciously allow Director authors to download their Xtras for free to experiment with them. However, they are shareware, and the downloadable versions work only in Author mode, so you need to register them to get them to work with projectors or Shockwave movies for distribution. Figure 10.3 shows an example of the Ripple Fade transition working on the Macromedia logo. This transition causes the stage to appear as if ripples of water are moving over it.

Working with Xtras

Figure 10.3   The Ripple Fade transition from the DM Xtreme Transitions pack distorts the
Macromedia logo in this figure.

The section called "Finding Xtras," later in this chapter, provides more sources for different
transition Xtras.

Cast Member Xtras

Even though Director can read a wide variety of file formats for importing cast members, it
would be nice to have even more to choose from. Cast Member Xtras extend the capabilities of
Director, enabling you to create and use cast members with different file formats, such as an
animated GIF file.

After a Cast Member Xtra is installed, the files it supports become like the native files that
Director supports by default. This provides a powerful alternative to converting a set of files for
inclusion in a Director project. If the appropriate Xtra for using a different file format exists,
there is no need to translate the files (using an external program) to one of Director's natively
supported formats.

The main difference between default file format support and Cast Member Xtra support is the
method used to import the files into casts. Instead of using the Import command from the File
menu, you use the Media Element command from the Insert menu (see Figure 10.4). Select the
type of file to import here, and then locate the file in the dialog box that appears. The selected
file is imported completely and appears as a new cast member.

Note

Several file types that are also available using the normal Import command also
appear in this menu by default. These are formats that still require a Cast
Member Xtra, but they have been more closely integrated with Director as native
formats. In versions 6 and 6.5 of Director, they could be imported only by using
the Media Element command.

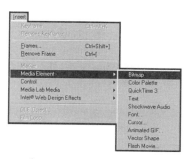

Figure 10.4   Cast Member Xtras appear as new media types on the Media Element submenu.

The capability to import QuickTime VR (QTVR) movies is an example of the use of a Cast Member Xtra. (QuickTime VR movies show a section of a panorama scene that can be manipulated by the user.) These movie files are not native to Director, but using the QTVR Xtra allows them to be used like other cast members. The Xtra also provides options that are specific to working with QTVR movies. These are accessible from the Cast Member property dialog box.

Import Xtras

Import Xtras are related to Cast Member Xtras, but they're different in one important way: This type of Xtra exclusively creates linked cast members. Just as the linked files must be distributed with any movie that uses them, so must the Xtra that is used to link to them.

This Xtra type is responsible for importing linked assets as the movie is playing. All the linked asset types that Director supports natively use this type of Xtra. The Media Support and MIX folders in the Xtras folder contain many Xtras that demonstrate this. Using Import Xtras is transparent to the movie author. The normal Import command provides the option to link to external files. When that option is selected, the appropriate Import Xtra is called on.

Playing a streaming MP3 audio file from Director is an example of using an Import Xtra. Director cannot read the format without the appropriate Xtra. The Import Xtra required for streaming MP3 files is included with version 7.02 of Director.

Script Xtras

Script Xtras extend the Lingo language with new commands. They are used for specialized features such as file manipulation, network functions, or functions not built in to Lingo. You need some knowledge of Lingo to use these Xtras properly, but the exact requirements vary depending on the Xtra.

The Lingo to control Script Xtras can take two forms. One is the use of simple commands that behave exactly like built-in Lingo functions. The other is to create objects from the Xtra and then use the object much as you'd use an object created from a parent script. Chapter 8, "Understanding Scripts," page 183, contains more detailed information about parent scripts and objects.

The standard Lingo function `interface` queries a Script Xtra for all its available commands. It returns text that the Xtra author provides, commonly copyright information, and then the list of commands. TaskXtra from Kent Kersten is a freeware Script Xtra with one command. It is used to get a list of all the applications currently running on the computer. Figure 10.5 contains the Message window information, showing the use of the `interface` command with this Xtra.

Figure 10.5   The TaskXtra has a single command, `SystemTaskList`, as shown by using the `interface` function with the Xtra name as a parameter. The absence of any parameters in the function list of the `SystemTaskList` function implies that it does not take any parameters.

Once installed, using this Xtra is straightforward. Put the results of the `SystemTaskList` function into a variable. It returns a list of strings that represent the names of the applications. One use for this Xtra is to check whether a projector is already running when a new one is started by the end user. If `SystemTaskList` returns two strings with the name of the current projector, the movie can choose to quit immediately to avoid playing two copies of the movie. Figure 10.6 shows an example of the return value from the `SystemTaskList` function.

Tip

The `SystemTaskList` command must have parentheses, even though it takes no parameters. If not supplied, it simply returns a reference to the Xtra object.

> Note that in Director's Author mode, only the title DIRECTOR is returned, and not the name of the current movie. The projector must be playing to get the proper name of the application associated with the movie.

You can download the latest versions of this Xtra for both Windows and Macintosh platforms from http://www.littleplanet.com/kent/kent.html. If you use his Xtra, it's a good idea to send an email to the author to thank him for his contribution.

The Fileio Xtra included with Director has a myriad of commands available for file management. Follow these steps to use this Xtra as an object:

1. Open the Message window in Director. Use the interface function with the Fileio Xtra to display a list of the commands it supports. Type the following in the Message window:

   ```
   put interface(xtra "fileio")
   ```

   Figure 10.7 shows the results.

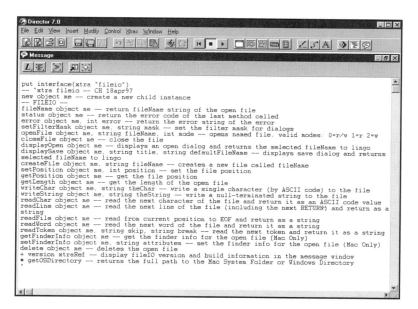

Figure 10.7   The interface for the Fileio Xtra, which provides a lot of advanced functionality, contains many more commands than TaskXtra does.

2. This Xtra requires the creation of an object to access its functions. Create an object and assign it to a variable by using the new command, the same as when creating a parent object from a parent script. Type the following in the Message window:

   ```
   fileObject = new(xtra "fileio")
   ```

Type the following to see what the variable looks like (see Figure 10.8):

```
put fileObject
```

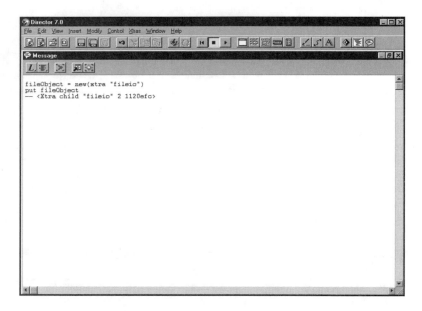

Figure 10.8 Setting the variable `fileObject` to the result of the new command puts the object created by the Xtra into the variable, and the strange information shown by `put fileObject` is the representation of the object.

3. To use the object created by the `Fileio` Xtra, specify the command to pass to the object, the variable containing the object as the first parameter, and then any other parameters. For this step, a new file is created in the main operating system folder. Type the following:

```
createFile(fileObject, "testfile.txt")
```

The new file, called `testfile.txt`, is empty.

> Make sure that the file does not already exist before executing the `createFile` command because the command will not work if a file of the same name is already in the directory.

4. Even though the file was created, it is still not open for use. Use the `openFile` command to open the new file. This command takes a parameter called the file mode; use 0 to open the file for both reading and writing. Type the following:

```
openFile(fileObject, "testfile.txt", 0)
```

5. Write a string containing your name to the file. Use the `writeString` command with the object variable and a string containing your name (or any other text). Type the following into the Message window:

```
writeString(fileObject, "Matthew")
```

6. It is always good practice to close a file when you're finished working with it. The Xtra provides the `closeFile` command for this purpose. It tells the Xtra to finish working with the file. Type the following:

```
closeFile(fileObject)
```

7. Open the file again to see what it contains. Use the same open command as in Step 4:

```
openFile(fileObject, "testfile.txt", 0)
```

8. The `readFile` command returns the entire contents of the file as a text string. In this case, it reads your name from the file and shows it in the Message window. Type the following:

```
put readFile(fileObject)
```

9. Because there is nothing more to do to the file, close it again. Use the same command as in Step 6:

```
closeFile(fileObject)
```

Also, destroy the object by setting the variable to `void` by typing the following:

```
fileObject = void
```

The results of Steps 3 through 9 are shown in Figure 10.9.

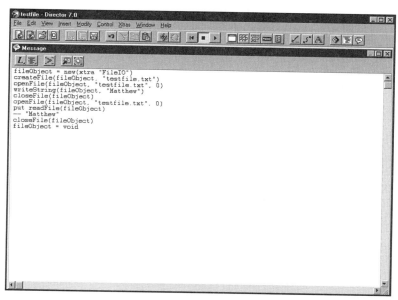

Figure 10.9   It is easy to see the power and usefulness of the `FileIO` Script Xtra, which allows any information the movie author specifies to be stored on disk in a file that can be read later.

Many Script Xtras are available. For information on where to find more, refer to the section called "Finding Xtras," later in this chapter.

Tool Xtras

The last type of Xtra is the Tool Xtra. It is used only during authoring time to provide functions for the movie author. A Tool Xtra may supply some capability that Director does not provide. Or it may make it easier to accomplish something than by using Director's built-in method.

Because these Xtras are for authoring only, they do not need to be distributed with the movie. Installation for Tool Xtras is the same as for other types of Xtras.

An example of a Tool Xtra from a third party is the `CodeCounter` Xtra, which is used to count all the lines of Lingo code in a movie and return a percentage representing how many of those lines are comments. This obviously has relevance only during author time. It is shareware that was developed by Jeff Bennett, available at `http://rampages.onramp.net/~bennett/devtools/`.

Finding Xtras

When movie authors are aware of the different types of Xtras and their capabilities, they often wonder what Xtras are available. Sometimes, a specific problem arises and it is possible that an Xtra may help solve it efficiently. Or perhaps Director developers are just looking for new and interesting features to add to their projects.

The Internet is the best source for information regarding what Xtras are available. Several Web sites devote pages to collected information about various Xtras. Mailing lists are also a good source of information because the person looking for an Xtra can ask a question of many experienced developers, all at the same time.

Finding Xtras at Web Sites

In general, it is best to look at the various Web sites when beginning a search for an Xtra. They are available all the time, and it does not disturb someone else to look there. The Web sites described in the following sections provide coverage of Xtras available on the Internet.

Macromedia Director Support

The Macromedia Director Support section of the Macromedia Web site (`http://www.macromedia.com/support/director/`) should be a first stop on any search for Xtras. Scroll down to the Download section on the left of the page, and select the Xtras link. This displays a new page with an alphabetical listing of many Xtras. Figure 10.10 shows an example of this page. You can use your browser's search command to help find specific Xtras based on a single keyword.

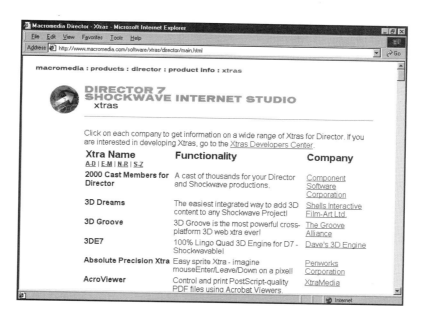

Figure 10.10 The Macromedia Xtra list provides the Xtra name, a short description, and a link to the developer's contact information.

Macromedia's page is kept up-to-date, but is not as flexible as the sites mentioned in the next section. There is no Web-based search feature and the descriptions are rather limited. Extensive contact information is kept on the site for each developer. This information also shows other Xtras by the same developer.

DirectorWeb

The DirectorWeb pages provide a lot of information about Director. The main page is located at http://www.mcli.dist.maricopa.edu/director/index.html, and the search page is located at http://www.mcli.dist.maricopa.edu/director/xobj.html. One section, the DirectorWeb XStuff page, presents a form for searching the site's Xtra database. Figure 10.11 shows how this form appears. You can use one of the four radio buttons in the platform area to specify only Xtras from the selected platform. The keyword search area limits the Xtras shown to those that contain only the specified words in their descriptions. You start a search by pressing the Show Me the Xstuff! button.

The search feature at this site is very useful for narrowing down the amount of Xtras shown. It is especially convenient to be able to specify what platform the Xtras must run on. You use the Dual option to display Xtras that work only on both platforms.

Finding Xtras with Mailing Lists

Chapter 2, "Why Director?" page 17, refers to three Internet mailing lists for general Director information in the section called "Community of Developers." Each list is also a good source for information on Xtras specifically.

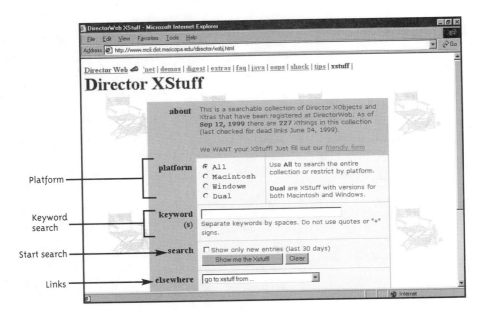

Figure 10.11 The DirectorWeb XStuff search page.

- Direct-L—For general Director information
- Lingo-L—For Lingo-specific issues
- Xtra-L—For information on Xtras, both included with Director and third-party

The Direct-L list is for general Director discussions. It is a good place to look for announcements of new Xtras and information on how to use them. The Director Web site mentioned previously in this chapter has a searchable archive of all the messages that are sent on Direct-L. Start looking there before asking a question about Xtras that may already have been answered.

For Script Xtras in particular, the Lingo-L list is good for reference. This more advanced list deals with Lingo exclusively.

Finally, there is a specific list for Xtras called Xtra-L. It is intended for people using Xtras, as well as for Xtra developers. This low-volume list is generally very good for information about almost any Xtra.

The information on how to subscribe to these lists is also in Chapter 2.

Other Sources for Finding Xtras

Other sources are also effective for learning more about availability of Xtras and what they can accomplish. For example, colleagues might have heard of an Xtra to help solve a problem on your project. A Macromedia user group in your area might be able to provide specific information as well.

Magazines and books can also lead to new Xtras. Trade shows and conferences provide a good overview of current commercial Xtras, and may even provide a chance to meet the developers in person.

Distributing Xtras with Movies

This chapter has already referred to the requirement of including Xtras with the Director movies for distribution. As mentioned, each projector application or Shockwave movie still requires the Xtras used during authoring. The movie fails to play properly without them.

The following sections cover the points to consider when distributing movies that require Xtras.

Logistics of Distributing Xtras

There are two methods for including the required Xtras in a title for distribution to end users. They may be bound directly to the movie used to make a projector, or they may be included individually in a special folder beside the application.

To include Xtras directly in a movie, use the Modify, Movie, Xtras menu commands. You get a list of all the available Xtras already included in the current movie. You can also add Xtras for inclusion with this dialog box. Figure 10.12 shows the Movie Xtras window. It starts with a generic list by default. All these Xtras will be included with any projector made from this movie. The Add button presents a new dialog box, showing a list of other Xtras that may be added to the movie.

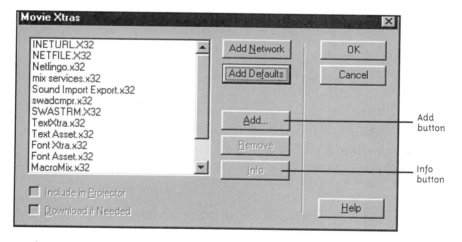

Figure 10.12 The Movie Xtras dialog box shows all the Xtras already assigned to the movie.

Whenever a cast member that requires the use of an Xtra is first imported into a cast, that Xtra is automatically included in the list of Xtras for the movie. This ensures that it will be available in the projector. The Xtra is not removed automatically if the cast member is deleted, however. You should periodically review the list of Xtras associated with a movie to verify that it contains only the Xtras that are actually used. This helps reduce the size of the resulting projector application.

Macromedia Director

You can click the Info button to open an Internet browser and go to the site referenced in the selected Xtra, which commonly contains more detailed information about the Xtra. It can also be useful for checking the latest version of an Xtra at the developer's Web site.

You can add more Xtras by clicking the Add button. This presents a list of all the available Xtras that are not already included in the movie. You can use this feature to add Script Xtras, which are not included by default.

You use the check box Download If Needed to allow the projector to automatically download an Xtra from the Internet if the application requires it. Use this option only under special circumstances because end users typically do not want to wait for files to download before they can use their applications. They might also become upset with the idea that unknown files are being downloaded to their computers. The exception to this is with Shockwave movies. Because users are already on the Internet, it is less of a burden to download Xtras. Keep in mind, though, that it will delay the user from starting the Shockwave movie.

Instead of including Xtras directly in a projector, an alternative is to provide them as individual files. If an Xtras folder exists in the same folder as the projector, it will look inside for any required Xtras. This is sometimes more convenient for the movie authors because they do not have to constantly update the projector as new Xtras are used. It also provides a reference area to the other developers on the project that lists which Xtras they need to have installed.

> **Note**
>
> Only one of these methods can be used with a given movie because they do not complement each other. All the Xtras must be in one place or the other, not in both places.

Licensing Xtras

With the advent of so much information about Xtras on the Internet, it has become difficult to track where all the Xtras were developed. Often an Xtra may be downloaded for free, but only for noncommercial use or perhaps for use for a limited time. It is important to understand the particulars of how each Xtra may be used.

There are three basic licensing models in use with third-party Xtras: freeware, shareware, and commercial. Hard work is required to make an Xtra, so always respect the wishes of the developer. Each model is explained in more detail in the following sections.

> **Note**
>
> Macromedia's license agreement allows the use of any Xtras included with Director. They may be distributed as needed and at no additional cost with the movies that require them.

Freeware Xtras

Freeware Xtras can be used with no compensation required to the developer. Sometimes, the developer may stipulate that documentation and the sample movie must always be distributed with the Xtra, as was shown with the TaskXtra previously in this chapter. As a gesture of goodwill, consider contacting the developer of any freeware Xtras used in order to give thanks or perhaps to send a copy of the product made by your team.

Shareware Xtras

Shareware Xtras are usually free to download and try for a limited time or within limited situations. After the free period is over or the situation has changed, you need to pay the developer if you continue to use the Xtra. This is a nice compromise because it requires no initial outlay of money to learn about an Xtra. If it does not suit the task, you can stop using it and pay nothing. If you do find it useful, though, you should reward the developer with whatever is stipulated in the license agreement. These types of Xtras commonly have a limited amount of technical support available.

Commercial Xtras

Commercial Xtras are similar to other types of commercial software. They must be purchased before they are initially used. Some commercial Xtras also require per-product or per-disc fees in addition to the purchase price. Demonstration versions of these Xtras are usually available for prospective purchasers to try before they buy the full version. Ask the developer about these if a demo is not readily available. The prices of commercial Xtras are commonly higher than for other types, and the level of technical support also increases, commensurate with the price.

In most Director development situations, the price of an Xtra is far outweighed by the cost of the time spent developing the movies. If a free Xtra does not work correctly, it can cost more in time or lost opportunities than an equivalent commercial Xtra. You should always consider this when figuring the total cost of an Xtra.

Creating Xtras

Throughout this chapter, Xtra developers have been mentioned. There is nothing magical about developing an Xtra. It just requires time, knowledge, tools, and the Xtra Development Kit (XDK).

The XDK is available for free from Macromedia. It is in the company's best interest to promote the development of as many Xtras as possible because each additional Xtra strengthens the overall value of Director in the marketplace. The main page for downloading the XDK and its documentation is http://www.macromedia.com/support/xtras/xdks/xdk_d7.html.

> **Note**
>
> Xtras are developed in C and C++. Thorough knowledge of these languages as well as the intricacies of Xtras in particular is required. This section does not attempt to cover this topic in detail, but only provides guidance on where to go for more information.

You need to develop Xtras specifically for each platform (Windows and Macintosh). You might be able to use some of the same code, but you need to have a compiler for both types of operating systems.

The Xtra-L Internet mailing list is a good source of information on the Xtra development process. Consider subscribing to this list if you're interested in the details of making Xtras from scratch.

Interactive Portfolio Project

The Portfolio Project used several Xtras without making explicit reference to them. The first section discusses some of these Xtras.

Two further examples of Xtras, in the form of transitions, will be added to the project. These add visual effects at specific points in the movie to provide additional layers of visual interest.

Working with Xtras

Xtras have already been used in the portfolio project section of previous chapters. All the animated GIF files that were imported require an Xtra, for example. When an animated GIF was first imported into each movie, the animated GIF Xtra was added to the movie's Xtra list.

Follow these steps to explore a movie's Xtra list:

1. For version control, create a Chapter10 folder on your hard drive and copy the files from your Chapter09 folder to the new Chapter10 folder. Final versions of the files from Chapter 9 are in the Portfolio_Project\Chapter09 folder on this book's CD-ROM.

2. Open the "intro.dir_" movie file. Open the Movie Xtras dialog box with the Modify, Movie, Xtras menu. Scroll to the bottom of the Xtra list, as shown in Figure 10.13.

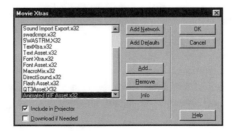

Figure 10.13 The Animated GIF Asset Xtra is at the bottom of the list because it was the last Xtra added.

Working with Xtras

3. Select the Animated GIF Asset Xtra. Connect to the Internet if you are not already connected. Click the Info button to open a Web browser at the information page for this Xtra, as shown in Figure 10.14.

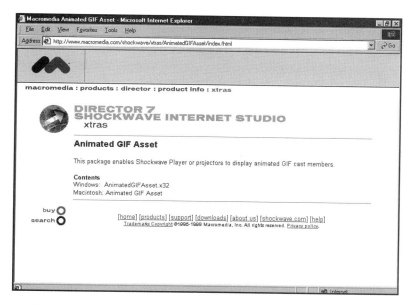

Figure 10.14 The information page for an Xtra provides a bit more detail about its purpose.

4. The project steps have not added Flash or QuickTime assets to any of the movies. (You may have added these yourself as optional content.) The Flash Asset and QuickTime 3 (QT3) Asset Xtras are in the Xtra list and don't need to be. If you are not using either of these two formats, select the Xtra name and click the Remove button. This way, they will not take up space in a projector made from this movie.

Note
You may also add Xtras manually to the list from the Movie Xtras dialog box. If you are using a script Xtra, this is a good idea because Director does not automatically add this type of Xtra.

Having superfluous Xtras in a movie's Xtra list does no harm, other than making the projector larger than it needs to be. You will make a projector for the movies in the portfolio project in the project section of the next chapter.

Adding a Transition

Transition Xtras were covered in their own section previously in this chapter. A collection of transitions from Dedalomedia Interactive (http://www.dmtools.com) was mentioned. If you haven't already downloaded one of its collections to try, do so in preparation for this section. If you prefer not to download the file, you may use one of the standard transitions instead.

Transitions provide an interesting visual for changing between frames. In this section, you will add a transition to the end of the introduction movie and the middle of the credit movie.

Follow these steps to add transitions to your movies:

1. Open the "intro.dir" movie.

2. Go to the frame script channel of frame 150. You will add a transition that occurs between the frame with the text and the next blank frame.

3. Move the script in the frame script channel from frame 150 to frame 151, as shown in Figure 10.15. This makes room for the transition before jumping to the "main.dir" movie.

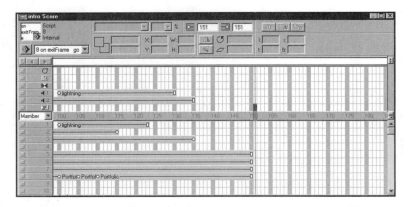

Figure 10.15 The information page for an Xtra provides a bit more detail on the purpose of the Xtra.

4. Double-click on frame 151 of the transition channel to open the Frame Properties: Transition dialog box, as shown in Figure 10.16. If you downloaded a package of transitions, click on the package name in the Categories list. If not, leave the All category selected.

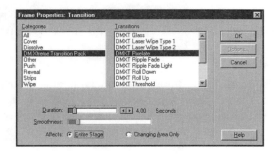

Figure 10.16 Choose one of the transitions from the Xtra package you downloaded.

5. Select a transition from the Transitions list. Set the Duration to the number of seconds (4.00 seconds is a good choice) that will let you see the effect of the transition. If your transition allows you to set the Smoothness (not all do), choose a value near the middle of the bar. Turn on the Entire Stage effect.

6. Close the dialog box. Rewind and play the movie. The transition will appear just before Director tries to open the next movie. Figure 10.17 shows the DMXT Pixelate transition in action.

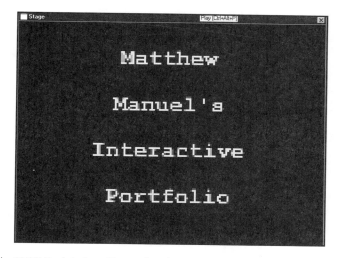

Figure 10.17 The DMXT Pixelate transition makes the sprites on the stage appear progressively more blocky. This image is from early in the transition.

7. Save this movie and open the "credits.dir" movie.

8. Open the Frame Properties: Transition dialog box on frame 16 of the movie. This is the first frame where the Macromedia logo appears.

9. Select a different transition from the list. Choose a suitable duration and smoothness. Select the Changing Area Only effect option, as shown in Figure 10.18. To be different, you will have this transition affect only the changing Macromedia logo. Close the dialog box to continue.

10. Rewind and play the movie. The Macromedia logo will replace the (click to continue) sprite with whichever transition you chose. Figure 10.19 shows one frame of the effect of the DMXT WormHole Out transition.

Macromedia Director

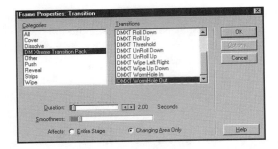

Figure 10.18 This transition will affect only the changing area of the stage.

Figure 10.19 The DMXT WormHole Out transition displaces the old area of the stage with the new area of the stage like a science fiction special effect.

Transitions are an efficient way to add interesting visual effects to any movie. To continue your experimentation, try adding transitions to other movies in your portfolio.

Wrap-up

The Portfolio Project was already using a Cast Member Xtra for working with animated GIF images. This Xtra was added to the movies' Xtras list automatically by Director the first time an animated GIF was imported. Extraneous Xtras can be removed from the Xtras list to make the resulting projector file size smaller.

Transitions are a useful and easy way to add visuals. Third-party transition Xtras are generally better quality than the ones included with Director, although they cost more.

In the next chapter, you will prepare your portfolio for distribution by creating a projector application so people without Director can view the movies.

Shipping a Title

Shipping a title is the last phase in any product development schedule. It is often overlooked because the effort required is typically underestimated. Good planning at this stage, both for procedures and schedules, can make the difference between shipping a good title on time and shipping a mediocre title late.

There are two main delivery methods for Director movies: projectors and Shockwave movies. Projectors are typically used for distributing products on traditional media such as CD-ROMs or floppy disks. Shockwave movies are the primary method of releasing Director movies on the Internet. The first two sections of this chapter cover the details of creating each type of application.

The last section of the chapter covers the important stage of testing and quality assurance for Director projects. Developers often wait until as late as possible before starting formal testing procedures, if they do them at all. This leads to poor-quality and error-prone products that must be rushed to manufacturing before they are stable. Proper planning and an understanding of the importance of testing can make this critical step operate smoothly.

Shipping a perfect product is the ideal goal of all development teams. However, no perfect software product has ever been released. Perfection, although a nice goal, should not be the yardstick of when to release a product. Rather, it should be shipped when it is finished. This is a difficult metric to define, but it involves satisfying the designers, testers, and management. It may also occur when people cannot work on the project any more. Regardless, you will know when your project is finished.

Working with Projectors

A *projector* is a standalone application that plays Director movies. It is used to distribute movies to end users for playback on their computers, without the need for the Director application. Windows and Macintosh require separate projectors.

There must be at least one Director movie incorporated into a projector application. The projector starts by playing the movie, and then the movie takes over and controls what occurs next. When the last movie plays or playback is stopped via Lingo, the projector application quits and returns control back to the operating system.

Before the advent of Shockwave, projectors were the only method available for end users to play Director movies without having Director. Projector applications can be shipped on traditional media such as floppy disks, CD-ROMs, and DVD-ROMs. They can also be downloaded from the Internet, either directly or in an archive package such as a zip or StuffIt file.

Some titles require the end user to install the projector from the delivery media onto the hard drive. This can be for performance reasons or to allow special settings that are dependent on the computer on which the projector is installed.

Hard drives have faster access times and transfer rates than CD-ROMs (or other removable media), so a projector can load and start running more quickly if it is installed on a hard drive. The installation procedure may also copy linked assets or external casts to the hard drive for increased performance. Interface cast members that are used frequently throughout a product are good candidates for being installed to the hard drive.

During installation, the application can probe the end user's system for configuration details. Items such as available memory, the bit-depth of the display, and the processor speed can all be used to tailor the projector's behavior to the current system. These settings are typically stored in a configuration file for access by the projector.

> **Note**
>
> An end user's system configuration may change after a program is installed. The end user may add more memory, upgrade the CD-ROM drive, or install a new video card. A well-behaved projector periodically checks the parameters it depends on for proper playback.

The process of creating a projector is covered in the following sections. It is not difficult, but the settings you use affect the playback experience to a large degree. For this reason, it is best to remake a projector as infrequently as possible. If the first movie in a project changes, the projector application that uses this movie must be created again.

By using a small stub movie, as explained in Chapter 6, "Working with Movies," page 113, the projector need not change with every change to the project. A stub movie has one Lingo handler or behavior that simply jumps to the first movie in the project. Projectors made from stub movies are relatively small and start playback quickly, giving the end user a good experience.

Projector Options for Multiple Platforms

Many of the options to create a projector are the same on both Windows and Macintosh platforms. This section explains the implications of each option.

Different types of titles require various selections that best fit the type of use expected. For example, reference applications work best as windowed applications, so they can be used in conjunction with other applications. In contrast, games should be full-screen applications so the end user is not distracted by other applications.

Creating the Projector

You select the Create Projector command from the File menu to start the projector-creation process. The Create Projector dialog box that appears is shown in Figure 11.1.

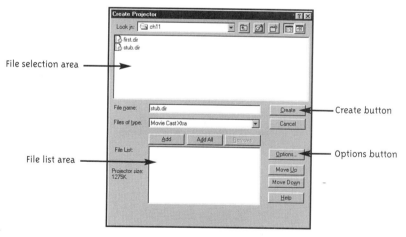

Figure 11.1   You use the Create Projector dialog box to select the movies and casts that are incorporated into the new projector application.

You double-click on the movie file in the file selection area to add it to the list of files that the projector will contain. You can accomplish the same thing by selecting the file and clicking the Add button. You can use the Add All button as a shortcut for including all the applicable files in the current folder to the file list. You can delete files from the list by clicking the Remove button.

Macromedia Director

The order of the movies in the file list determines their playback order in the projector—assuming that the movies themselves do not control the playback order with Lingo or behaviors. It is possible to create a projector from a series of unlinked movies and have them play back in order automatically. This is useful for slide shows or other relatively noninteractive applications.

Projectors with a single movie that links to external movie files are more flexible than projectors that contain multiple movies. As mentioned previously in this chapter, the projector does not need to be updated as often as each of the movies in the project are updated. Including a single movie in a projector is recommended unless there is a compelling reason to include multiple movies in a projector.

One possible reason for including multiple movies is that the title distribution is limited to one file. Rather than distribute many external movies, and possibly external casts and other asset files, the projector can contain everything that is required for proper execution. The Xtras required should also be included in the projector if you use this method. This is an excellent way of packaging a project for distribution over the Internet via end-user downloads.

> **Note**
>
> The Move Up and Move Down buttons in the Create Projector dialog box change the order of files in the file list. Select a file and then click either button to move it toward the top or bottom.

Setting Projector Options

Before making the projector by clicking the Create button, you should verify that the parameters of the projector are correct for the application. You can click the Options button to display the Projector Options dialog box shown in Figure 11.2.

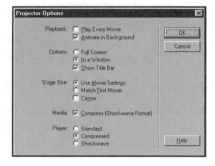

Figure 11.2   The Projector Options dialog box provides a host of parameters that affect how the projector plays the included movies.

The Playback section contains two options: Play Every Movie and Animate in Background. On the Macintosh, a third option, Reset Monitor to Match Movie's Color Depth, is also available. See Table 11.1 for a listing of Playback options and their uses.

Table 11.1 Playback options.

Option	Description
Play Every Movie	When checked, causes the projector to play each movie in the file list in order. This occurs whether they are linked via Lingo or not. When unchecked, only the first movie in the list plays automatically. The other movies may still play if they are referenced by the first movie.
Animate in Background	When checked, the movie continues to play if the application loses the focus of the operating system (for example, if the user selects another application or clicks on the desktop). When unchecked, playback pauses until the projector is the foremost application again.
Reset Monitor to Match Movie's Color Depth	This Macintosh-only option automatically changes the bit-depth of the monitor to match the stage bit-depth of the first movie in the projector.

Tip

The Reset Monitor to Match Movie's Color Depth is a Macintosh option because not all Windows video cards support changing the bit-depth automatically. The Lingo property the colorDepth can also be used to change the bit-depth during movie execution. In fact, this is preferable to using the projector option because it allows the movie to restore the previous bit-depth when playback is finished.

Note

Most Director titles are intended for interaction with the user, so this option is often unselected. However, if a projector requires an extended period of time to accomplish a task, it might be beneficial to allow background execution.

The Options section contains properties that affect how the projector application appears onscreen. It can be shown either full screen or in a window. If a window is chosen, then it might also show a title bar. These options are explained in more detail in Table 11.2.

Table 11.2 Projector options.

Option	Description
Full Screen	This option is used most often for games and entertainment applications. It shows the stage in the center of the screen, with a border around it that extends to the edge of the screen.
In a Window	With this option, the stage appears within a normal application window. Other applications and the desktop are visible beyond the edges of the stage, and the end user cannot resize the window. Figure 11.3 shows a window with a projector playing a movie that has a title bar.
Show Title Bar	The title bar, showing the name of the projector, appears at the top of the projector application (see Figure 11.3). (Note that in Figure 11.3, the filename of the projector is PROJECTOR, so that is what appears in the title bar.) The end user can reposition the screen using the title bar.

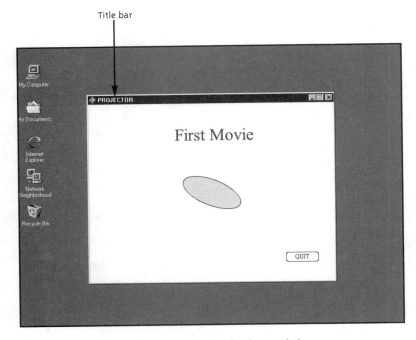

Figure 11.3 A projector playing a movie in a window that has a title bar.

The Stage Size section has two complementary options, Use Movie Settings and Match First Movie, plus the Center option, an option to center the projector window. Each option is covered in Table 11.3.

Table 11.3 Stage size options.

Option	Description
Use <u>M</u>ovie Settings	Each movie in the projector plays according to its own settings. This means that the projector application window changes size if the movies use different stage sizes.
Match <u>F</u>irst Movie	The stage settings of the first movie in the file list are used for all movies in the projector if this is selected. Subsequent movies have their stages repositioned and scaled, if needed, to match the first movie's location and dimensions.
Ce<u>n</u>ter	This is useful for having projectors start in the middle of the screen. Otherwise, the projector window appears onscreen according to the stage location in the movie file. Full-screen projectors are always centered.

Warning

The Use <u>M</u>ovie Settings option can be disconcerting to the end user and should be avoided unless required for a specific reason, such as an application that chooses movies with larger stages when played on fast computers.

The Media section has only one option: <u>C</u>ompress (Shockwave Format). If this option is selected, all the cast members in the movies and casts in the file list will be compressed. The compression method is equivalent to making the movies or casts Shockwave files. This reduces the size of the resulting projector at the expense of extra time required to decompress the cast members at playback time.

Note

External movies and casts not included in the projector are not affected by the Compress option. They should be processed separately using the Update Movies command from the Xtras menu. This is explained in more detail later in this chapter, in the Interactive Portfolio Project section.

The Player section of the dialog box has new options with for Director version 7.02 of Director. The projector can use the Standard method, be Compressed, or use the Shockwave plug-in option. Each option is covered in Table 11.4.

Table 11.4 Player options.

Option	Description
Standard	This is the default option. The projector itself is full size and has all the components required to run built in. This option is ideal for CD-ROM projects.
Compressed	The projector itself is compressed like a Shockwave movie. The resulting projector file is noticeably smaller in size, ideal for download applications. However, as with Shockwave cast members, the decompression step does add to the startup time required.
Shockwave	The Shockwave option creates projectors that have the smallest file size possible. They use the Shockwave plug-in from the end user's system to play the movies. If the plug-in is not installed on the system, the end user is prompted to download and install it from the Internet.
Use System Temporary Memory	When the Use System Temporary Memory check box is selected (available on Macintosh only), the projector attempts to use memory from the operating system. This occurs only in low-memory situations in which the projector has already used all the memory available in its own allocation. More information about this topic is available in the "Memory Partitions" section of this chapter.

Note

You should use the Shockwave projector option only if you face severe file-size restrictions because end users are likely to be annoyed if they have to spend too much time downloading a component before they can use the application. This option works with only version 7.02 or later of the Shockwave plug-in.

After you have selected all the options for the projector, you can click OK and then move on to creating the projector itself. You click the Create button in the Create Projector dialog box to open a new dialog box, in which you can save the projector with a specific name in a selected folder (see Figure 11.4). The filename defaults to `Projector.exe`, but you can change it before saving the projector.

After you save the projector, it is important to test it for proper operation. Close Director and run the projector as you would any other application, by double-clicking on it. It should appear onscreen with the proper options and start playing the first movie. Navigate to any movies that are complete. They should play back as expected.

Later in this chapter, in the section called "Creating Projectors," you'll find a step-by-step example of creating a projector.

Figure 11.4   In this dialog box, you can select where to save the new projector and what
filename to give it.

Memory Partitions

Windows and Macintosh handle assigning RAM to applications differently. It is important to
realize the implications of the distinctions for better projector movie playback.

Development machines used for asset creation and movie authoring typically have much more
physical memory than most consumer computers. Therefore, the projectors and movie files
should be tested extensively on computers with less memory to identify and fix any problems
that result from low-memory situations.

Windows

Windows has a highly refined virtual memory system. *Virtual memory* is essentially space on
the user's hard disk that acts like RAM from memory chips. When all the *physical RAM* (that is,
the RAM on chips installed in the computer) is used up, Windows allocates more memory by
using the hard disk. Applications do not need to know the difference between physical and virtual memory because Windows looks after allocation and control.

The availability and use of virtual memory means that even if a computer has only 32MB of
physical RAM, it can simultaneously execute several applications that require more than 32MB
of RAM in total. The drawback is that virtual memory is very slow compared to physical memory. The operating system takes portions of physical RAM and saves them on the hard drive. If
the information in these portions is required again, they must be reloaded into physical RAM,
displacing other portions to the hard disk.

Although an application will not likely run out of RAM, it might begin to execute very slowly if
it has to use virtual memory. When determining a project's minimum hardware requirements,
you need to consider the RAM requirements of the projector and the operating system to
decide on the amount of physical RAM required. For example, Windows 95 and Windows 98
can operate minimally on 8MB of RAM, so a projector that requires 8MB of RAM needs a
machine with at least 16MB of physical RAM to operate at optimal performance.

Windows NT (or Windows 2000) requires substantially more memory for just running the operating system than either Macintosh or Windows 95/98. A base amount of RAM for just the
operating system is approximately 32MB. Therefore, the 8MB projector requires a system with
at least 40MB of physical RAM, or 48MB, which is a more common multiple.

Macintosh

The Macintosh, on the other hand, allocates a portion of RAM to applications immediately when they are started. This portion must be taken from the total amount of RAM available on the computer, and other applications cannot share it. Macintoshes also have a virtual memory system, but it is not as advanced as the Windows system. Macintosh projectors should rely on having the minimum amount of physical RAM available that they need in order to operate.

You use the File, Get Info menu option (Cmd+I) on the projector file to set the minimum and preferred memory partitions. If the projector requires 8MB to operate, you should use that as the minimum, and consider setting the preferred amount to 10MB or 12MB for even better operation.

The Macintosh typically requires more physical RAM than Windows 95 or Windows 98. A normal installation and setup of the Macintosh may require between 12MB and 16MB of RAM. This leads to the minimum requirements of Macintosh systems being roughly 8MB higher than the same program on a Windows system. So, an 8MB projector that requires 16MB on a Windows system would require 24MB on a Macintosh computer.

Warning

The option Use System Temporary Memory, described in Table 11.4, is used to cheat a little on the projector's memory allocation. If this option is selected, the projector will try to use some extra memory from the system's area in low-memory situations. This should normally be avoided because it has the side effect of destabilizing the operating system somewhat, possibly making it prone to crashes. It is far better to not use this option and specify the proper amount of RAM required.

Tip

On Macintosh computers, it is possible to partially simulate a computer with less memory. First, change the minimum memory requirement for a common application, such as SimpleText, to a very high number. Use a partition size that will leave only the amount of free RAM typically found on a minimum system. The projector is then forced to use its minimum allocation of RAM, and memory problems may become evident.

Including Xtras in a Projector

To include Xtras in the projector, you need to specify all the required Xtras in the movie parameters. This is explained in greater detail in Chapter 10, "Working with Xtras."

The projector depends on the movies in its file list to determine which Xtras to include. If you're using only a stub movie to make the projector, you need to ensure all the required Xtras are referenced in it. External movies that require Xtras do not work correctly unless the Xtras are included in the projector.

Creating Projectors

Use the following steps to create two projectors that demonstrate the available options:

1. Open the file "stub.dir" in Director from the Chapter 11 folder on this book's CD-ROM. This file has only one script, which is in the Script channel of frame 1. The behavior Play Movie X from the Navigation library takes a movie name as its parameter. Figure 11.5 shows the parameter dialog box for this behavior.

Figure 11.5   The behavior parameter dialog box for the Play Movie X behavior.

2. Type the filename of the movie to jump to when the script is executed (which, in Figure 11.5, is @\first). The @ symbol tells the script to look in the current directory. The \ symbol delineates the folder and the movie file. Leave off the extension so that the script is not dependent on it being present.

3. Open the "first.dir" file from this book's CD-ROM and examine its contents. It has a text sprite, a vector image sprite, and a button sprite. There is also a behavior, Go Loop, at the last frame of the sprite span that causes the movie to loop forever. The vector image has the Rotate Continuously behavior attached. The button labeled Quit has a behavior that causes the movie to stop on a mouseUp event. (The Quit button simply stops the movie but does not quit Director in Author mode.) Play the movie and notice how it works.

4. Choose the Create Projector command from the File menu. Select the file "stub.dir," and add it to the file list. Figure 11.6 shows the dialog box that appears.

Figure 11.6   The movie "stub.dir" is selected and added to the file list for the projector. The main movie, "first.dir," is not added to the file list and remains external.

5. Select the Options button to open the Projector Options dialog box. Set the parameters so that they are the same as those shown in Figure 11.7. This projector will operate in a window with a title bar, and will animate in the background.

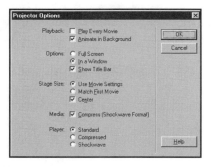

Figure 11.7   The projector's options. Note that the Media option is set to Compressed, even though it does not matter very much for this movie because it has only one script.

6. Click OK to return to the Create Project dialog box. Click Create to bring up the next dialog box. Name this projector Window, and save it in a folder on your hard drive (see Figure 11.8). (Note that Windows users do not need to add the extension .exe because it is appended automatically by Director.) The projector is created, and all the files being included in the application are shown in the progress dialog box. Note that several default Xtras are included because they were not specifically removed. Close Director before continuing.

Figure 11.8   This projector application is named Window as a reminder that Window mode is used.

7. Locate the new projector and run it. It starts in a new window and goes directly to the "first.dir" movie. Try selecting the desktop to verify that the animation continues even when the projector is not the application with the focus. Use the title bar to move the window around the screen. Figure 11.9 shows an example of this projector running.

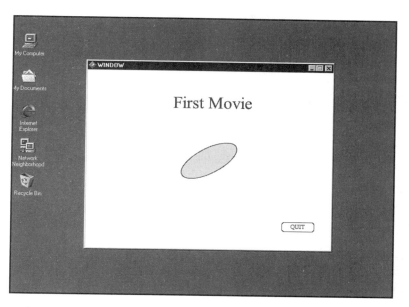

Figure 11.9   The projector runs in a window with a title bar, and continues execution in the background.

8. Quit the projector and reload "stub.dir" in Director. Open the Movie Xtras dialog box by selecting Modify, Movie, Xtras. Uncheck the Include in Projector option for all the Xtras except TextXtra, Text Asset, and Flash Asset, which are required for this movie (the projector will not operate without them). Figure 11.10 shows an example of this procedure.

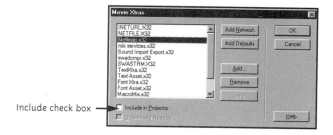

Include check box ⟶

Figure 11.10   The selected Xtra, NetLingo.x32, has the Include in Projector option unchecked, meaning that it is not automatically added to projectors created using this Director movie.

9. Save the movie with the name "stub2.dir" in the same folder in which you earlier saved the projector application. Start creating a projector and add "stub2.dir" to the file list. Open the Options dialog box and match its settings to those in Figure 11.11. This time, the projector will be full screen and not animated in the background, and the projector itself will be compressed. The file "stub2.dir" is also on the CD-ROM in the Chapter11 folder for reference.

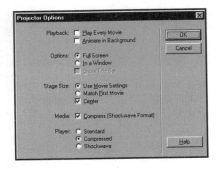

Figure 11.11   A projector, showing different settings for contrast.

10. Click OK to confirm the projector options. Click Create to make a new projector. Name this projector FullScreen to differentiate it from the first one. Click Save, and watch as fewer files are added to this projector. The Xtras that were deselected are not included when this projector is built.

11. Compare the file sizes of the two projectors Window and FullScreen. On my system, Window is approximately 2.5MB and FullScreen is around 1.4MB. This is a substantial savings, which is a result of eliminating unneeded Xtras and compressing the projector. You might notice that this projector takes a slightly longer time to start running because it has to decompress itself before playback starts.

12. Run the new FullScreen projector and notice that it completely covers the desktop. The stage color is used as the border color beyond the stage area for consistency. Figure 11.12 shows an example of this projector running.

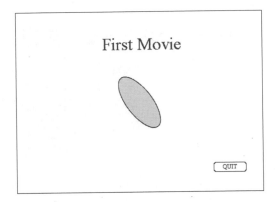

Figure 11.12   A full-screen projector that is centered, creates a border to the edges of the screen, and is set to have playback paused in the background.

13. Try bringing another application to the foreground, and watch as the spinning ellipse stops until the projector is selected again.

In this example, you created two projectors from stub movies. The first projector played in a window and included all the default Xtras. The second projector was full screen, only included required Xtras, and was compressed. The file sizes between the two were markedly different. You should now have a frame of reference from which to base your own projects when you make decisions on compression and projector options.

Projectors are versatile applications that can be set to provide the best playback experience for any movie. You can use the available options to customize how the projector appears onscreen and what files it contains. Always try to minimize the file size of projectors, but remember the tradeoff in startup time as well.

Exploring Shockwave Movies

Shockwave movies are compressed versions of Director movies. They are intended primarily for Internet use, although they are not restricted to this. Shockwave movies on the Internet play back inside a Web browser. The browser must have the proper Shockwave plug-in installed. If the plug-in is not installed, the end user is prompted to download and install it before the movie can play. The plug-in download and installation process has been improved in recent versions so that it is increasingly easier for people to install it successfully without much knowledge of the process. Also, with the prevalence of Shockwave content on the Internet, it is likely that the end user has encountered a Shockwave movie previously and has the plug-in installed.

The Shockwave compression process reduces the file size of any movies and external cast files. External asset files are unaffected by this compression, and you should handle them separately so that you can determine their compression requirements. For example, you may want to compress linked JPEG images so they are even smaller files.

The Shockwave plug-in automatically displays the Shockwave logo as a movie downloads in a browser. A progress bar, just below the logo, is also presented to give the user feedback on the download progress, shown in Figure 11.13.

As with a projector, using a stub movie with Shockwave content can be advantageous. The stub movie can be as simple as a link to the next movie. In this case, the Shockwave logo does not appear in the browser while the next movie is downloading.

A more advanced stub movie might contain a small loading screen. This provides feedback to the end user about how long it will take to download the main movie. The advantage to this over the standard Shockwave logo is that it can use the same theme as the main content. For example, the company logo or character animation could be shown as the next movie downloads.

The following sections explore considerations specific to Shockwave movies.

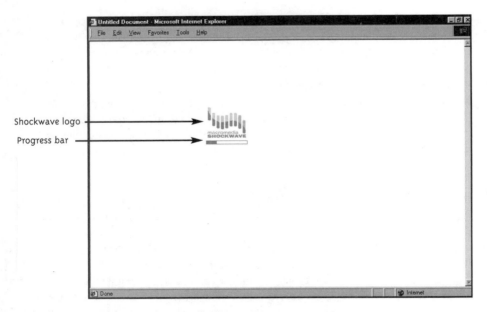

Figure 11.13   The Shockwave logo appears in the browser as a Shockwave movie downloads, and the progress bar at the bottom of the logo shows the percentage downloaded graphically.

Creating a Shockwave Movie

You start creating a Shockwave movie by selecting the Save as Shockwave Movie command from the File menu. This brings up a dialog box that prompts you to save the current movie in Shockwave format (see Figure 11.14).

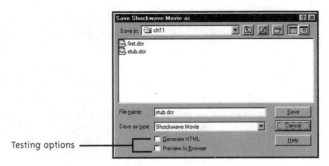

Figure 11.14   The Save Shockwave Movie as dialog box presents the name of the current movie with the .dcr extension.

You can use the testing options in the Save Shockwave Movie as dialog box to create a sample Web page and automatically load it in a browser. The Generate HTML option creates a Web page document with the same name as the Shockwave movie. This document has rudimentary HTML code that references the Shockwave movie. It can be used to manually preview the movie in a browser, and it could also form the basis of a Web page posted to the Internet.

The Preview in Browser option automatically opens the default browser to view the movie immediately. If the Generate HTML option is selected as well, the new Web page is opened in the browser. Otherwise, the Shockwave movie is loaded directly into the browser for preview.

> **Note**
>
> The load times of both the sample Web page and the Shockwave movies in Preview mode are not representative of Internet bandwidth. The files are loaded from the hard drive and likely appear almost immediately. They take significantly longer to load from a server on the Internet, especially using a standard analog modem.

Optimizing Download Times

Shockwave movies on the Internet depend on the end user's available bandwidth to the Internet for their load times. Because typical Internet bandwidth is a mere fraction of even the slowest CD-ROM transfer rates, this has a major effect on load times.

The majority of Internet users still access it via analog modems. Even with the advent of 56Kbps modems, the transfer rates are very slow. Shockwave movies are compressed so that they can load as quickly as possible over slow connections.

The file size of a Shockwave movie, and therefore the time required to download it, is directly proportional to the size, in bytes, of the cast members it contains. You should make cast members as small as possible by reducing their dimensions or bit-depth. Remember that vector images typically are smaller than equivalent bitmap images. Additionally, you should remove all cast members that are not used by the movie before converting to Shockwave format.

The effects of low-bandwidth connections can be mitigated somewhat by the organization of Shockwave movies. As pointed out already, a stub movie can be used to present something to the viewer almost immediately.

Also, you can choose to have the entire movie download before it begins to play or to have it start to play before it is completely downloaded. Downloading the entire movie before playback begins provides for the best performance during actual movie playback. This is achieved at the expense of starting quickly: It takes longer to download but there will be no pauses from additional downloading during playback. Action games where playback performance is key to their enjoyment should be set up this way. If a fast playback start is desired, you can set the movie to download additional cast members in the background. Pauses in playback may occur if the movie progresses to a point in the score where cast members are required before they are downloaded. Reference or information-heavy movies are a good choice for this method. The end user may spend enough time reviewing material that the next cast members are already downloaded before they are needed.

Macromedia Director

The settings that control this aspect of Shockwave movie playback are contained in the Movie Playback Properties dialog box, which you access by selecting <u>M</u>odify, <u>M</u>ovie, <u>P</u>layback (see Figure 11.15).

Streaming options

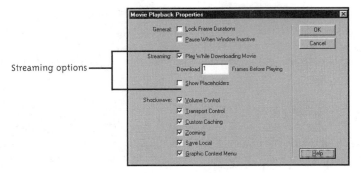

Figure 11.15   A dialog box that presents options to control how the movie downloads.

The options in this dialog box that you should be most concerned with are the streaming options, which are as follows:

- Play While Downloading Movie—This setting is the main control for determining when playback starts. If it is enabled, the movie will begin playing before the entire movie file is downloaded. When disabled, the entire file is downloaded before playback starts.

- Download *x* Frames Before Playing—You can select a number of frames to download before the movie starts by using this option. You cannot use this option unless the <u>P</u>lay While Downloading Movie is selected. Playback does not start until all the cast members in the specified number of frames are downloaded. This always starts with frame 1, so cast members to be downloaded first should be in the early frames of the movie.

- <u>S</u>how Placeholders—This option also applies only when the <u>P</u>lay While Downloading Movie option is enabled. If this option is checked, sprites are shown as rectangles before their associated cast members are downloaded. Normally, this option should be disabled for best control over the look of the movie.

Enhancing Shockwave Performance

Shockwave movies that execute inside browsers do not have access to the entire computing power of the system on which they are running. The browser uses the CPU and memory for itself. It also controls how quickly the Shockwave movie plays back.

Shockwave and projector movies that are otherwise equivalent movies have different playback performance. A projector has access to the host computer just as any normal application does: It can use the full capabilities. The same movie, saved as a Shockwave file, plays more slowly than the projector file. Almost all movies can play back successfully in Shockwave format, but the minimum requirements of the system may have to be increased to achieve the same level of performance.

In practice, the performance variation between machines and operating systems is greater than the performance variation between Shockwave and projectors. For example, the performance difference between a Pentium and Pentium III (or a PowerPC 601 and G3) computer is much greater than between a Shockwave movie and projector on the same computer. It is important to be aware of the performance penalty of running a movie inside a browser, and you should test playback on a wide variety of systems before the Shockwave movie is released.

Shockwave Limitations

The capabilities and features that are available for projectors are not all available for Shockwave movies. The fact that they run inside a browser limits Shockwave movies and restricts them from performing certain tasks. For example, Shockwave movies are not allowed to change the bit-depth of the end user's monitor. A projector can use the `colorDepth` Lingo to control this, but it has no effect in a Shockwave movie because a Shockwave movie is a secondary application inside the browser, unlike projectors, which are full, normal applications.

Note

Lingo commands that access the end user's hard drive are also restricted. These commands can access only the specific area of the browser's cache folder allowed by Shockwave. This is a security measure to prevent Shockwave movies from causing damage to a computer system.

Controlling Playback with Shockwave Remote

Macromedia introduced a new Shockwave controller with the `shockwave.com` Web site. The Shockwave Remote gives end users control over the playback of Shockwave movies and enables users to save Shockwave movies on a hard drive for playback at a later time without downloading again.

The Shockwave Remote, shown in Figure 11.16, has playback controls much like the Control window in Director. The end user can rewind a movie to the beginning, pause a movie, start it again, and fast-forward it. Additionally, the end user can set the volume of the movie. The Save button near the playback controls enables the user to store the Shockwave movie in one of five slots. Stored movies do not need to be downloaded every time they are played.

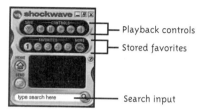

Playback controls

Stored favorites

Search input

Figure 11.16   The Shockwave Remote application appears automatically whenever an end user encounters Shockwave movies on the Internet.

The stored favorites area is used to access one of the five downloaded movies. Clicking a number opens the associated movie in the default browser. For storage of more than five movies, end users can purchase Macromedia's ShockMachine application, which allows virtually unlimited storage of movies.

The search input area is used to find Shockwave movies with the specified content. Only Shockwave movies on Macromedia sites are included in this search function. Third-party developers can submit their movies to Macromedia for inclusion. For example, if you search for *arcade games*, a new browser window opens, and you see the results of the search in typical search-engine format.

Movie authors have control over how their movies respond to the Shockwave Remote. The Movie Playback Properties dialog box in Figure 11.15 includes the following Shockwave options:

- Volume Control—When enabled, this option allows the Shockwave Remote to influence the movie's volume.

- Transport Control—When enabled, this option allows the Remote to execute rewind, pause, play, and fast-forward commands on the movie.

- Custom Caching—This option is currently unused.

- Zooming—The ShockMachine application offers full-screen playback for Shockwave movies. When enabled, this option allows ShockMachine to increase the stage area of the movie.

- Save Local—When enabled, this option allows the end user to save the movie in one of the positions in the Remote or Machine.

- Graphic Context Menu—When enabled, this option presents a graphical menu to users when they right-click and then press Ctrl+click on the Shockwave movie. A standard text menu is shown if this option is disabled.

The Shockwave Remote and ShockMachine applications provide more control over Shockwave movies for the end user. You can set which aspects of this control apply to end users of your movies. The Remote will likely make Shockwave content even more popular on the Internet.

Testing and Quality Assurance

All multimedia titles should have thorough testing and quality assurance performed on them. These procedures help find problems the developers may have missed before the title is released to the public.

Testing a product involves searching for errors or omissions in functionality and compatibility, including incomplete or wrong assets, error conditions, and program crashes. Testers work with the movie authors to find bugs, report them, and verify that they are fixed.

Quality assurance, in contrast, is the process of evaluating a product for the excellence of its content. This type of evaluation tries to determine, before a product is released, whether it will be successful in the marketplace. Often, publishers have a wide range of concerns regarding quality that developers must adhere to. These include suitability of material, adherence to a licensed character or property, and number of features.

Testing occurs near the end of the development process, after most of the product is implemented. It is the last stage before release. Quality assurance should happen as early in the schedule as possible. Problems found during the quality assurance phase require more involved fixes and can alter the basic structure of a title.

The remainder of this section covers the phases of testing, operating system concerns, hardware compatibility, and browser compatibility.

Phases of Testing and Quality Assurance

A product goes through many different phases during overall development. Play testing, alpha, beta, and release candidate phases are covered in this section. Various levels of completion define the phases. Many different definitions of each phase exist, and they vary among development teams. The definitions in this section are merely suggestions intended to provide a broad understanding of the phases.

Play Testing or Focus Testing

As part of the quality assurance process, games and other entertainment titles should go through some form of play testing. This consists of different people playing the game and making suggestions for improvements. The game may be too easy or too hard for its intended audience. There may not be enough levels to keep players interested, or the control methods may be too frustrating. Play testing can help discover these problems and lead to appropriate fixes.

Focus testing is more general than play testing and can apply to many different types of projects. It is usually done by people who are not associated with the product, but who fit its intended audience. Feedback is solicited regarding the suitability of the product and whether it accomplishes what the developers intend.

Both play testing and focus testing provide great feedback, but the window of opportunity for completing this type of testing is small. The product must be complete enough to be representative of the final version, and the testing must happen early enough in the schedule to allow for changes. Prototypes may be used for either type of testing, provided that they accurately show how the product will eventually behave.

> **Warning**
>
> It is important to use the results of focus or play testing appropriately. Development team members are responsible for the ultimate design of the product, and they should carefully incorporate the suggestions of the testers, understanding their ramifications. For example, one person might suggest that his or her favorite control scheme be implemented for a game. If this scheme is used by a significant minority of the potential players and negatively affects the enjoyment of other players, it should probably not be incorporated.

Alpha Phase

There is no one standard definition of *alpha*. The following requirements are common to many people's definitions, however:

- Users can navigate through the entire product and are able to reach all areas. This implies that all areas are present and that no errors prevent testers from visiting them all.

- Some versions of all the assets are in place, even if not the final version. They should be representative of final versions, but can be tweaked during the alpha phase.

- No new features are added past this point. The product should start to stabilize, and new features will likely introduce new problems.

The alpha phase of a product can last a variable length of time, depending mainly on the size of the title. Larger products are generally more complex and take longer to test thoroughly. It can be as short as a few days or as long as several months on extremely large projects.

Beta Phase

Like the alpha phase, the *beta* period of development has no universally accepted definition. The transition between alpha and beta phases is often vague and declared at a somewhat arbitrary point. The important aspects of the beta phase are as follows:

- All assets are final and implemented. No new assets are introduced, and no existing ones are changed.

- All major bugs that have been found are fixed and verified. The program should not crash or otherwise quit unexpectedly.

- Director movies at the beta phase should be in their final format. Before this point, it is acceptable to use normal movies (.dir) for ease of testing. Either protected (.dxr) or compressed (.dcr) movies are used during the beta phase so that final performance is accurately reflected. External casts are in the same format as they would be in the actual movies.

The length of time for the beta phase is also variable. It can be one week or less for small projects, or more than a month for larger ones.

Release Candidate Phase

The release candidate phase is the final step before the product is ready for its end users. The definition of a release candidate is fairly consistent across development teams:

- The movie authors report that all known bugs are fixed. The testing process continues in order to verify the fixes and determine whether any other bugs exist. New bugs may be introduced by the latest fixes or more subtle bugs could be found for the first time, even if they existed in previous versions.

- Some open bugs may be deferred rather than fixed. The development team may decide that a bug is insignificant or would simply take too much time to fix.

Many publishers require a release candidate to be tested for a specific number of days without finding new bugs before it is declared final. This allows testers to work with a stable version for a longer period of time and gives a better chance of finding more obscure bugs. This period should last at least three days, but not more than about 10. The period chosen should partially reflect the number of people testing the product: A greater number of people will test a product for more total hours within the same number of days. Fewer days of testing are required when more people are involved.

Operating System Considerations

Director supports playback on Macintosh and Windows operating systems. Separate projectors must be created for each platform. The title should be tested thoroughly on all operating systems on which end users might use the project.

Minor versions exist within the major versions of each operating system. General functions and compatibility are maintained between these minor versions, but a good testing process should experiment with the product by using each version. This leads to fewer surprises with customer support calls after the product is in the marketplace. Table 11.5 outlines the minor versions of each major operating system.

Table 11.5 Operating system versions.

Major Version	Sample Minor Versions
Macintosh System 7	7.1
	7.5
	7.6
Macintosh System 8	8.5
	8.6
Windows 95	First version
	OEM Service Release 2
Windows 98	First version
	Second Edition
Windows NT	4.0
	Service Pack 4
	Service Pack 5

In addition to testing on the minor versions, the product should also be tested on international versions of the operating systems. If the product is intended for release in other countries, it is important to know that minor differences in the operating system will not cause new errors.

Finally, the customization settings of each operating system should be changed from their default values for periods of testing and quality assurance. The program should not depend on these options being set in a specific format. Monetary units, date and time formats, as well as personalization touches such as custom sounds may all be different on end users' computers. In one situation, a developer relied on the date being formatted as "Day, Month, Year," and a bug was found that caused the program to not behave properly if this was changed to "Month, Day, Year." Fortunately, it was discovered and fixed before release to the public.

Hardware Compatibility Issues

At least minimal hardware compatibility testing should be performed during the testing phases. Even though Macromedia tests Director's projector applications and Shockwave plug-ins thoroughly, the development team is held responsible for any problems that arise from the product on different types of hardware.

Consider sending the product to a company that specializes in large-scale compatibility testing. These companies have many more configurations available because they make their living from testing on a wide variety of hardware. This testing should occur late enough in the process that the version represents the final product but also early enough that problems can be fixed before it ships.

Two examples of these types of companies are

- Veritest—www.veritest.com
- PCTest—www.pctest.com

If a hardware compatibility problem appears, it is often helpful to work directly with the hardware manufacturer for resolution. You might need only a driver update to eliminate the problem, or the manufacturer might already know about the problem and have a workaround. Manufacturers are generally supportive of developers because they want to ensure that their products work with a wide variety of software.

Browser Compatibility Issues

Like operating systems, Internet browsers are available in major versions as well as different minor revisions. The Shockwave plug-in works as a Netscape plug-in with the Navigator series of browsers and as an ActiveX control with the Microsoft Internet Explorer browsers.

Shockwave movies should be tested for performance and compatibility on as many different browser variations as possible. Because of intense competition, browsers have been updated more often than operating systems. Therefore, many more variations exist and it is almost impossible to test them all. You should select a representative sample and research any possible issues before making the movies available for download.

The Final Product

Perhaps the most satisfying part of any project is delivering a finished product. All the hard work, sacrifice, and compromises are forgotten when the team realizes that it has finished another great product.

This chapter covered the important aspects of shipping a finished product. Whether you are creating movies for CD-ROM or the Internet, the options chosen in these final phases of development are critical.

Product testing and quality assurance are vital for eventual success. Ample time and resources should be dedicated to play testing (or focus testing), and the alpha, beta, and release candidate phases. Hardware and browser compatibility should be covered as part of any testing plan.

The last few phases of product development are both critical to its success and also the most stressful. Decisions made at the end affect the overall success of the product as much as those made near the beginning. It is important to know when to release a product: not when it's perfect, but when it's finished.

Interactive Portfolio Project

This is the final Portfolio Project section. At the end of this chapter, you will have a working set of movie and cast files that can be distributed with a projector.

The first section demonstrates how to make a stub Director movie and link it to the introduction movie.

You will also convert the normal Director movies, with the extension .dir, to protected movies with the extension .dcr. Protected movies are used for shipping with a final project. All of the information required to play the movies remains intact, but they cannot be opened in Director. This means that all the scripts and other cast members are inaccessible.

In the last section, you will create a projector from the stub movie. This projector is the main application for viewing your portfolio.

Making the Stub Movie

A *stub movie* consists of a minimum number of cast members that open another movie as soon as it starts playing. Typically, the only cast member is a script to load the next movie.

The purpose of a stub movie is to minimize the number of times a projector must be created for a project. Because the stub movie is so simple, it is unlikely to be modified during development. Therefore, the projector based on the stub movie will not have to be modified.

Follow these steps to create a stub movie for the portfolio:

1. Perform the usual version control step of copying the files from the Chapter10 folder to a new folder, Chapter11, on your hard drive. As always, completed versions of the previous chapter's files are in the Portfolio_Project\Chapter10 folder on this book's CD-ROM.

2. Open the "intro.dir" movie file in Director. Immediately save it under the new name "stub.dir." This copies the movie settings to the stub movie rather than having to re-create them.

3. Switch to the internal cast window and select everything in the cast by using Edit, Select All or [Ctrl+A](Cmd+A). Remove all the cast members with Edit, Clear. Now, the cast is empty.

4. Switch to the score window and select everything by using Edit, Select All again. Remove everything with Edit, Clear. Now, the score is clean of all sprites, sounds, scripts, and transitions.

5. Select frame 1 in the script channel. Type go to movie "intro" in the script window. It will appear as soon as you type the first letter. The exitFrame handler is automatically generated, shown in Figure 11.17. Close the script window to continue.

Figure 11.17   This script causes Director to jump to the introduction movie as soon as the frame is finished.

6. Save the movie and play it. It should open the intro movie immediately.

You have created the stub movie for the portfolio project. This file will be used to make a projector in a following section. A finished version of this movie is in the Chapter11 folder inside the Portfolio_Project folder on this book's CD-ROM.

Converting to Protected Movies

Protected movies should be used for shipping with the final project. They cannot be opened in Director, so your hard work is protected from prying eyes. Creating a backup of your movies is critical before you protect them. If you don't, or if you lose the backup, there is no way to ever edit the movies in Director again.

Director provides a useful command for converting a list of movies in batches. By default, it will create backups of the movies before converting them. You can override this backup feature, but it is not recommended.

The following steps show how to protect all the movies, except the stub movie, in the portfolio project.

1. Select the Xtras, Update Movies command. The Update Movies Options dialog box, shown in Figure 11.18, appears.

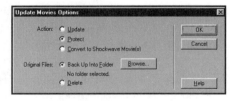

Figure 11.18   The Update Movies command is used to process multiple movies in one step.

2. Select the Protect option in the Action section. The Update option simply opens each movie and resaves it. The Convert to Shockwave Movie(s) option saves each movie as a Shockwave movie. This can be used on multiple movies as an alternative to the File, Save As Shockwave Movie command.

3. Click the Browse button to open a standard file dialog box, shown in Figure 11.19. Navigate to the folder on your hard drive containing the movies and casts for this chapter's project section.

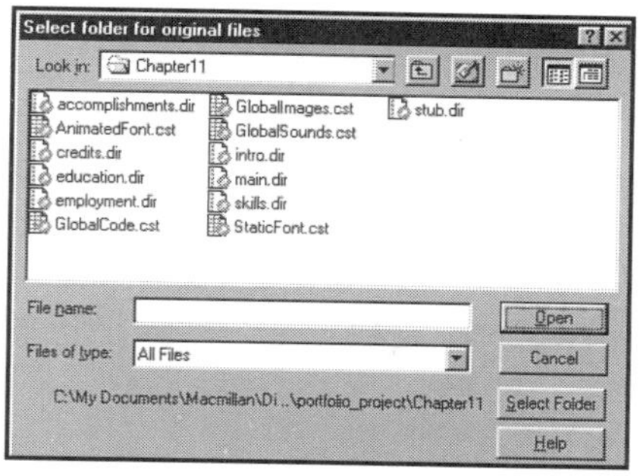

Figure 11.19 Create, open, and select a backup folder in this dialog box.

4. Create a new folder named backup in the folder with the movie and cast files. Double-click the backup folder to open it and click the Select Folder button. This tells Director to place the backup files in this folder during the protection process. Click OK to continue.

5. The Choose Files dialog box appears, as shown in Figure 11.20. You can select which files will be processed by the Update Movies command.

Figure 11.20 Add files to be converted to the file list in this dialog box.

6. Select each of the movie and cast files except the "stub.dir" movie. You haven't created the projector from the stub movie yet, so it should not be converted. Click Add to add them to the file list.

7. Click Proceed to continue. Director confirms one more time that you actually want to proceed with the conversion. Choose to continue and watch as all the files are backed up and then converted to protected versions.

Macromedia Director

8. Open the folder on your hard drive that contains the working files for this chapter's project section. Notice that all the files have changed to .dxr and .cxt extensions for movies and casts, respectively. Verify that you cannot open one of these files in Director.

9. Open the backup folder and confirm that your original movie files are still available.

You have created protected versions of the movie and cast files that will ship with your portfolio. The end user will not be able to open or modify these files, even if they own Director.

Tip

Use the Update Movies command to convert a number of movies and casts to Shockwave versions. This is much easier than saving each file in the Shockwave format, one at a time. Remember to use the backup option because Shockwave files, like protected files, cannot be edited in Director.

Creating the Projector

The final step in the portfolio project is to create the projector that will be distributed with the movie and cast files. The projector will allow end users to view the portfolio by running it as a normal application.

For the portfolio, you will create a full-screen projector because it is best to present the portfolio without other distracting applications onscreen.

Note

In the project section of Chapter 10, "Working with Xtras," you may have chosen to download the demonstration versions of some transition Xtras. These Xtras will not work in a projector unless you have purchased the full versions. Before starting these steps, modify any movies that use these transitions to use the built-in transitions instead.

The following steps lead you through the creation of a projector from the stub movie:

1. Open the "stub.dir" movie in Director.

2. Check the Xtras that are associated with this movie in the Movie Xtras dialog box, accessible with the Modify, Movie, Xtras command (see Figure 11.21).

3. Locate the demonstration version of the Transition Xtra if you chose to download it in Chapter 10. Uncheck the Include in Projector option, so it will not be bundled in the projector. Uncheck this option for any other Xtras, such as Flash and QuickTime, that you know are not used in your movies. Click OK to dismiss this dialog box when finished.

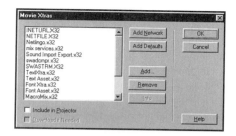

Figure 11.21 The Movie Xtras dialog box lists all the Xtras associated with the current movie.

4. Save the movie, and choose the File, Create Projector command. The Create Projector file dialog box appears, shown in Figure 11.22. Locate the "stub.dir" movie on your hard drive and add it to the file list.

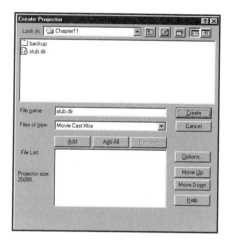

Figure 11.22 This projector will contain only the stub movie.

5. Select the Options button to open the Projector Options dialog box, shown in Figure 11.23. Match the settings for your projector to those shown in this figure, or choose different settings if you want. For example, you might want a compressed player to make the projector application smaller. When finished with your selections, click OK to continue.

6. Click Create and save the projector in the folder containing the protected movies. Use an appropriate filename such as portfolio or your name.

7. Close Director and try running the projector by double-clicking it. The introduction movie should play, followed by the main movie. Explore the portfolio to ensure that all the movies are accessible.

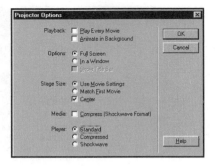

Figure 11.23 Use these settings as a guide for creating your own projector.

You have created the last piece of the Portfolio Project. Now, anybody can view your interactive portfolio on his or her computer.

The next step is to package it for distribution. You may want to bundle the protected files and the projector into a zip or StuffIt archive. Or, you may want to make a CD-ROM with your portfolio on it. Remember that the projector must be in the same folder as the protected files for it to operate correctly.

Wrap-up

In this chapter's project section, you finalized your interactive portfolio, enabling it to be viewed by anybody with a compatible computer.

First, you created a stub movie that was used as the basis for the projector. Then, you protected the entire set of movie and cast files so they couldn't be opened in Director. Finally, you made the projector to play the portfolio movies.

You may want to enhance your portfolio by using other media, such as Flash or QuickTime movies. If you are a visual artist, try creating a slideshow of your best work in one of the movies. You could even create a little game inside the portfolio to show off your new Lingo skills. No matter how you choose to customize this project, you are now on your way to producing professional-quality products using Director.

What's on the CD-ROM

Author Example Files

The author has provided files on the CD-ROM to be used with the step-by-step examples found in the chapters. These files correspond with the short chapter examples that introduce you to the concepts being covered and are not part of the interactive Portfolio Project section at the end of each chapter.

These files are located on the CD-ROM under the \EXAMPLES directory, with each chapter having its own subdirectory. Examples are provided in Chapters 3–9 and Chapter 11.

Interactive Portfolio Project Files

The workshop format of this book walks you through the creation of an interactive portfolio—from beginning to end—which you can later modify to fit other purposes. To help you with this process, the author has provided the files for this project at each stage of creation. Some of the longer listings from Chapter 8 have also been provided for you in text format, which you can copy and paste into Director.

The Portfolio_Project files are located on the CD-ROM under the \PROJECT directory, with each relevant chapter having its own subdirectory. There are files from Chapters 4–11.

Software

Following is a list of software products that will be useful to you as you put the information you learn in the book to work. (Note: Where available, Macintosh versions have been supplied. However, some of the software listed as follows may be available only for the Windows platform.)

Macromedia Director 7.0 Trial Version

Adobe's Acrobat Reader 4.0

Photoshop Tryout Version

Eye Candy 3.0 Demo Version

Xenofex Demo Version

CaptureEze 97 Trial Version

HVS Animator Trial Version

HVS ColorGIF Trial Version

HVS ColorJPEG Trial Version

HotText Tryout Version

Microsoft Internet Explorer 5

Netscape Communicator 4.61

Xtras

Third-party Xtras are "add-ons" that extend Macromedia Director's functionality. Under the \XTRAS directory is a collection of demo and free versions of Macromedia Xtras from MediaLab and Penworks. Please see the documentation provided with the Xtras explaining their use.

Images

Included in the \GRAPHICS directory is a 500-piece sample of "Imagine It! 111,000 Premium Graphic Images 2.0." With sample graphics, including some animated GIFs, you have a starter resource for building your projects. Please see \graphics\start.html for more information.

Index

F

J

Index

331

properties

    of behaviors, 168-169

    changing using Lingo, 205

protected movies, converting to, 314-315

prototypes, 18-19

puppetSound command, audio files, 251

put command (Lingo), 190

put statements, debugging using, 216

puzzle adventure games, developing, 24-25

Q

quality assurance

    browser compatibility issues, 312

    description of, 308

    hardware compatibility issues, 312

    operating system considerations, 311

    phases of, 309-310

QuickTime behavior library, 157

QuickTime format for digital video, 253

QuickTime VR (QTVR) movies and Cast Member Xtras, 273

R

raster images, 230

Real Pool (Digital Fusion and Wizard Works), 27

real-time 3D capability and Director, 14

reference applications, developing, 21-22

release candidate phase, 310

Remap Palettes When Needed option, 118

repeat while structure for loops, 210

repeat with structure for loops, 210

repeat with...in structure for loops, 211

Reset Monitor to Match Movie's Color Depth option (Projector Options dialog box), 293

resources, community of developers, 19-20

responding to user input, 207-209

RETURN keyword, 222

Riven, 24

Rotate Continuously (time-based) behavior, 239

Run Length Encoding (RLE), 253

S

sample rate of audio files, 250

Save as Shockwave Movie command (File menu), Shockwave, 304

Save Local option (Movie Playback Properties dialog box), Shockwave Remote, 308

Save Shockwave Movie As dialog box, Shockwave, 304

Save-as-Java option, introduction of, 7

Save-as-Java techniques, 161

saving movie properties settings, 119

schedules, 33-34, 46-47

score

    as state machine, 91

    customizing

        color coding, 90

        magnification, 89

        number of channels, 88-89

        overview of, 87

        size and position, 88

        sprite label options, 90

    description of, 10, 81-82

Macromedia Director

Index

Transport Control option (Movie Playback Properties dialog box), Shockwave Remote, 308

truncating sprite spans, 95

U

underline behavior, 227

unItalicize subroutine handler, 225

unload priorities for cast members, levels of, 65-66

Update Movies command, Xtras menu, 314-316

Update Movies Options dialog box, 314

UpdateStage, 20

updateStage function call, 190

Use Movie Settings option (Projector Options dialog box), 295

Use System Temporary Memory option (Projector Options dialog box), 296-298

user input, responding to, 207-209

V

vectors
advantages of, 237
comparing to Flash movies, 256
creating, 237-240
disadvantages of, 241
overview of, 235-236

Veritest, 312

version control
media management and, 261
overview of, 42-43

versions of operating systems, 311

Video Compression dialog box, 101

Video for Windows format, 253

VideoWorks (Macromind), 6

virtual memory, 297

Visual SourceSafe, 43

Volume Control option (Movie Playback Properties dialog box), Shockwave Remote, 308

W

Walt Disney World Explorer (Disney Interactive), 28

Watcher window and debugging, 217-218

WAV files, 248

waveform audio, 248

Web 216 palette, 117

Web sites
Adobe Premiere, 103
Asymetrix, 15
Authorware, 14
Behaviors.com, 157
Buried in Time, 28
Clevermedia's Resource Page, 20
Clevermedia's Shockwave Arcade, 25
Cyberflix, 15
Dedalomedia Interactive, 271
Director Online, 20
Director Web, 20
Director7.com, 20
Equilibrium DeBabelizer, 51
Macromedia, Inc., 20
Macromedia Fireworks, 51

Index

339

Notes

Notes

Notes

Notes